D0427038

SOUL SHIFTS

Also by Barbara De Angelis

HOW DID I GET HERE?:
Finding Your Way to Renewed Hope and Happiness
When Life and Love Take Unexpected Turns

SECRETS ABOUT LIFE EVERY WOMAN SHOULD KNOW:
Ten Principles for Total Emotional and Spiritual Fulfillment

WHAT WOMEN WANT MEN TO KNOW

REAL MOMENTS: Discover the Secret for True Happiness

REAL MOMENTS FOR LOVERS

PASSION

CHICKEN SOUP FOR THE COUPLE'S SOUL

CHICKEN SOUP FOR THE ROMANTIC SOUL

ASK BARBARA: The 100 Most-Asked Questions About Love, Sex & Relationships

*CONFIDENCE: Finding It and Living It**

THE REAL RULES: How to Find the Right Man for the Real You

ARE YOU THE ONE FOR ME?: Knowing Who's Right and Avoiding Who's Wrong

SECRETS ABOUT MEN EVERY WOMAN SHOULD KNOW

HOW TO MAKE LOVE ALL THE TIME

*Available from Hay House

Please visit:

Hay House USA: www.hayhouse.com®
Hay House Australia: www.hayhouse.com.au
Hay House UK: www.hayhouse.co.uk
Hay House South Africa: www.hayhouse.co.za
Hay House India: www.hayhouse.co.in

SOUL SHIFTS

Transformative Wisdom
for Creating *a* Life *of* Authentic Awakening,
Emotional Freedom, *and* Practical Spirituality

DR. BARBARA De ANGELIS

HAY HOUSE, INC.
Carlsbad, California • New York City
London • Sydney • Johannesburg
Vancouver • Hong Kong • New Delhi

Copyright © 2015 by Barbara De Angelis, Ph.D.

Published and distributed in the United States by: Hay House, Inc.: www.hayhouse
.com® • *Published and distributed in Australia by:* Hay House Australia Pty. Ltd.: www
.hayhouse.com.au • *Published and distributed in the United Kingdom by:* Hay House UK,
Ltd.: www.hayhouse.co.uk • *Published and distributed in the Republic of South Africa
by:* Hay House SA (Pty), Ltd.: www.hayhouse.co.za • *Distributed in Canada by:* Raincoast
Books: www.raincoast.com • *Published in India by:* Hay House Publishers India: www
.hayhouse.co.in

Excerpts from "If the Falling of a Hoof" and "An Infant in Your Arms," from the Penguin
publication *The Gift: Poems by Hafiz.* Copyright © 1999 Daniel Ladinsky and used with his
permission.

Photo of Barbara De Angelis on page 313: Charles Bush

All rights reserved. No part of this book may be reproduced by any mechanical, pho-
tographic, or electronic process, or in the form of a phonographic recording; nor may it
be stored in a retrieval system, transmitted, or otherwise be copied for public or private
use—other than for "fair use" as brief quotations embodied in articles and reviews—without prior written permission of the publisher.

The author of this book does not dispense medical advice or prescribe the use of any
technique as a form of treatment for physical, emotional, or medical problems without
the advice of a physician, either directly or indirectly. The intent of the author is only to
offer information of a general nature to help you in your quest for emotional and spiritual
well-being. In the event you use any of the information in this book for yourself, the author and the publisher assume no responsibility for your actions.

Cataloging-in-Publication Data is on file with the Library of Congress

Hardcover ISBN: 978-1-4019-4442-1

10 9 8 7 6 5 4 3 2 1
1st edition, March 2015

Printed in the United States of America

*Offered with the Highest love in honor of
my beloved Teachers.*

*Offered with the Highest love in honor of
my beloved students,
who have given me the privilege of being their teacher
and who have also been my teachers.*

*Offered with the Highest love in honor of all
who are courageously remembering.*

CONTENTS

Part Four
LIVING YOUR SOUL SHIFTS

PREFACE

In Service to Your Highest

"Your own Self-realization
is the greatest service you can render the world."
— Ramana Maharshi

My Highest welcomes your Highest to this great journey of awakening!
I'm overjoyed that you remembered our appointment with each other,
and, even more important, that you kept your appointment with yourself
and with the unfolding of your own emotional and spiritual freedom.

I've been preparing for your arrival for many years, creating a sanctuary of healing, revelation, and remembrance in the form of this book.
Now it's complete, and everything is ready for you. It's finally time for me
to joyfully fling the doors open and invite you in.

**This is what teachers do—we prepare ourselves to serve the stu-
dent, and then we wait for the student to arrive.** So it's a great moment
of celebration when we can finally deliver what we've been saving for
you. My own teachers were in service of my greatness. I'm honored to
have the opportunity to offer myself in service of your greatness, in service of your freedom, and in service of your Highest.

For 40 years, I've been an author, a speaker, a radio and TV host, and
an educator. *Mostly, however, I am a mystic.* A mystic is someone who un-
derstands, contacts, and maps the invisible roads inside of us. Since I was
a child, I've always felt as comfortable navigating these inner highways
as I have moving on the external plane of existence. It seems that I show

up in people's lives when they're ready to cross a threshold into more consciousness, healing, and awakening.

Over the past four decades, my work as a transformational teacher has undergone several major paradigm shifts. Each time, these external shifts have been birthed by my own foundational spiritual shifts, significant inner transformations that made it possible for me to be a more powerful and transparent channel for love and wisdom, and, subsequently, to be able to actively transmit these healing energies to my students for the purpose of the upliftment of their vibration and the acceleration of their return to wholeness.

Now I'm at a place in my life where I find myself with an abundance of harvested, ripe wisdom. This kind of authentic wisdom can only be born from a mysterious process of the alchemy between profound contemplation, deep mystical and personal experience, the passage of time, and the careful articulation of all of these.

Imagine an explorer who knows there is an amazing destination that will take them years to get to, years to explore, and then years to travel back from, but the promise of what they will find there is irresistible. They depart, and when they return, they aren't the same. This is the exciting adventure I've been on—I've taken eight years away from writing to immerse myself in teaching and a serious deepening of my own journey. Out of this, *Soul Shifts* emerged.

This is the most important work of my lifetime. It has transformed me, it has transformed my students, and now I'm hoping it will transform you. The nature of this kind of wisdom is that it yearns to be transmitted to others. **For a true teacher, the feeling of passionate enthusiasm that accompanies this is not "Look at me," but "Look at *this! Look at this golden goblet of wisdom! Look at this sparkling jewel of understanding! I want you to have it!"**

Books arrive in our lives like gifts delivered by mysterious benefactors—a friend, an article, an e-mail, a store display. Something inside of you whispers, *"You need to read this."* You sense that it contains messages and guidance you've been waiting for. It's the answer to a prayer, a question, or a longing, sometimes especially those longings you haven't allowed yourself to fully acknowledge or articulate. It's as if your soul decides it wants the book before your mind can intervene. It recognizes a piece of the puzzle you've needed, and grabs it.

Some books offer us information, and some books take us on a journey. I've designed *Soul Shifts* to do both. When I write, my highest intention is to create a virtual "Ashram of Words," a refuge, a place to which all of my students—past, present, and future—can come for guidance, inspiration, and practices to help them on their own path to freedom.

"The fruit ripens slowly, but falls suddenly and without return."
— Nisargadatta Maharaj

When I was 20 years old back in 1971, I spent six blissful months in residence on the island of Majorca off the coast of Spain with my first spiritual teacher, His Holiness Maharishi Mahesh Yogi, as part of a meditation teacher–training program. Maharishi was a great enlightened master and a radiant being. Every night, he'd sit with us and share profound, life-changing wisdom. During those six months, I wrote down every single word he said in a series of large hardbound notebooks.

Yesterday, something prompted me to find one of these precious notebooks and page through it. As I did, I came upon this beautiful sentence I'd noted that was part of a talk he gave to our group the day before our course was over, as we were about to leave for different parts of the world to teach meditation. He said:

"When the fruit comes on the branch, the tree bows down."

There are so many layers of wisdom woven into this seemingly simple but stunningly profound sentence. The ripe fruit creates a triumphant heaviness on the branch of the tree, helping it to bow down so that it can more easily offer itself to whoever is waiting to receive it. The fruit blossoms on the branch and the tree does not feel proud, but bows in humble awe at the miracle of what has been revealed.

My teacher was teaching us how to be teachers: *to always remember that teaching is an act of service; and to not feel elevated, but rather to be humbled by the ripening of our own awakening that he knew would unfold for many of us as the years passed.*

Forty years later, I am awed by the fruits of wisdom and awakening that have appeared on my branches, and I bow down in humble gratitude for the opportunity I've had to serve others on their path and be a channel for healing. "The instrument is blessed by that which flows through it," said Paramahansa Yogananda. This book is my ripened fruit, offered to you with great love. I feel so deeply blessed to have been the instrument for the delivery of *Soul Shifts,* and I am honored and delighted to pass the gifts, guidance, and grace it contains on to you.

**Our responsibility as conscious beings, sincere seekers,
and planetary transformers
is to rebirth ourselves over and over again.**

May these Soul Shifts bless and free you as they have blessed and freed me.

Offered with great love and in service to your Highest,

Barbara De Angelis
August 2014
Santa Barbara, California

INTRODUCTION

Before We Begin: Some Guidance That Will Help You Receive the Most from This Book

*"All truly wise thoughts have been thought already
thousands of times; but to make them truly ours,
we must think them over again honestly,
till they take root in our personal experience."*
— Johann Wolfgang von Goethe

There is a mysterious but unmistakable alchemy that takes place when you allow yourself to experience a book as more than an enjoyable collection of words, but rather as a powerful "vibrational spaceship" that's waiting to take you on an amazing journey to places within yourself that you haven't visited before. I suppose, then, you could say I am in the *spiritual transportation business!*

For me, writing is the final phase of what is a profound, mystical, and sacred process: the creation of a living vortex of transformational energy that will be called a "book." I spend years structuring that transformational energy into "rooms" of wisdom, awakening, clarity, and healing, sort of like reverently designing and decorating a beautiful sanctuary or retreat so that all who enter will be uplifted and shifted. **The words acting as this vibrational spaceship are not the destination, though. They are just energetic vehicles or entry points, verbal doorways into the actual experience of transformation that is contained within the vortex known as the book.**

So what can you expect to find here? *Soul Shifts* contains two kinds of content: **informational and vibrational.** The informational content I offer you is *designed to impact your mind,* and is what you traditionally expect to receive when you read a book such as this—ideas, concepts, and explanations that offer you new ways to understand yourself and the world.

Vibrational content, on the other hand, is designed not to simply be understood by your mind, but to actually be experienced by your heart and your consciousness in such a way that it creates a real and significant energetic impact. It is the difference between the process of your intellect gathering information about something (a mental encounter) versus your actually having a *visceral experience* of that thing (a vibrational encounter). You will be learning much more about vibration later on, but simply put, *the purpose of this vibrational content is to help you make real shifts from the inside out.*

Imagine the difference between hearing about a bowl of ice cream versus eating the delicious, creamy treat, or the difference between hearing about a tropical turquoise sea versus floating peacefully in the warm water. *The first experience sounds good; the second experience feels good.* It does something to you. This is my highest intention for you as you read *Soul Shifts*—that it doesn't just sound good but feels good, that you allow it to do something to you, and to deliver the many transformational experiences it's designed to offer.

More Than Information:
Receiving the Transmission of Energy

I'd like to suggest that you be open to experiencing the book as *not only information, but also as transmission.* There is a lot woven into these pages that your mind won't be able to locate simply by comprehending the words. Perhaps you've read books by me or other authors and already understand what it means to experience the alchemy I'm describing. If you haven't, I invite you to open to experiencing this book differently, and see what happens.

Words that are produced not from the level of the intellect,
but from within the expanded consciousness of
the writer or teacher and are then offered to you
as a reader, are not simply inert words—
they are enlivened, activated, and vibrating with
an actual frequency of transformation and awakening.

Receiving them with this understanding can connect you
to the wisdom and experiences and attainment
from which they emerged,
which will then activate these same experiences
inside of you.

Another way to understand this is to think of it as if you are plugging yourself into an electrical socket so that your own electrical device can work, or establishing a connection with a Wi-Fi network so that you can tune in to the Internet and receive downloads.

If you'd like to experiment with this, *you can simply have the intention of opening to the vibrational energy contained in the book,* even if you aren't sure right now what that means. You might imagine as you read that your eyes are not only physically looking at the words, but are absorbing the energy from the words, as if streams of pulsating light are pouring off the page and into your eyes.

You can also *have the awareness that the book is not just a collection of words and ideas, but a living being with whom you are visiting, a benevolent energy that has come into your life to offer you guidance, compassion, and love.* When you read, you can imagine that you are quietly sitting with that wise being. You could have the sense that the pulsating energy of the words is pouring into your heart.

You might also *visualize a golden cord connecting the book and the wisdom it contains to your heart* or, if you like, connecting your heart to mine. You will feel something profound happen.

Of course, you're welcome to do none of this and read *Soul Shifts* just for the information it offers, which I sincerely hope you will find to be helpful, inspirational, and uplifting. There is, however, a lot more available to you than just information on these pages, so don't be surprised if you feel something else taking place.

LOOK FOR THE GATEWAYS

Soul Shifts contains actual energetic and *Vibrational Gateways*. I use words, phrases, or a flow of ideas to assist in creating vibrational openings inside of you, which I will be explaining more as we go forward. These Vibrational Gateways will present themselves as you read, so look for them and give yourself permission to pass through them.

How should you do this? ***Simply notice when something you're reading stirs an emotion in you, or creates a sense of expansion, excitement, or even agitation. This means you're having a vibrational reaction to the words. You've come to a Gateway:***

**The words in this book are more than just words—
they are Vibrational Bridges created for you to cross over,
and Vibrational Gateways for you to pass through.**

I don't want you to miss any Gateways. Often I'll bring your attention to what I consider an important Gateway by setting the words by themselves in bold type, just as I did above.

My suggestion is that when you sense you might be at a Gateway, take a moment to read those parts out loud to yourself, or if you and a friend or loved one are both reading the book, take turns reading passages to each other. Hearing yourself say the words will infuse your vibration with the vibration of the wisdom that is being offered and open you to the energy that is trying to come in. I also invite you to read the book through many times at your convenience to give yourself a chance to experience the fullness of what it has to offer. You may want to have a journal nearby, so you can jot down notes or insights that come to you while reading.

Like any gift, a book such as *Soul Shifts* is meant to not just be looked at and admired, but to be unwrapped, used, and lived. Throughout these pages, I will offer you many practices and techniques. As you start using some of the techniques I share, you'll begin to understand the information you've read from the inside out, rather than only from the level of your intellect. **Your realizations and awakenings will happen not because of my words, but because of your own experiences of integrating the concepts into action.**

MAPPING YOUR SOUL SHIFTS JOURNEY

I've designed *Soul Shifts* as what I hope will be a smooth, easy, clear, and exciting journey for you. The content systemically unfolds one layer at a time, each concept building upon the previous one, so that when you're reading, you feel like you're climbing a fascinating stairway that keeps taking you higher and higher.

I've structured *Soul Shifts* in four sections:

Part I: Gateways to Authentic Awakening

This first section is like the staging area at the beginning of our journey, where we're given our maps, our supplies, and an orientation to the road upon which we're about to travel. You'll learn about why real transformation can only happen from the inside out, and how there's nothing missing inside of you—you're already wired and ready for awakening! Consciousness is the control panel for your life, and you'll discover how to shift your consciousness *so you can stop trying to control and manage your life, and instead live with real mastery.*

Part II: The Technology of Transformation

Transformation doesn't just happen—there's actually a technology that can make it faster and easier. I call this "spiritual physics." In Part II, you'll learn why both modern science and ancient spiritual texts say the same thing: that you're in fact a vibrational being, and how everything that happens to you is a vibrational experience. *To shift your life, your thoughts, and your relationships on the outside, you have to recalibrate your vibration on the inside by making the Soul Shifts I'll explain.* You'll learn how to cultivate true vibrational credibility, which will have a profound effect on your own confidence and radically transform your relationships with everyone around you.

Part III: Soul Shifts for Practical Spirituality

This section of the book offers you many powerful Soul Shift techniques that will guide you to connect with, and live in and as, your Highest not just some of the time, but all of the time. *You'll discover how to put everything you've learned in Parts I and II into practice in ways that produce real and lasting changes in all aspects of your life.* Practical spirituality will explain how you may be sabotaging your happiness without realizing it, and how you can instantly recalibrate your consciousness to your most enlightened self no matter how you're feeling or what's happening.

Part IV: Living Your Soul Shifts

How can you live your purpose every day? What needs to happen so that you can experience more love and freedom under all circumstances? In Part IV, you'll discover how to live your Soul Shifts. *You'll learn about your "soul accomplishments" and your own "cosmic curriculum," and I'll share more Soul Shifts Practices that will open your heart and uplift your spirit.* These final chapters will inspire you as you realize that you can and are making more of a difference in the world than you can possibly imagine.

My Panoramic Style of Teaching

Imagine that you've come to a museum to see a famous ancient sculpture that is enormous in size. You want to experience it fully, to understand its beauty. Would you pick one spot and remain standing there, looking at the sculpture from only the same angle without moving to see it from the side or back? Of course the answer is no.

Most people, however, tend to look at themselves and their life in just this way, from the same vantage point where they've been standing for a long time—sort of like staring at the sculpture from only one place, or parking in the same spot each time you want to enjoy the view of a mountain, or a city skyline, or a scenic area. **We think we are seeing all there is to see, and base our understanding of reality on that assumption, but in truth, we're just seeing the sculpture or the mountain or ourselves from one angle. I call this** *"seeing the world through the eyes of your issues."*

My teaching style is what I have named "panoramic." I take my student, or audience, or reader, "move them over" a few inches in perception and contemplation, and say, *"Now look at yourself or the situation from here. This view gives you a totally different perspective, doesn't it?"* Then I create another new vantage point that "moves" the student over to another angle, and invite them to look from there. Then I take them on what we can call a "conceptual helicopter ride" up to a vantage point high above the issue or situation, and say, *"Now look down at it from up here!"* Once we've done that, we take an elevator deep down to the roots of the issue, and look at it from its foundation.

This panoramic style of teaching is like being given a very thorough tour that allows you to see the wholeness of yourself and your issues, including what's keeping you limited in any way, and to *discover the pathways that already exist to lead you out of those limitations into more freedom.* You'll notice that I use many teaching metaphors as part of this "tour," since they offer you different ways of looking at the same thing. These are great tools for helping you take principles and understand them in a practical, grounded, everyday way.

Honoring All Paths to the Highest

On my own personal and spiritual journey, I have gained great value and inspiration from the wisdom, symbols, and stories offered by many cultures and religions, and I'll be sharing these with you throughout *Soul Shifts.* You'll notice that some of these stories and images will reference my own background and study in Eastern thought, but I want to emphasize and reassure you that this book is not based on any one spiritual path, nor is it derived solely from the teaching or the philosophy of any one person but myself. It is universal in that it invites you into more permanent wakefulness, which I believe is the goal of all spiritual practice.

This is not about you following my pathway, but rather a respectful offering of tools that I hope will help you better navigate your own individual path and more successfully put your own beliefs into practice. I have students from every religious background imaginable—Christians, Jews, Muslims, Hindus, Buddhists, agnostics, and more. Over the years, many of them have found themselves being drawn back more deeply into their own religion, experiencing it more fully from the heart. I honor all paths that lead us to the Highest, whatever your name for that Highest may be.

Allow Yourself to Go Deep

One summer when I was in my 20s, I was returning from a meditation retreat in Europe and decided to visit some sacred sites with a friend. Something happened at one of our stops that I'll never forget. We'd been told about a beautiful, secluded monastery, and traveled there to experience the serenity and see the exquisite art. Arriving at the property, we split up and went our separate ways. For about an hour I explored the many small chapels and peaceful prayer gardens, hoping to absorb the sanctified atmosphere that saturated the monastery from hundreds of years of prayer and worship.

At the appointed time, I reunited with my friend, who was just glowing. "Wasn't that lovely?" I asked. "I'm so glad we came."

"Unbelievable," she replied. "Of course my favorite was that candlelit room with the huge statue of the Blessed Virgin."

"Candlelit room with the Blessed Virgin? You're kidding." I sighed. "I didn't see it. *How could I have missed it?*"

"It was all the way downstairs at the very bottom. There's a small doorway on the floor below where we are now that leads to a narrow set of stone stairs, and if you keep going down, there's the most sacred part of the monastery."

"I went down one flight, but didn't know there was *another* downstairs below that," I answered sadly.

My friend looked at me sympathetically and said: *"I guess you just didn't go deep enough."*

Years later, when I began my career as a transformational teacher and a writer, I remembered that poignant moment, and those meaningful words: *I guess you just didn't go deep enough.* I couldn't have imagined back then how much this understanding would become a significant part of my message and offering to my own students. Looking back on that day, I realize that I did receive the grace of the Blessed Virgin after all!

As we embark on this journey together,
I lovingly invite you to find the courage to go deep—
deep into the places this book takes you inside of yourself,
deep into the wisdom offerings I've gathered here for you,
deep into the hidden sanctuaries of grace
and hidden shrines of truth buried in your own heart.

This deep exploration, deep opening, and deep surrender is what true healing, true transformation, and true awakening requires.

This is what awaits you.

You deserve nothing less.

PART ONE

GATEWAYS
TO
AUTHENTIC
AWAKENING

❀ 1 ❀

Stepping Over the Threshold

"If [the teacher] is indeed wise,
he does not bid you enter the house of his wisdom,
but rather leads you to the threshold of your mind."
— Kahlil Gibran

In all religions, on all spiritual paths, one of the most sacred and mystical physical places is the threshold one crosses to enter the temple, cathedral, prayer hall, synagogue, teepee, or space of worship. A threshold is a doorway between worlds, a mystical border between the everyday and the Divine, and, therefore, a place of potency and grace.

In most Eastern cultures, one honors this understanding of the threshold by never stepping directly on it, but always stepping over it, and by leaving one's shoes outside as a sign of reverence and respect. On my pilgrimages to Indian temples, I have often seen a temple attendant squatting on the ground next to the threshold leading into the temple proper, to make sure no one, particularly no uninformed Western tourist, makes the terrible mistake of stepping on the raised divider.

Many years ago when I began my spiritual journey, I was taught that whenever I entered a temple, or a hall in which the teacher was seated, I should bend down to touch the threshold or entrance with my right hand, and then raise that hand up to touch my heart. It was also suggested that I do this on the way out of the temple or hall. No one explained the significance of this to me, but I did it anyway because that was what everyone else was doing—and because I was always a very dutiful student!

In time, however, as I had the direct experience that my teacher was giving me the gift of entrance into my innermost realms of consciousness, I understood that gesture of respect, and why my hand went from the floor to my heart. For me, it became a way of saying, *"May what awaits me in this room, over this threshold, go directly into my heart."* On the way out, it was a way of saying,

3

"I am so grateful for the grace that I have received while in this sacred space. May it unfold fully within me."

This metaphor of stepping over the threshold is a beautiful mirror for your journey of personal and spiritual transformation: **You have been on a path since the moment you were born into this world, and you've already courageously crossed many significant thresholds.** All seekers must travel these invisible roads within, distances that cannot be measured in miles, yet are the hardest and most challenging part of the human adventure: the distance from the habit of turning away to the insistence on turning toward; the distance from the frightened part of you that says, *"I don't want to look at myself, I don't want to face things, I don't want to feel things,"* to the fearless part of you that finally proclaims, *"I will do whatever it takes to be free."*

We step over the threshold of our resistance, back into the sacred space of trust.

We step over the threshold of our fear, back into the sacred space of vision.

We step over the threshold of our confusion, back into the sacred space of truth.

We step over the threshold of our forgetfulness, back into the sacred space of remembrance.

And with each bold, brave step, we come closer and closer to the great reunion with the fullness of our own awakened self.

As you stand at this threshold of your Soul Shifts journey,
I welcome you to your pilgrimage.
I honor you as a great seeker.
I offer you a virtual garland of flowers,
  and respectfully place them around your neck as one would do
  to a long-awaited and revered guest who has finally arrived.

Enter . . .

"When one realizes one is asleep,
at that moment one is already half-awake."
— P. D. Ouspensky

For all human beings, life is a long series of questions. It's our nature to want more and to wonder how to achieve those things. These questions are there from the time we can speak, and evolve as we do. When we are children, our questions are focused on our own comfort and pleasure:

"Can you carry me? Can I have more candy? Why do I have to brush my teeth? Why do I have to go to school? Why can't I have that toy? Why can't I stay up and watch TV?"

As we move into adolescence, our questions shift their focus from our isolated world to include the world around us:

"Why can't I stay over at my friend's house? Why does that teacher hate me? How can I get that boy to like me? Why is that person acting so mean to me? If I join that club, will people think I'm a nerd? What do I have to do to get into that college? Why don't I ever like the way I look? What do I want to do when I grow up?"

Our adulthood brings more serious questions into view:

"Where do I want to live? Is this the right person for me? How can I create my own business? Are we ready to start a family? Am I spending too much money? Why can't I get through to my son? Should I quit this job and look for another one? Why can't I lose this extra weight? Do I have enough put aside in my savings?"

Sometimes our questions are the wrong ones, because they aren't real questions—they're actually complaints disguised as questions that aren't waiting for real answers:

"Why is this happening to me? Why is he such a jerk? When is this going to stop? Why can't my kids just behave? Why does everything always go wrong? Why does everyone always let me down? Why can't people get it together?"

One way to know that you have truly begun your journey as a seeker is to recognize that the kinds of questions you've been contemplating have changed. You begin to ask what I call "sacred questions," those questions whose focus shifts from wondering about the outside of your life to wondering about the realm inside of you:

"What is my purpose in this life? Why is it so hard for me to love myself and allow others to love me? Why aren't I living as the person I'm supposed to be? Why do I react to people and situations in ways I know aren't from my Highest? What is the truth about existence? How can I find a refuge of peace inside myself? What is the Source of everything, and how am I connected to it?"

And perhaps the most important question of all: ***"What do I have to do to find the answers to these questions?"***

Some of you have been asking these questions all your life, as I have. Some of you just began these contemplations in the past few years, or months. These questions come from deep within your being, and whether you realize it or not, they signal that something profound has already taken place inside of you.

**The courage to ask yourself sacred questions
is what identifies you as a seeker of truth,
and is an auspicious sign that your journey of awakening
has already begun.**

TIME TO WAKE UP:
YOUR COSMIC ALARM CLOCK HAS GONE OFF

What is this powerful inner turn of events that starts us off on a serious path of growth? I call it *the Cosmic Alarm Clock.* It's as if an alarm suddenly goes off inside of you, and it dawns on you that you've been asleep in your life, and need to get up. Often you are awakened with a start: *"Oh—have I been asleep? Wait a minute—what am I doing here on this planet? Wasn't there something I was supposed to do? I feel like I've been in such a daze. I can't waste any more time! I have to get up now!"*

The thing about the Cosmic Alarm Clock is that once it goes off, no matter how many times you push the snooze button and try to ignore the alert, it is going to keep ringing until you pay attention. Perhaps some of you are reading this now because you finally realized that you couldn't keep pushing the snooze button!

This brings us to the next important question:

**Who set the alarm in the first place?
The answer, of course, is: *You did!***

Your Highest Self, your soul, set your own cosmic alarm to make sure you got up in time to participate in the great shift that is happening on our planet. You had an appointment to wake up now, at this moment, in this life, at a time when so many others are waking up, and when so many others are in need of being woken up by those who got up first.

Recently in my own spiritual studies, I was astonished to discover that this concept I've taught for some time of a Cosmic Alarm Clock going off inside of you is actually described in the ancient texts of Kashmir Shaivism, a Hindu philosophy originating around the 9th century in Kashmir, which is in the northwestern part of what we now know as India. These texts were written over a thousand years ago, and explain that there comes a profound moment in the life of a soul when the individual suddenly begins to have what they describe as the "thought of awakening":

"I should learn more about the truth of life. I think I am here for something, to do something, to search for something. I must find out. I need a teacher. I need wisdom. I must wake up."

These thoughts of awakening occur, the texts explain, **because an inner awakening has already spontaneously occurred as a cosmic event in the deepest regions of your individuality, an awakening that generates a turning toward enlightenment, toward wisdom, toward freedom.** This inner event manifests within you as a rising up of the impulse to begin searching for truth, and is what actually sets you in motion toward a guide or teacher, toward spiritual or religious pursuits, toward reading, toward study, and ultimately toward attainment.

Just as an earthquake deep within the ocean generates powerful tsunami waves on the surface, so an "earthquake" on the soul level suddenly generates your questioning, your longing, your seeking, and, ultimately, your finding.

I remember how excited I was when I first heard these ancient verses explained, because the significance was mind-boggling: According to these texts, *there is no such thing as a random encounter with a teacher, a helper, a minister, a healer, a path, a transformative event, or even a book such as this.* You wouldn't have come into proximity with these kinds of experiences had a profound inner shift not *already* taken place within you, even if you don't remember or realize it! Because of that inner shift on your soul level, you are then drawn, guided, or magically "led" to individuals, teachers, teachings, or situations that will help you unfold that awakening.

> **If you've begun your outer journey
> toward a state of awakening, then you must have
> *already* experienced an inner awakening.**

In my life, I had my first conscious "thoughts of awakening" at a very early age, even though at the time, I didn't understand what I was experiencing. I remember being 10 or 11 years old and writing beautiful but depressing poetry, wondering what life was all about, wondering where I could find someone to help me discover the truth, and feeling certain that something was wrong with me because no one else I knew seemed to think about the same things I did.

I recall believing, somewhat naïvely, that the more I learned, the quicker I'd become enlightened. I'd go to our local library each week and check out 10 to 15 books on philosophy. Late at night, when my mother thought I was sleeping, I'd read my books by flashlight. I can still smell the cloth bindings of the old volumes, see my library card with the handwritten titles and date stamp, and feel the excitement of taking my first intoxicating journeys into wisdom. Even then, I was desperately hoping to find some answers to questions I didn't know how to articulate.

This was the early 1960s, and there was no personal-growth movement, no self-help literature, no transformational seminars, no popular awareness about anything that is commonplace today. My mother was so worried about me that she sent me to a child psychiatrist, who, of course, could not relate to my soul-searching, and explained it away as "prepuberty disturbances." **Inner awakenings, however, do not disappear with time, and thankfully do not reverse themselves,** and as I'd come to understand from reading those ancient texts 40 years later, my trajectory toward the spiritual path had been set in an inevitable motion toward a cosmic and blessed rendezvous.

In the fall of 1969, when I was 18 years old, I left home to attend college at the University of Wisconsin. I'd only been there for two weeks when, one afternoon, I saw a poster on a bulletin board that said LEARN TO MEDITATE along with a photo of a beautiful, smiling Indian man wearing white robes. I had absolutely no clue what meditation was; I had absolutely no idea who the Indian man was; I'd had absolutely no exposure to any kind of Eastern philosophy. Yet in that moment, *my heart somehow recognized what I was seeing as what I'd been seeking,* and I knew without a doubt that my formal spiritual journey had begun.

Perhaps you can remember when you first had your own thoughts that propelled you onto a path of transformation. For some of you it may have been a long time ago, and you have been consciously transforming ever since. For others, it may have been just recently that you found yourself longing for more understanding, more learning, and deeper spiritual experiences. It has been over half a century since I began my search for meaning, and now in the 21st century, there are so many doorways available through which seekers can enter a path of exploration. One of my greatest feelings of accomplishment in this life stems from having been one of the first individuals to popularize the idea of self-help, beginning in the early 1980s, and to have my books and television programs be there waiting when so many people's Cosmic Alarm Clocks went off.

It was not by accident that I went to that particular university, or saw that poster and decided to attend the lecture that would lead me to my first spiritual teacher and to a profound mystical path of awakening, without which you would not be reading these words. It is not by accident that perhaps you happened to open an e-mail announcing a personal-growth seminar, and decided to attend the weekend that would lead you to a whole new path of understanding. It is not by accident that perhaps you began dating someone who happened to practice meditation, and decided to begin yourself, which would lead you to great inner self-exploration. It is not by accident that perhaps you hurt your back and decided to take the yoga class offered through your church that would lead you to becoming a yoga instructor yourself. *It is not by accident that you are reading this book.*

**This is a great moment of celebration
on the journey of your soul.
Your first, and most important, Soul Shift
has already happened:
You remembered that you had
an *appointment for remembrance.*
And you kept it!**

Take a minute to really try on this understanding, and see how wonderful it feels. The hardest part of your journey is already over. You woke up! *The rest is just remembering what you forgot.*

**Something miraculous and profound
has already taken place inside of you.
It is a cosmic event of the greatest importance.
The fact that you're seeking
means that you have already found something.
Your seeking *is* your inner awakening in action.
The thought of awakening means you are, finally,
already on your way home.**

I know that this is all very intense and serious stuff to consider, in our first chapter no less! Since humor is a great way to ground ourselves, here is a little joke I wrote just for you:

A soul came into a new body, and immediately forgetting what he was here for, fell asleep at the beginning of his life.

The personality he became went about the business of being human, completely unaware that anything was wrong.

Seventy-five years passed, and the soul's time on Earth was over.

The angels responsible for escorting souls back to the Other Side arrived at his deathbed, and took the still-sleeping soul in their arms.

Suddenly, the soul woke up and saw the angels.

"Whoa, I must have dozed off," he said. "What did I miss?"

My hope is that the answer for all of us will be: **Less and less every day.**

Introducing Soul Shifts

"Once the soul awakens,
the search begins and you can never go back.
From then on, you are inflamed with a special longing
that will never again let you linger in the lowlands
of complacency and partial fulfillment.
The eternal makes you urgent."
— John O'Donohue

A golden moon was just rising over the shimmering water of Back Bay when I stepped into the car I'd hired to take me from my hotel to the international airport in Mumbai. I was returning to California from a magnificent trip to India, and although I was happy to be going home, I wasn't looking forward to the 30 hours of traveling ahead of me. I spent the next 20 minutes gazing out the window to take in my last glimpses of this fascinating city.

Suddenly I snapped out of my reverie, realizing that for some time our vehicle had been going at half the speed of other cars on the road, and we were still far from where we should have been by then. If we continued at this rate, I'd miss my flight.

"You're driving awfully slowly, sir," I said. "Can you please go faster?"

"Don't worry, missus," the driver responded cheerfully. "Please relax yourself. We are sure to be getting there eventually."

"I don't doubt that," I replied. *"But I don't want to get there eventually. I want to get there much sooner than eventually."*

There are pivotal moments in the lives of all seekers when we realize that we've been moving along on our path of transformation but, simply put, *we want to go faster.* Staying where we are, or proceeding at the pace we've been used to, is no longer comfortable or even acceptable. We know we're being called to something more significant, authentic, and expanded, and, like me on the way to the airport, we want to get there *sooner than eventually.* We have become spiritually impatient.

In these pivotal moments, what is needed is not simply more change, but profound transformation; not simply an adjustment in our outer life, but a repositioning from the inside out. We don't just want to rearrange the pieces of ourselves so that they look better temporarily. We want nothing less than rebirth. *We are ready for Soul Shifts.*

What are Soul Shifts? They are *transformative inner actions originating from and in alignment with the highest spiritual truths.* **Rather than focusing on rearranging or revising things on the outside, we learn how to take these auspicious inner actions, to make powerful shifts in understanding, feeling, and consciousness from within, thus transforming our lives from the inside out.**

This is the difference between simply *changing* and actually *shifting.* Most of us attempt to change either ourselves, our relationships, or our circumstances by dealing with things on the surface level—managing, controlling, or even covering up what we're unhappy with. To truly shift, we need to go beneath the outer, visible manifestation of our life to the "roots." For transformation to be significant and lasting, *it must originate from the inside out,* so that instead of constantly micromanaging everything, we operate from true mastery at the deepest level of who we are— the soul level.

Soul Shifts are not adjustments in thinking or behavior that we make and have to remember to keep on making. Instead, they are radical, vibrational shifts originating from inside that spontaneously and inevitably transform the way we relate to ourselves, to others, and to the world.

What are the "inner actions" that create a Soul Shift? You will be learning about this in detail throughout this book. A simple understanding to begin with is that an inner action isn't a behavioral action in the way we understand the term *action*—trying to "act" more caring, for instance—nor is it a mental action, such as a shift in attitude, like trying to think more positive thoughts.

The inner actions that I call Soul Shifts are inner choices, pulsations of feeling, and perspectives that, by nature, have a higher vibrational frequency because they're in alignment with the highest spiritual principles. Therefore, the vibrations of these inner actions are expansive, life enhancing, uplifting, and liberating, and create conditions for profound and permanent recalibrations of our energy field.

When we learn how to make these Soul Shifts, our inner position or internal vantage point inevitably shifts position, and automatically our way of seeing and experiencing ourselves and our life fundamentally shifts, too. *It's as if we put on a new pair of glasses and are seeing ourselves and the world differently, not because we're trying to, but because that is now what we see!*

Suddenly, what we perceive when we examine our work, our relationships, our external world, and ourselves looks radically different. Places where we have felt stuck or stagnant, or issues about which we have been unclear or confused all become illuminated with new, enlivened understanding. Pathways emerge where none seemed to exist, obstacles turn into possibilities, dead ends transform into doorways, challenges convert into astonishing maps leading us to exciting new territories, all because we have made Soul Shifts.

You have already experienced many Soul Shifts in your life without realizing it, changes on the outside propelled by internal shifts or "inner actions":

Perhaps after years of trying to control everything, you were forced to "let go" in a particular situation, and soon found a new road presenting itself.

Perhaps you had been very hard on someone you loved, and finally became exhausted from trying to change them so stopped pushing, and it was then that the person began to look more deeply at themselves.

Perhaps instead of trying to talk yourself into how much you should like your job, you gave yourself permission to feel how unhappy you were, and suddenly you saw a solution that had been hidden from view.

In all of these examples, something energetically shifted inside yourself, something invisible and unexpressed to anyone but yourself, or something even you weren't conscious of occurred, and because of that, a significant external event was able to take place.

The Soul Shifts and transformations you make on the inside
will manifest in profound transformations on the outside
in all areas of your life.
This is the formula for mastering your life
from the inside out.

Are You Suffering from Divine Discomfort?

"The eternal makes you urgent," wrote the late poet and priest John O'Donohue in the beautiful quote I offered earlier. Put more colloquially in the context of what we've been contemplating, once the Cosmic Alarm Clock goes off, you wake up, you get up, and then you realize that you're impatient to rise up to do whatever you're here to do and learn whatever you're here to learn. I've felt this "divine urgency" for as long as I can remember. **I call it "Divine Discomfort," an inner pressure from something in you trying to bring itself forth into your life and the world that, in its efforts to move out, collides with your own inner walls and obstacles.**

What creates Divine Discomfort? I believe that all of us come to this planet with what I call bundles of cosmic deliveries—bundles of wisdom, bundles of service, bundles of offerings, bundles of love. We promise to make these deliveries during our lifetime as our contribution to the planet. Just as a delivery person who loads up their truck in the morning knows that by 6 P.M., they need to have delivered everything and come back with an empty truck, so too we come in with "truckloads" of packages that we are committed to delivering by the end of our "day."

However, doing our cosmic "job" of delivering these packages isn't as simple as it sounds. We have problems with our "vehicle"; we have delays on our route that discourage us; we become distracted by the superficial and forget that we're making deliveries; we misplace our maps and lose our way; we get tired of driving around and just want to take a long nap; we feel no one is appreciating the things we deliver, and go on strike.

As we get older, it becomes later in the cosmic day, and we realize that we haven't made the deliveries we were supposed to. They begin to feel heavy and burdensome, and the sense of frustration becomes more intense. We know we are behind schedule, and become frightened that we've failed. We have a bad case of Divine Discomfort.

Whenever I speak about Divine Discomfort, people in my audience react very strongly. Some cry. Some start to laugh. Some look like the weight of the world has just slipped from their shoulders. Some stare at me with their eyes as wide as saucers. I have named something that they've been experiencing without knowing what it is. Afterward, I always hear the same comments:

"I've never been depressed before in my life, but lately I can't seem to shake off this sensation that something inside of me is stuck."

"I've been feeling like I'm going to explode, but haven't known why."

"My husband keeps telling me I'm having a midlife crisis, but I knew that wasn't what was wrong. I just feel like I want something to come out of me. No wonder I've been overeating—it numbs me to how uncomfortable I feel."

"No matter how much I meditate or pray, I haven't been able to calm my anxiety down, but I can't figure out what's making me feel so crazy."

"I have a great wife and terrific kids, and have pretty good financial success, so being this unhappy hasn't made any sense to me."

If you suspect you've been suffering from a case of Divine Discomfort, don't despair—you are not alone. I firmly believe that we are in the midst of a Divine Discomfort epidemic, particularly among those of us on a conscious path of growth who are feeling the pressure to deliver more and deliver now:

**The accelerated times we're in are propelling you
to your next level of "delivering"—
of serving, of offering, of helping, and of loving.
More people are trying to wake up,
and they need their "packages."**

**The cosmic energy within you is building up,
and so an internal battle ensues between that which wants
to express itself out through you,
and those habits, patterns, outdated psychological
programs, and emotional blockages that are in the way.**

**The collision between what's trying to emerge
and what's in the way
creates tremendous inner agitation,
discomfort that has a "divine" source.**

Like so many teachers and guides who have gone before me, I've suffered through my own long bouts of Divine Discomfort in order to birth myself into who I am today. In the process, I've developed powerful technologies for transformation that have become the "deliveries" I am making now through my work. *Soul Shifts* is the most recent of those deliveries, which I am overjoyed to be offering to you.

This, then, is the loving intention behind this book: to help you move more gracefully through your own Divine Discomfort and bring forth all that is waiting inside of you out into the world. It is an invitation to accelerate your personal and spiritual transformation in these times of intensified planetary velocity when stepping up into your Highest Self is desperately needed.

You may believe that you need to wait for the passage of time or the impact of significant outside circumstances in order for something remarkable or magical to occur for you, but this is not true. **You can accelerate this process of meaningful transformation, learn how to invite it, to open to it, to identify and relinquish your resistance to it, and to masterfully navigate through it to create a new way of living, loving, and serving your world that will go beyond anything you ever imagined or hoped was possible.**

A Message from Bell Rock

"Soul development should take precedence over all things."
— Edgar Cayce

One of my favorite spots on Earth is Sedona, Arizona, where I often give retreats. Sedona is an exquisitely beautiful area characterized by impressive and otherworldly configurations of red rocks, and is known for being a place of metaphysical healing because of what is said to be the mysterious power that emanates from its vibrational vortexes. Simply put, a vortex is believed to be a location at which highly concentrated, subtle spiritual energies are radiating from the surface of our planet, creating a conducive environment for prayer and meditation, and strengthening our ability to connect with our Highest Self.

My preferred vortex in Sedona is a towering red-rock formation known as Bell Rock. I've been to Bell Rock dozens of times, and when I'm there, I always feel as if I'm hooking myself up to an enormous cosmic antenna through which I receive a powerful spiritual recharge. The intense vibration is unmistakable and pretty hard to miss.

Recently I was teaching a seminar in Sedona, and decided to visit Bell Rock before my students arrived. There's a walkway that leads to the base of the mountain, and as I proceeded along the path, I was already feeling a definite sense of upliftment and expansion. Just then, I noticed a couple coming toward me. They caught my eye because it's highly unusual to see unhappy people at Bell Rock, especially when they're on the way down, and the man looked really angry and disgruntled. He was walking ten feet behind his wife, scowling, shaking his head, and muttering under his breath, while she scurried along ahead of him, nervously glancing back every few seconds. It was clear to me, even from a distance, that he had not enjoyed Bell Rock at all!

As they approached me, I heard the man say something I've never forgotten.

"I don't get what the big deal is," he complained. "I didn't feel a damn thing!" And just to make sure his partner got the point, he repeated: "Did you hear me? *I don't get what the big deal is; I didn't feel a damn thing!*"

Realizing that I'd overheard her husband's comments, the woman gave me an embarrassed, apologetic smile as she passed by, probably noticing from the beatific look on my face that I was one of those people who certainly *had* felt something!

Suddenly, I understood how although I hadn't even begun my climb, the vortex had already offered me a profound teaching: Our existence on this planet is just like a trip to Bell Rock. *We arrive and prepare to climb up and see what awaits us.* Everything is possible on this massive spiritual vortex called Earth: beautiful vistas; experiences of wonder, upliftment, and delight; innumerable moments of joy; and the opportunity for deep healing. At the end of our lifetime, we descend from the vortex. Our visit is over.

What will we say as we come down from the mountain of this existence? How many of us go through life missing what is happening because we don't allow ourselves to see, to feel, to tune in, or to be moved? How many of us end up feeling just like the man that day: *"I don't know what the big deal was. I didn't feel a damn thing. What was so great about being a human being? What was so great about love? What was so great about having a body? What was so great about making a difference in the lives of others? What was so great about the planet?"*

That day, I felt so much compassion for that man. He'd showed up expecting something to happen but couldn't receive what was right there waiting for him because *he didn't open himself to what was happening.* This is how so many people live. They wait for something to open them, rather than opening first to whatever awaits them.

**Instead of waiting for something to open you,
open yourself first.
Only then will you be able to receive
what is there to be received.**

OPENING TO THE WISDOM THAT IS WAITING FOR YOU

Imagine that there is a great treasure hidden within you—your own remembrance, your own power, your own peace, all there patiently waiting to be discovered. Now, imagine that there is a great, wise teacher living within you—your own wisdom, your own love, your own wholeness, waiting for your arrival.

How do you locate this treasure, or this teacher? Your mind tells you that you have to search, to look, to run after every clue and not give up until you succeed. **But what if I told you that you don't have to search for anything, or run after anything? All you have to do is open to it.** You just have to open to the wisdom that is waiting for you.

Try holding this phrase gently in your consciousness for a moment:

"I open to the wisdom that is waiting for me."

Now take a deep, slow breath in, and as you exhale, say it out loud if it is comfortable for you to do so: *"I open to the wisdom that is waiting for me."*

Repeat your breathing cycle and say the phrase again. Do this a few times, and then relax. Notice how you feel.

The words "I open" create a powerful shift in your vibration. When you say "I open," something in you does just that. Your mouth opens. Your energy opens. Your heart opens. In that moment, you are inviting in healing. You are inviting in grace. You are also pushing down the walls of fear, anxiety, skepticism, resistance, and mistrust. You are clearing the way to receive.

"I open to the wisdom that is waiting for me, within me as my Highest." You are calling it forth—not wisdom you need to run after; not wisdom that is far away; not wisdom that is resisting coming to you; but wisdom that is waiting for you to open to it, to receive it.

Now, for our first Soul Shift:

SOUL SHIFT

SHIFT FROM SEARCHING TO OPENING

**You're not waiting for your wisdom.
It's been waiting for you.
You're not waiting for it to reveal itself.
It has been waiting for you to *open* to it.**

This book has a destination, a reunion with something inside of you that's already there waiting for you—your own wisdom, your own love, your own Highest. So we aren't searching for anything that is separate from who you already are, but rather we're remembering how to open to it. As we learned from the disappointed man at Bell Rock, *by looking too hard for something, you will miss everything.*

When you read, remind yourself that you're opening not only to my wisdom, but to your own. The maps and keys I share in these pages are meant to help point you in the right direction, and to assist you in unlocking those places of guidance and revelation that already exist within yourself, clues to your freedom that have been patiently waiting to be discovered.

As you journey through the vortex of this book, allow this new understanding to guide you:

Tell yourself that you do not have to do anything now but receive what these pages will offer to you. You don't have to try to understand; you don't have to try to learn because you think you need to fix yourself; you don't have to work hard to attain anything.

Just open, and then receive. Just open, and then receive.

The Teachings of the Tuberose

*"There's only one corner of the universe you can be
certain of improving, and that's your own self."*
— Aldous Huxley

I love flowers, and the tuberose is one of my favorites. Its delicate
white blooms grow on a long stalk and emit an intoxicating tropical fragrance that reminds me of Hawaii and India—two of my most sacred
pilgrimage destinations. My students always lovingly offer me tuberose
garlands, and whenever I can find the flowers here in Santa Barbara, I fill
the house with them.

One thing that always puzzled me about tuberoses was that I felt they
were teasing me by only offering a few open flowers on each stem. When
I'd buy them and bring them home, there were always some blossoms
opened, but many more of the tiny buds were closed and never opened
at all. I couldn't figure out why this was the case, and would stare at the
closed buds with longing, wondering what I could do to entice them
to open.

One day while visiting the local farmers' market, I saw a man behind
a table surrounded by buckets and buckets of tuberoses. He was the Tuberose Man! I became very excited as I approached his stall and basked in
the abundance of so many beautiful flowers, as I imagined putting not
just a stalk or two, but bunches in every room of my home.

I introduced myself and told the man about my love affair with tuberoses, which delighted him since that was his profession—growing tuberoses on his farm. "It's so nice to meet someone who really appreciates
them," he said, smiling. "I'm going to get you several really good bunches." In a moment he returned, and handed me about 50 tuberose stalks
bunched together. "Here, these will be perfect," he said proudly.

I looked at the stalks he gave me, and tried to hide my disappointment. They looked just like the ones I always bought, each containing
only a few opened blossoms, with the remainder of the buds tightly
closed. The farmer must have seen the sad look on my face, because he
asked me if there was a problem.

"I'm sorry to appear so ungrateful," I answered. "It's just that I was
hoping for a better bunch with more opened flowers. These only have a

few blooms on them, and since I know the buds will never open, they won't be as fragrant as I wished."

The Tuberose Man stared at me for a moment. Then he said, "You don't understand how tuberoses work, do you? Here, let me show you their secret."

He took one of the stalks from my hand and pointed to a bud. *"See this bud? It looks closed, but it's actually ready to open.* This little pink spot on the top of the white bud means the top of the bud has softened. If you just gently press on it like this, see . . . the blossom opens."

I watched in delighted amazement as he delicately opened bud after bud with his finger. My tuberoses were blooming before my eyes.

"They just need your attention, and a little help to open at the right time," he explained. "Then you'll have many more blossoms. *But you have to be careful—if you press the buds too soon before they're ready, they're not going to open, and in fact they will break off. So timing is everything, plus remembering to always be gentle."*

By now, I was smiling so much that the Tuberose Man was encouraged to continue his lesson. "Here's another secret," he said. "See these little buds that look kind of brown and crusty? They're draining energy and nourishment from the stalk. *You need to pinch off the old buds that didn't bloom so they stop draining the sap, and then the new buds can have more nourishment and open."*

"I had no idea this is what I was supposed to do."

"That's why we have teachers in life," he told me with a wink. "Though I guess most people just think of me as a flower farmer. So, you said you live here in town. You seem like a nice lady. May I ask what you do for a living?"

I smiled back at him. "Well, since you ask, I'm a teacher," I replied, "and I guess you could say I am also a flower farmer. Except my flowers are my students. And what you just taught me to do with the tuberoses is exactly what I've been teaching people to do with themselves so that they can blossom."

"I'll have to think more about that, but it sounds good," the Tuberose Man said.

I paid for my stalks and enthusiastically thanked the farmer. As I said good-bye, I told him that from now on, I was going to share the wisdom he'd taught me about making tuberoses bloom with all of my students, and write about it in my next book. *And so I have, and so I did.*

That day, I realized why I'd always loved tuberoses. I must have unconsciously sensed that they contained a powerful teaching about transformation.

Even the humble flower delights in being a teacher . . .

So we return to where we began, to our sacred questions:

How do we rebirth ourselves? How do we move through our Divine Discomfort? How do we prepare ourselves to make our cosmic deliveries? How do we proceed more rapidly, not eventually but now, down the road toward our freedom? And once we are awake, what do we do to fully blossom?

Tuberose wisdom offers us the answer. We need to pinch off the old, dry, stagnant parts of ourselves that are draining the energy and nourishment from our entire being. **Our intention to grow isn't enough—we have to learn how to locate what is no longer serving us energetically,** those things sucking the nectar from the garden of our soul, and remove them. Then, we need to redirect that energy of the life force so that it can flow where it is needed, to those parts of us waiting for new nourishment in order to blossom.

At the same time that we're letting go, we need to be helping ourselves open. We learn to look for those places that are ready to shift, just like the buds on the verge of blossoming. *Soul Shifts* will teach us how to stare at what appear to be walls until we see the hidden doorways, how to gently push against those places ready to open, how to understand divine timing, and be on the lookout for the signs of a transformation in progress so that we can align ourselves with it, and bloom.

Wisdom is everywhere.
Opportunities for revelation are everywhere.
Soul Shifts can happen anywhere, if we are open to the wisdom
that is waiting to reveal itself to us.

The more we wake up, the more we will have
the wondrous experience that everything and everyone
is somehow mysteriously conspiring to cooperate with
our ultimate awakening.

"Yesterday I was clever, so I wanted to change the world.
Today I am wise, so I am changing myself."
— Attributed to Rumi

Whether on a metaphysical mountaintop in Sedona, a midnight drive on a Mumbai highway, a farmers' market in Santa Barbara, or wherever you are right now, your Cosmic Curriculum is already waiting and ready for you. As you cross threshold after threshold on these pages, you will discover your own inner temple of wisdom, and arrive at the true destination of this Soul Shifts journey, which is nothing less than your own wholeness, fulfillment, and freedom.

Stepping over the threshold,
May all you know you are seeking,
     and all that you don't yet know you are seeking
Be waiting to joyfully greet you on the other side,
     welcoming you back Home . . .

❧ 2 ❧

Turning Walls into Doors:
Shifting from a Seeker to a Seer

"He who knows others is wise,
But he who knows himself is enlightened.
He who overcomes others is strong,
But he who overcomes himself is mightier still."

— Lao-tzu

Everyone is a seeker. Even those people who don't consider themselves seekers spend their lives seeking. We seek power, success, money, advancement, relationships, possessions, and prestige. We seek to acquire things, accomplish things, do things, and experience things. We seek love, happiness, respect, acceptance, agreement, and admiration. We seek justice, forgiveness, redemption, recognition, approval, and praise. If we consider ourselves spiritual seekers, we also seek enlightenment, inner peace, wisdom, answers, revelation, and connection with God or Spirit.

To truly be fulfilled and free in this life, however, **we have to make an important Soul Shift from just *seeking* to *seeing*.**

Seven years ago, during a time of deep introspection and awakening, I was away teaching an advanced seminar, and after a long day of work, I fell into a deep sleep. That night I had a profound and life-changing Soul Shift dream.

As the dream began, I found myself in the midst of a very complicated and difficult obstacle course. I didn't remember why I had to go through the obstacle course, but somehow I knew I had no choice. There were large hurdles I had to jump over, mazes I had to find my way out of, and holes I had to avoid falling into. It was all very hard, but I kept going.

All of a sudden, I came to this enormous structure made of wood and steel that rose high up into the sky. It was so tall that I couldn't see the top of it, as if it just went on and on forever. It was so wide that I couldn't see where it ended on either side of me.

I knew that I had to get to the other side of the wall, and that it was a matter of life and death. I couldn't go back to where I'd come from, so I had to go forward. I also knew that something miraculous would occur if I could get beyond this obstacle, that something amazing was on the other side waiting for me, but that a terrible tragedy would take place if I stayed where I was. I became very frightened because I could not imagine how I'd be able to accomplish this impossible task.

I approached the enormous wall, and as I got close enough I saw that embedded into it were little looped ropes hanging down like footholds or handholds. *I guess this is how I have to climb up,* I thought. So I began to climb up the wall, looking for places to put my feet and hands as I slowly inched higher and higher.

For a while, even though my climb was treacherous, I was making progress. Soon, however, as I got to a certain height, I noticed that there were fewer and fewer of the little looped ropes I was using to climb, and I began to worry. Then I got to a place on the wall where the footholds and handholds completely disappeared, and I was stuck. There was nowhere to put my feet. There was nothing to hold on to. I thought to myself, *This must be a mistake. I know I'm supposed to climb up. I have to go over the wall and get to the other side! I must be going up the wrong part of the wall. I need to climb back down and find a better spot.*

I climbed all the way back down the wall to the bottom, just as I'd climbed up. I was exhausted, but I walked for a while to another section of the wall that looked promising, and started to climb all over again. Everything happened exactly the same as before. I'd climb up to a certain height, and all of a sudden the ropes would disappear. I'd be stuck and have to climb back down, and start again somewhere else. Over and over I tried other sections of the wall. Over and over I would get to the same spot with no ropes, and feel total despair.

Then, as I was about to start climbing up yet again, I heard a mystical voice in the dream say to me: "**This time when the ropes disappear, look more carefully.**" I didn't know where the voice came from, or what the message meant. I just knew I could not stop. With my last ounce of strength, I began climbing until I got to the place where there was nothing for me to hang on to, and I couldn't go any farther without backtracking again.

I remembered what the mysterious voice had said to me: *"This time when the ropes disappear, look more carefully."* I looked up above me as carefully as I could, but didn't see any ropes. I looked to the sides as carefully as I could, but didn't see any ropes. I was about to give up and surrender to whatever horrible fate I felt certain was waiting for me. "Look more carefully," I kept repeating to myself, when it dawned on me that I hadn't looked directly in front of me at the wall I was facing and clinging to.

I took a deep breath, and stared carefully at the space before me. There in the wall, where before I'd thought was nothing, I saw a tiny, tiny crack. And to my amazement, there in the crack was a tiny key. Then I realized that a few inches over, practically invisible, was a tiny keyhole.

In the dream, the voice appeared again and, with so much kindness, said:

> **"Dear one, this isn't a wall—it's a door.**
> **This isn't a wall—it's a door."**

All at once, deep within my heart, I understood the truth of what I hadn't seen before: ***The wall was not there for me to climb over, but to go through!* It looked like a wall, but it had been a doorway all along. It appeared to be solid and impenetrable, but if I had the right key, it would open.**

I took the tiny key in my hand, placed it into the tiny keyhole, and opened what I had thought was a wall but was really a door. *Instantly, the wall vanished, and I was flooded with ecstasy and bliss and radiant light. There was nothing but light. There was nothing but love. I was light and love.*

And then, I woke up.

As I came back into present time, in my body, in my bed, in my house, in this life, I instantly knew that I had just undergone a powerful inner initiation, and received a profound teaching from my own invisible guides and masters. **The dream was a gift, a Soul Shift. The dream itself *was* the key.** And now I offer that key to you.

SOUL SHIFT

SHIFT FROM SEEKING TO SEEING

Many of us live just as I was functioning in my dream. We see life as a series of obstacles to be surmounted, climbed over, dominated, vanquished, worked around. We set our goals and then go about seeking to accomplish them, just as I set out to climb over the wall.

In my dream, I was seeking to get to the other side of the wall, but I was approaching it in the wrong way. *I didn't realize that there were doorways in the wall, because I wasn't looking for them. I wasn't actually looking for anything at all because I was too busy trying to reach my goal. I was seeking a result—to climb over the wall.* When I failed, I tried seeking in a different way from a different place, and failed again. Only when I listened to the voice and the message it offered me did I stop seeking and start seeing, and that's when the profound opening took place. **I had to shift from being just a seeker to becoming a seer.**

The walls that you think are in front of you right now are not walls—they are doorways. You're not meant to go over them, or around them, but rather you need to go through them.

> **We think we need to climb over our obstacles**
> **and challenges, to seek ways to conquer them,**
> **but actually, we need to go through them.**
> **We need to see the doorways hidden in the wall.**
> **We need to shift from being just a seeker to being a seer.**

The very issues you would like to get rid of are doorways to tremendous wisdom about yourself, tremendous healing, and tremendous freedom. They are not blockages or walls to be cursed, fought with, or wrestled to the ground. They're to be moved into, and to be moved through.

*"It is not the easy or convenient life for which I search,
but life lived to the edge of all that I may be."*
— Mary Anne Radmacher

One bright and sunny day in the middle of the ocean, two young fish were swimming along looking forward to the yummy breakfast of algae they were about to consume, and chatting about fish types of things.

An older fish was swimming by in the other direction, and being a gentleman, decided to be polite to the youngsters and greet them. "Good day, fellows," he said as he swam past them. "How's the water?"

The two young fish didn't respond to the older fish, and swam on for a while in silence. Eventually, one of them looked over at the other and said, "What the heck is water?"

I heard a version of this story many years ago. The person told it as a joke, but I experienced it as something much more significant. For me, it illustrates that our true journey of awakening and self-discovery always begins when we first realize that we aren't sure where we are, or who we are, or why our life looks like it does. *First we have to wake up and see what it is that we haven't been seeing.*

> **Until we wake up and begin to be conscious,
> we don't realize how much unconsciousness
> we've been living with.
> Realizing that you've been lost
> is the first step toward being found.**

This process of discovering that you have wandered far from home *is* the journey home. The grief of asking, "What happened? How did I get into such forgetfulness? How did I stray off the path?" is the first turn toward the road to freedom. When you realize it, it's already passing. Like the fish, when you don't realize that you are in water, you can't have the thought, *Why am I in the water?* You're just in it.

When you ask what the heck is water, you're beginning to realize that you've been swimming in something you didn't even know existed. *You're no longer just seeking—you are seeing.*

"Why have I been disconnected?" *is* the beginning of connection.

"Why have I been so stuck?" *is* the beginning of being unstuck.

"Why do I avoid facing the truth?" *is* the beginning of the truth.

"Why is it so difficult for me to love?" *is* the beginning of love.

*"People travel to wonder at the heights of mountains,
at the huge waves of the sea, at the long courses of the rivers,
at the vast compass of the ocean, at the circular motions of the stars,
and yet they pass by themselves without wondering."*
— Saint Augustine

A while ago I was watching a beautiful documentary about one of the world's greatest cellists, Yo-Yo Ma. Perhaps you've seen him perform on television or in person, as I've been privileged to do. He is a musical genius who possesses a loving and expansive spirit. In this interview he said something profound and important:

"Every day I make an effort to go toward what I don't understand."

When I shared this with a group of my advanced students, they humorously confessed what their mottos used to be before doing this work:

"Every day I try to run from what I don't understand."

"Every day I try to cover up what I don't understand."

"Every day I pretend to understand what I don't understand, and hope no one notices."

These are funny, but unfortunately true—*most of us do not run toward what we don't understand about ourselves, but away from it.* We become impatient with what we don't understand, or resistant to what we don't understand, or frightened of what we don't understand. Sometimes we pretend that what we don't understand doesn't exist, even when someone else points out to us that we seem to be uncomfortable.

We're going in the wrong direction. **Something is calling to us when we feel an inner discomfort. Something is asking us to address it, to see it. We must not ignore it. It is a signal. It is a doorway. In fact, it is a bridge.**

SOUL SHIFT

SHIFT FROM MODULATING YOUR SEEING TO SEEING EVERYTHING

Recently, I took a flight from San Francisco to my home in Santa Barbara. I boarded the plane, and settled into my assigned seat next to the window. It's a beautiful ride when you fly down the coast of California, because you see the mountains and the ocean, and I always enjoy looking out at the spectacular view.

As the plane took off and circled around the city, my attention became drawn to the man sitting in the seat directly in front of me, who was behaving in a very odd manner. His window shade was pulled down almost to the bottom, with only a few inches of the glass showing. And yet this fellow had hunched over with his head bent sideways, straining to peer out the window through the four-inch section.

Perhaps he's about to go to sleep and just wants to catch a quick peek at the view, I thought to myself. To my amazement, however, the man remained just like that, bent over and craning his neck in the most uncomfortable manner so he could look out through the narrow slit of glass not covered by the shade. By this time, I had forgotten all about looking out of my own window, transfixed by this bizarre scenario. I just couldn't make sense of what I was seeing.

My mind began to try to solve this mystery with a series of ridiculous explanations: *Maybe he's from another country and doesn't understand how to pull a window shade up. Maybe he has a disability and cannot use his hands. Maybe he's never been on a plane before. Maybe he is a contortionist in a circus act.* These theories were all nixed when the flight attendant asked him if he wanted her to pull his shade up, and he assured her in perfect English that it was fine the way it was. I saw him take out his iPod and put in his earbuds, so I knew that his hands were functional. What was going on?

Time passed, and this fellow remained in his tilted, twisty position, looking out the tiny slice of window. The longer I watched him in that uncomfortable posture, the more uncomfortable I became! To make it worse, each time he adjusted his bizarre position, he banged against my seat.

Now I began willing him to take action: *"Put your shade up. Please! Put your shade up,"* I silently broadcasted with my most powerful inner voice. I tried visualizing him lifting the shade up. *Nothing.* Finally, mercifully, the hour flight was over. This fellow had never lifted the shade, and yet had stared out of the tiny opening for the entire duration of the trip. As we stood up to leave, I looked at him to see if I could gain any insight into the baffling situation, but he was a completely normal-looking young man wearing jeans and a backpack.

Suddenly, I realized what I'd been seeing, and why it had such a powerful effect on me. This incident had illustrated how so many people live their lives. *We lower the shade of our perception, of our willingness to see. We look at situations through a small sliver of consciousness and wonder why we feel lost or confused.* **We forget that we can pull the shade up.**

**Many of us live our lives with
the shade of awareness pulled down,
the shade that covers up the window of truth,
the window of seeing, the window of feeling.**

**Rather than lifting our shade up,
we shape-shift and contort ourselves
to try to look out at where we are
through the narrow slit of the truth,
the narrow slit of our limitations,
rather than just pulling the shade up.**

It simply didn't dawn on the man to lift up the shade so he'd be more comfortable. Like this, it often simply doesn't dawn on us to widen our view so we can see more of what there is to see, or to realize that what we think we're seeing may only be a very limited perception of the wholeness that exists.

At times, we do have the thought *"I have a feeling I should raise my shade, but I'm not sure how to go about it,"* or *"I know it's time to raise my shade, but I'm afraid if I do, I won't like what I see, so I'm going to keep it down."*

The result is that we condemn ourselves to being hunched over, strained, uncomfortable in how we live, how we relate, how we do everything.

Perhaps you grew up with a lowered shade. Maybe somebody lowered it by telling you who you were or weren't, what you were allowed to see and feel, or what it wasn't safe to express. Maybe you lowered your own shade at some point in your life to protect yourself, because you didn't want to face the pain of seeing what was going on in your childhood, or later, with someone you loved. Maybe you've kept your shade down to avoid confronting circumstances in your life that you know need to change, or that are daunting for you to face.

It is natural to protect ourselves by turning away from pain or discomfort. **The problem is we forget that we put our shade down, and like the passenger on the airplane, we think that it's perfectly normal to keep seeing life through the tiny slit of consciousness that we've allowed ourselves.**

I always say that teachers are everywhere if we are ready to recognize them. I am very grateful to that passenger for demonstrating this principle to me, one I have since shared with tens of thousands of people, and am now sharing with you. Thank goodness my own shade of consciousness was pulled all the way up so I could see and receive the delightful gift of a teaching gateway that Cosmic Intelligence was offering me that day!

The journey of this book is designed to help you raise your shade so that you can see more of what there is for you to see, and *begin to live not just as a seeker, but as a seer.* You can begin now by looking at your relationship with your "shade of perception." Maybe you can already feel your shade inching up higher even as you've taken in these words!

Here are some questions for study, journaling, discussion, and contemplation that will serve you as a Soul Shift Gateway:

Soul Shift Gateway Questions

In what areas of my life is the shade pulled down?

How long has it been down?

When did I pull it down?

Why did I pull it down?

When I have my shade pulled up,
what kinds of things happen that make me
quickly pull it down?

What do I tell myself would happen
if I raised the shade all the way up?

What am I afraid I would see if my shade
was pulled all the way up all the time?

Am I comfortable with people whose shades
are pulled up higher than my own?

Do I keep my shade down in order to make people
more comfortable around me?

WHAT YOU CAN SEE, YOU CAN SHIFT

"We usually don't look. We overlook."
— Alan Watts

"You are awesome!"

I had just given a speech at a business conference a few years ago and was on my way back to the workshop I was offering when a man standing nearby passionately shouted those words out, and began quickly walking toward me. "I mean it—you're awesome!" he repeated with a huge smile. "I'm your biggest fan, and I'm so excited to be able to learn from you in person. Your talk was a home run!"

"Thank you," I replied. "I'm glad you feel that way. I'm on my way to the workshop, so since we're both going there, you're welcome to walk with me."

"Oh no, I'm not attending the workshop," he said almost proudly. "I'm what you'd call a 'get-it-done' kind of guy. I'm not much into spending time trying to understand things about myself or see into myself. I'm into action! I'm into results! I'm into progress! Anyway, it was great meeting you, and don't forget: *You're awesome!*"

Many of us are just like "Mr. Awesome"—*we like the idea of being a seeker, but we don't want to be a seer.* We like the idea of transformation, of living a bigger, more successful life, and tell ourselves we are ready for a shift, but we want to bypass that which is required in order for us to make truly authentic shifts: *Before we shift, we have to see.*

Before you can accurately consider what you want to shift about yourself or your life, something else has to take place: *You have to see.*

What you can see, you can shift.

Here is how shifting works:

First, we become courageous enough to raise our shade of consciousness, or perception; *we see what there is to see* about ourselves, or a situation. Next, *we feel how we feel* about what we see, and then we get motivated to shift. This is how it works. We see. We feel how we feel about seeing. And then we say, "Okay, I'm ready to shift it."

What's the opposite?

What you can't see, you can't shift.

What you can't see, for instance, about your business and how you're running it, you can't shift. What you can't see about what is creating emotional collisions in a relationship, you can't shift. What you can't see about yourself, you can't shift.

Put this way, it sounds so obvious. It only makes sense that, in order to know what to shift, we have to be willing to see what is not balanced, not in alignment with our Highest, and not serving us. Whether we realize it or not, *our resistance and reluctance to seeing our self and our life with total honesty and clarity will inevitably create a resistance to shifting and transforming.* It won't serve us to have an attitude like the one expressed by Mr. Awesome: "I want to shift, but I don't want to see." We must make the Soul Shift from seeker to seer.

> When we have the attitude of
> "I don't want to see anything,
> I don't want to look at the truth,"
> it is as if we are saying,
> "I don't want to shift. I don't want to grow.
> I don't want to expand.
> I don't want to be free."

Some of us, as we'll see, were psychologically programmed in such a way that, in order to emotionally survive, we had to not see. *Often we had to stop seeing things as children that we could do nothing about—except we forgot that we've turned off our seeing, and that we need to turn it back on again so we can rediscover our knowingness, our power, our ability to engage fully with the world.*

To begin making this Soul Shift from seeker to seer, we can remind ourselves that seeing is grace. Shedding light on yourself is grace. Is it uncomfortable temporarily? Sometimes. Is it more uncomfortable and treacherous to live in the dark? Absolutely.

Here's a question to contemplate: ***Do you get in trouble in life and make more mistakes because of what you don't see, or because of what you do see?*** Think about this for a moment. Of course, we know the answer: All of us have been hurt more, suffered more, or misstepped more because of what we have not seen, not faced, and not dealt with. We've all had experiences of this in the physical world—we don't see our child's toy on the floor and trip on it; we don't notice a hole in the concrete sidewalk and stumble. We get hurt because of what we cannot or did not see.

> Wanting *not* to see is dangerous.
> What you can't see controls your life,
> and is the cause of much of your suffering.

How many times have you found yourself saying, *"I didn't see it coming." "I didn't see that he was lying." ""I didn't see that she really just wanted my money." "I didn't see that my boss was threatened by me." "I didn't see that company had no room for growth." "I didn't see that she was working against me behind my back."* And because you didn't see it, something undesirable happened.

None of us would feel comfortable wandering around in the dark without a flashlight, or walking down a completely unlit street in a strange neighborhood. In the same way, it's natural to be reluctant to venture into the house of our consciousness and our inner being when we feel that we will be stumbling around in the dark. It is natural to have an aversion to raising our shade of perception to see and explore ourselves if we fear that we won't be able to safely navigate in a place that seems poorly lit, shadowy, and unknown. Of course we're afraid to proceed into what we cannot see without enough light.

How many times in your life have you traveled a path that was not well lit—not a physical path, but a relationship, a career choice, or an important decision? It was like going down an emotional dark lane inside yourself without the comfort of any illumination. Danger awaited you on the dark roads of the heart and the mind if you were not guided by light. *How many times in your life have you stumbled because there was not enough inner light, inner consciousness, inner wisdom?*

**We need as much light as possible
so that we don't stumble on the path of growth.**

The Soul Shifts Mantra

In my dream about the wall, the voice guided me to look more closely, and I was given the key that allowed me to move through the wall by discovering the doorway I hadn't known existed. Now, it's time for me to offer you a very powerful vibrational key that I call "the Soul Shifts Mantra."

Mantra is a Sanskrit word describing sacred syllables or sounds that, when recited or used in silent meditation, have a profound vibrational impact on the practitioner. The word contains the root *man*, which means "to think" or "meditate" or "the mind," and the suffix *tra*, which refers to the idea of instrumentality, or a "vehicle" or "tool." So a mantra could be thought of as *an instrument or tool for thought, contemplation, and meditation.*

A disclaimer: Over 40 years ago when I began my practice of meditation, the word *mantra* was something I had only heard from my own spiritual teacher, and was certainly not part of our popular culture. To me it was and still is something incredibly sacred, and my own rituals include traditional mantra repetition. These days, I always have mixed feelings as I see "mantra" used in TV commercials, discussions about the stock market, and just about everywhere in a very colloquial way. Yet I realize that it has come to mean something much more general and secular, that most people understand it to be like a "saying," so I am using it in that way here.

Here is the Soul Shifts Mantra:

TODAY I AM GOING TO SEE WHAT THERE IS TO SEE, TO FEEL WHAT THERE IS TO FEEL, AND TO KNOW WHAT THERE IS TO KNOW.

The Soul Shifts Mantra is a map of understanding for you to work with in your life. It is a credo and a tool, and the most powerful technique I'll be offering that you can use as a practice for recalibrating your consciousness. *It serves as a powerful Gateway—a vibrational door through which you can pass that will lead you to places of truth, authenticity, and freedom.*

This is the core practice used by all of my advanced students. By *practice,* I do *not* mean these words are supposed to be chanted or repeated like a mantra or thought you'd use in meditation, or proclaimed as positive affirmations. *This is definitely not what this is meant for.* Think of it more like a phrase of commitment and intention you can use to point yourself in the right direction on your journey.

My experience, however, and that of so many students who have used this, is that these are not just words. **They are vibrational keys that will make it easier for you to raise your window shade and find the doorway in the wall.**

Let's explore each part of the Soul Shifts Mantra:

"Today I am going to see what there is to see"

"Going to" means that I am committing to seeing. This is why it is phrased this way. "Going to see" means something different from "I will try to see, I will do my best to remember to see, I might see if I feel like it." These are all conditional statements. *But "I am going to see" is not a hope, or even an intention—it is unconditional.* The vibration of those words elicits something different in you. Can you feel that? Say, "I am *going* to see" out loud, and emphasize the word *going.* It is an empowering energy that takes your inner will and purposefulness and moves it out into action. You are making a promise to yourself.

"What there is" means just that—*whatever* there is that I need to see, whatever there is that I am confronted with, whatever is happening, I will see it. This includes things I haven't wanted to see, things that have been trying to get my attention, things that will emerge throughout the day and poke at my awareness hoping I notice them. That is the "what." It is neutral.

It means I will not pick and choose what I see based on whether or not I like it. It means I won't just allow myself to see those things that aren't challenging to see, but I will stop ignoring and pretending that I don't see what is upsetting to me. **To see what there is to see means to be open to seeing, but with no judgment, no prejudice, no editing, no resistance, no pushback. No matter what, I *will* see it. Even if it collides with my self-image or what I've been telling myself is true, I *will* see it. Even if it scares me, I *will* see it.**

First, I'm going to see what there is to see about myself. I'll pay attention to what's going on within me, how I behave, the choices I make, how I act and react.

I'm also going to see what there is to see about everyone around me—wisdom they have to offer me, reactions they have to what I've done, behavior I notice that I can learn from—*everything.*

"To feel what there is to feel"

I am going to feel *what* there is to feel, whatever it is. This follows the same pattern as the first phrase we just analyzed. **It means not to pick and choose what I am going to feel.** It means not to just feel what is enjoyable, or *not* scary or uncomfortable, but to feel it all. *It means not to* *notice what wants to be felt and push it down or away; or minimize it, hide from it, or pretend I don't feel it.* It means not to try to drown out the fire of what I am feeling by drenching the emotions with my intellect's excuses, rationales, and reasons.

It means to embrace whatever I am feeling, to allow the energy of that feeling to move through me and out of me. It means to invite my feelings to reveal themselves to me for the purpose of helping me to see more, understand more, and course correct whenever necessary. **It means to have the courage to feel everything, and to remember that it is only by feeling things that we can heal them, and transmute them into love and wisdom.**

Later on I'll share more with you about the kind of "seeing" that the heart does. To really be accurate I'd have to say that *what takes place when we allow ourselves to fully "see what there is to see" in any given moment is that we will also be seeing what is happening in our heart.* That "seeing" of the heart's events will automatically tune us into "feeling what there is to feel."

"And to know what there is to know"

This part of our mantra is the result of the first two phrases. First I need to see what there is to see. Once I see what that is, I can notice how I feel about it. Then, when I am conscious of how I feel about what I'm seeing, I will have automatically arrived at a place of knowing. I allow my seeing and feeling to come together in a profound alchemy, out of which knowingness naturally arises.

"To know what there is to know" doesn't mean coming to an understanding from your mind or intellect. It is not the same as "figuring something out."

When you see enough and feel enough,
knowingness will spontaneously rise up within you.
Your Soul Shifts will come because of
your willingness to see and feel,
and the wisdom that what you see and feel produces.

Many people live by a different commitment mantra. I call it the "anti–Soul Shifts mantra":

"Today I am going to *totally ignore everything that is unpleasant or uncomfortable, completely shut off anything I feel that upsets or disturbs me, and pretend that I don't know what's going on with me or with those around me as much as I possibly can."*

Perhaps this sounds painfully familiar? Maybe it is how you used to live, or are trying to shift from living now. Maybe it is how someone you know lives. It is sad but true that literally billions of people go through each day this way: *I am not looking at that, not dealing with that either, nope, not feeling that, whoa, I definitely don't want to go there . . .*

Here's something important to bring into our contemplation:

**When you have the intention that you don't want to see,
you don't want to feel, and you don't want to know,
then your mind, your will, and your choices
structure your life to cooperate with this
intention to be unconscious.**

When you don't want to look at things, you need to create habits and activities that will successfully keep you from seeing, feeling, and knowing. So you might eat too much, drink too much, sleep too much, shop too much, party too much, distract too much, rescue too much, exercise too much, argue too much, and dramatize too much. Who has time to see or feel with all of this going on?

I'm not judging these behaviors. I'm simply pointing out that they'll become increasingly necessary and difficult to let go of if they are serving your unconscious intention to not see what there is to see, feel what there is to feel, and know what there is to know.

Sometimes you may find that you've attracted people into your life who you know will cooperate with your not seeing, not feeling, and not knowing. After all, if you don't want to see, feel, and know, you're not going to hang around with somebody who wants to do those things, correct? Even the environments in which we choose to work, the friends with whom we choose to spend time, and the activities or hobbies in which we engage *may* reflect our own willingness or unwillingness to see, feel, and know.

Using the Soul Shifts Mantra

The Soul Shifts Mantra might seem deceptively simple, but I assure you that it is a powerful transformational Gateway. **The verbal commitment to see, feel, and know instantly raises your window shade of** consciousness, opens your heart, and recalibrates you in profound and essential ways.

I invite you to begin using the "SSM," as my students call it, as one of your first Soul Shifts Practices. Here are some suggestions:

* **Each morning before starting your day, take a moment to read the SSM and, if possible, to speak it out loud.** Start by taking a few deep breaths. Think carefully and deeply about the meaning and intention behind each phrase as you read or recite it slowly and deliberately. You may do this several times if you wish. Three recitations builds up strong energy.

Remember—the words aren't magical. Saying them without feeling and awareness won't do anything. *This is not an affirmation. It is a verbal Vibrational Gateway that will realign you to your Highest Self.*

* **Keep the Soul Shifts Mantra in your consciousness by placing reminders of it where you can easily see them—on your computer screen, on your desk at work, on your refrigerator, in your car, anywhere.** I've included a graphic template of the SSM at the back of the book if you'd like to make copies to place wherever you wish.

* **Whenever you're feeling stressed, confused, upset, or frightened, you can use your SSM** *to help you see and feel and know more clearly what is actually happening.* Follow the same procedure I offered for the morning, but change the words in the first phrase from "today" to *"right now."* This will pull your own energy of consciousness into the moment, and steady you:

> *Right now,* **I am going to see what there is to see,**
> **to feel what there is to feel,**
> **and to know what there is to know.**

I've had students tell me stories about doing the SSM while driving to an important business presentation, in a restaurant restroom during a first date, in the waiting room of a hospital during an emergency, and in every other possible situation. I've heard of couples stopping themselves as a conversation begins to escalate into an argument, taking each other's hands, and saying the words together out loud. You may be surprised to discover how quickly this can lift you up from the swirl of agitation or drama, and bring instant illumination to whatever you are dealing with.

* Children love the Soul Shifts Mantra. Many of my students have introduced the SSM to their families and incorporated it into a ritual with their children. They teach them the words and say them together, and then later on they sit with them and everyone takes a turn sharing what they saw and felt and knew. How wonderful for a child to begin understanding what it means to see what there is to see and feel what there is to feel!

* Use the Soul Shifts Mantra to help you open more fully to high-energy positive experiences. Sometimes we have a difficult time staying open and present when we are interacting with a lot of intense positive energy. We can emotionally "short-circuit" and shut off when we're feeling too much intimacy, excitement, or even happiness. I often receive notes from students who share that they used the SSM to ground themselves right before a big event such as a special vacation, a family celebration, a wedding, or even the birth of a child!

If there's nothing else you take from this book, use this Soul Shifts Mantra. It will bring you back home to yourself.

**Waking up is for the brave.
Becoming a seer, and not just a seeker,
is not for the faint of heart.
It is for the visionaries, the awakeners, the Soul Shifters,
the courageous members of the cosmic advanced team.
It is for you.**

Seeing is not always easy. It isn't particularly pleasant to face the things that we're not happy with about ourselves, or where we're stuck, or what lessons we need to learn. But to authentically shift, transform, and awaken, *we have to see.* Just like in my Soul Shifts dream, once we do, we *will* find the keys to our freedom.

We are blessed to do this work. I am blessed that you are reading these words. We are blessed to be waking up.

From Darkness to Light

*"From the Unreal, lead me to the Real.
From Darkness, lead me to Light.
From Death, lead me to Immortality."*
— Brihadaranyaka Upanishad

In 1968, when I was 17 years old, I came upon this verse from the Brihadaranyaka Upanishad. The Upanishads are a collection of Vedic texts revealed between the 9th and 3rd century B.C. in what we now know as India. The word *Veda* in Sanskrit means "knowledge," and the Vedas are believed to be the oldest spiritual literature in the world. They were originally passed down as an oral tradition until approximately A.D. 1000, and are understood to contain revealed truths about the nature of reality and human existence. The Vedas were composed or revealed by sages known as "Rishis"— divinely inspired seers or poets, whose knowledge was being revealed directly from the Universal Source, or the soul level.

At the time when I first read this verse, I was still in high school. I knew absolutely nothing about Eastern thought or philosophy, and frankly couldn't relate to it. I had yet to meet my own spiritual teacher, or even understand what a spiritual path was. Nonetheless, I immediately felt the power of these words, as if they were mysteriously resonating with something deep inside myself that I'd forgotten—*and of course they were.*

Let's take a closer look at each line of the verse:

"From the Unreal, lead me to the Real"

What is unreal and inaccurate about your perceptions of yourself and the world? What old programming is still operating inside of you that keeps you from seeing clearly? Where is your window shade of consciousness pulled down? What old emotional baggage are you still carrying around? In what ways do you not see how magnificent you are, how much you deserve to be loved? *These things are the unreal.*

From the unreal, lead me to the real—my wisdom, my wholeness, my authenticity, that which is exquisite and untarnished within me.

"From Darkness, lead me to Light"

When the Vedas refer to darkness and light, they mean ignorance and true knowledge. Ignorance comes from unconsciousness, those habits that drag us from our natural state of love and expansion into the darkness of limitation and forgetfulness. Just as darkness obscures light, ignorance and unconsciousness obscure true wisdom and understanding.

When we want to remove the darkness, we bring in the light. When we want to remove ignorance, we bring in truth, not truth we get from a book, or through the mind alone. This truth is the knowledge that arises from "seeing."

From darkness lead me to light: May I see all I need to see so I can live in and *as* the truth.

"From Death, lead me to Immortality"

This isn't about eternal life in the religious sense. Death here means the forgetfulness, the blindness, and the death of understanding that deludes us into thinking we are small, limited, and disconnected from the Great Consciousness.

From that, lead me to remembrance of who I truly am, which will be my freedom. May I fully and permanently awaken from the sleep of forgetfulness.

This is what we're doing on this Soul Shifts journey, shifting from the unreal to the real, and from darkness to light.

First, you ask yourself: *"What is unreal, unnecessary, unsupportive, inaccurate, incorrect about how I see the world, how I see myself and others? Where do these unreal perceptions come from? How can I find the path within me that leads me from the ways I've been identified with what's unreal back to what is real, back to my Highest and most true Self?"*

Next, you ask: *"Where am I in darkness? Where am I suffering or living a less than expanded and fulfilled life because of that darkness? Where has light been shining, but I have turned away from what it's been trying to show me? What can I do to bring in more light so that I can see what there is more clearly?"*

And finally: *"What parts of me have been hidden or dormant, as if dead, and how can I rise up to live in freedom?"*

This is what it means to be a seer!

The more we choose to see,
the more we wake up.

The more we wake up,
the more we discover the truth.

The more we discover the truth,
the more we remember who we really are.

The more we remember who we really are,
the more we become truly free.

Where there once was confusion, may you discover keys.
Where there once were walls, may you discover doors.
Where there once was darkness, may you discover Light.

❧ 3 ❧

From Forgetfulness to Remembrance

"The cosmos is also within us. We are made of star stuff.
We are a way for the cosmos to know itself."
— Carl Sagan

Imagine if someone were to tell you that there was a treasure of an unimaginable worth hidden somewhere on the other side of the world in an unmarked cave deep in an unknown mountain. This person explains that no one else but you has this information, and if you can figure out how to somehow find that location, the treasure will be yours. How would you feel? Frustrated? Confused? Anxious? *Where is the cave? What country is it in? How am I supposed to find it? I want the treasure, but don't even know where to begin looking for it.*

Now, imagine if another person were to come to you with a different story. He announces that buried beneath your house there's a chest containing unimaginable wealth. You don't have to travel anywhere to find it. You don't have to figure out any clues that will reveal its location. You just have to dig, and the riches will be yours.

This second story is true. What, then, is that treasure? **It is your Great Remembrance.** If you're remembering, what is it that you've forgotten? **It's the truth of who you really are: a human container for Divine Cosmic Intelligence.**

The truth is that you are not your body, personality, skills, or talents. The truth of who you are is not even the events of your life, or what you know, or what you've done. The truth of who you are is not the thoughts in your mind, or the emotions in your heart. The truth of who you are transcends all of these things.

Who you think you are is just
the disguise of your individual ego,
your particular costume that serves as
a unique container for the Ultimate Consciousness.

The disguise says, *"This is my name. I live here. I look like this. I do this."* However, something outrageous is underneath the human costume you're wearing. It is your core: Consciousness, Light, Divine Energy, Spirit, God—whatever word you resonate with. Everything you think you are emanates and vibrates out from that center.

If you'd like, let those words and the transmission of this energy come into you now, and touch the deepest part of your soul as you acknowledge to yourself that somehow, you've always known this. *You've always been seeking the Great Remembrance.*

THERE'S NOTHING MISSING INSIDE OF YOU

*"The moment people remember that they've forgotten
is a moment of grace."*
— Barbara De Angelis

When I was a young girl, and in the years that followed, I experienced an inexplicable sensation that something wasn't right about my life: *There's something important that I've forgotten and am supposed to remember. There's something I'm not seeing that I need to see. I feel like something is missing. Maybe other people understand something I don't, or have something I don't. If I could just remember what's missing, or find it, I could be truly happy.*

Perhaps you too have experienced this at some time in your life, **the feeling that you're supposed to remember something or do something, or that things aren't as they should be, but you're not sure what it is that is missing. You want to go "home," but you aren't sure where home is.**

When I began my formal travels on the path of awakening, I realized that what I had been feeling all along was *spiritual homesickness.* Some part of me knew I had forgotten the secret of life and the truth of who I really was. That's what was missing. *I was disconnected from my own wholeness, and trying to find my way back to it.*

My longing was a spiritual longing, not an emotional one. The ultimate truth had somehow been hidden from me, and I knew I needed to find it. *The place I was homesick for wasn't to be found anywhere outside of myself. It was not "there," but right "here."*

This is the second half of the story about the treasure: Some part of you has always sensed it was "here." Some part of you has always felt there was something you'd forgotten. Spiritual wisdom from all traditions tells us that this disconnection from your Highest, this split from your true home of consciousness, this cosmic forgetfulness, is the cause of all of your suffering. In your heart, you know this is true.

> **There's nothing missing inside of you.**
> **We suffer not because of what we don't have**
> **and who we are not,**
> **but because we've forgotten what we do have**
> **and who we are.**

I have a saying: "All ignorance is just memory loss." *I forgot that I'm divine and magnificent. I forgot that I know how to love. I forgot that I have something important to share with the world. I forgot that I have so much wisdom inside of me.* And remembering it is the best feeling in the world. **It's like coming home, because it is coming home.**

SOUL SHIFT

SHIFT FROM SEARCHING TO REMEMBERING

We started our Soul Shifts journey by waking up. Then, we realized we needed to shift from being just a seeker to a seer, and to learn to see what there is to see. Now, what's that first thing we need to see to continue on our journey? It's this:

> **There is nothing we are missing that we need to get.**
> **We just need to remember what we've forgotten.**

The path of awakening is not about finding anything we don't have, but remembering what is already there inside of us. This is the understanding that forms the foundation of my own journey, the heart of my service to others, and the offering of this book.

All transformation is not a search for something, but a return to something you already are. It's a discovery of what is already there and intact inside of you, as you. It is a remembrance of what you truly are as a part of that Great Oneness.

This Soul Shift in understanding radically changes the dynamic of our process of growth. *When we believe we need to find something that we don't have or are missing, we're operating from the assumption that we are deficient. If there is, indeed, something missing, then there's also the possibility that we will fail to locate it. Fear and deficiency fuel us forward.*

When you make the Soul Shift from searching to remembering, you begin to understand and experience that you aren't searching for an unknown destination, but returning back to your wholeness, your home. It is already intact inside of you—it can't *not* be intact! It is impossible that you would be less than divine.

All awakening is remembrance.
You're not trying to change into something you're not.
You're not searching for something you've never had.

You're rediscovering the wholeness of who you really are.
You're retrieving something you forgot that you lost,
and remembering that you had it all along.

Have you ever seen ads for those companies that help people find money they've forgotten about? They pitch the idea that we all have bank accounts we forgot existed, investments we've never cashed in, or refunds we've never collected. There's always a photo of someone cheerfully claiming, "The XYZ Company helped me find $1,500 I didn't even know I had!"

You're probably thinking, "This can't be for real—who could forget about their money? Who could have something valuable somewhere that they didn't remember?" The answer to that question is: You could! You have a great treasure located within you waiting to be claimed. **So one way to look at the path of personal transformation is that you're remembering and locating your misplaced cosmic assets, and reconnecting yourself with your lost cosmic bank accounts.**

THE GREAT RETURN

One of the first lectures I heard when I was just beginning my spiritual path as a teenager was called *"The Path of the Great Return."* I didn't know what it meant at the time, but it sounded exotic and exciting! And it is.

The spirituality of the East often uses the phrase "the Path of the Great Return" to refer to our soul journey. Are you beginning to understand what the Great Return is? It's returning to your cosmic center, returning to your wholeness, which is not far away, but is your very essence. *It is the journey home.*

Most people have had glimpses of this. Perhaps you're sitting in prayer or meditation, or taking a quiet walk, or lying next to someone you love, or holding your child in your arms, or listening to your church choir, or stroking your cat or dog, or gazing out at a spectacular moment in nature—when all of a sudden you feel as if you have just expanded out from who you normally are, melting into something greater, something exquisite. Waves of peace, love, and knowingness wash over you without being prompted by any particular thoughts. *In fact, you're not thinking at all—you're just being.*

**When sacred moments occur, it is usually because,
for a mysterious moment, you "forget your forgetfulness"
and experience remembrance.
You transcend the limitations of
your own container of consciousness,
and become consciousness itself.**

I remember the first time I experienced this remembrance, this expansion into consciousness. I was 18 years old, and had just been initiated into my meditation practice. I was sitting with my eyes closed, and distinctly remember thinking, *This is outrageous. I feel so blissful. But the strange thing is that it feels perfectly normal. In fact, this is the most normal I've ever felt.*

For the first time in my life, I didn't feel like anything was missing; *I had temporarily bypassed the forgetfulness of my limitations, and slipped into remembrance.* At last, I had finally glimpsed the truth of my soul, and my overjoyed heart sighed in relief and whispered, "There you are."

In that moment, I had shifted my identification from being the individual container of consciousness known as "Barbara" to being the consciousness that was contained within it. Nothing had actually changed. It was just a shift in identification.

All spiritual transformation and awakening is just a shift in identification— not an intellectual shift, but a vibrational shift.

That first experience of connecting with my Highest Self didn't occur because I made a shift in thinking. It didn't happen because I was telling myself, "I am divine." It was not an understanding or a mood, but a vibrational reality. *It was an actual experience of vibrating with my wholeness rather than vibrating as my limitations.*

All authentic transformation is just this: a shift in identification from who you thought you were to who you are in your fullness, a shift from forgetfulness to remembrance. This is why it is called the Great Return, and *why I say that the path of growth is more about undoing than it is about doing.* We learn how to undo our forgetfulness, undo our numbness, undo our habit of contraction that is keeping us from experiencing our true nature as expansive. Once you undo and remove the layers that have covered up your wholeness, you reveal the radiant consciousness that was always underneath.

We'll talk much more throughout the book about how to shift your identification. This is such an important Soul Shift concept. It answers the question we often ask ourselves about why we feel something is wrong with us. Here's how I put it to my students:

All suffering is a case of mistaken identity!

Matted Over: Uncovering Your Shimmer

Recently, I wanted to update some of the woodwork in my house, and decided to have it painted a beautiful, glowing, golden color. I hired someone to help supervise the project while I was traveling, and before I left, we painted a section with special metallic gold paint to make sure the color was what I envisioned, and it looked beautiful. I left to teach a seminar and was excited to receive a message that the painters had finished the job, and it would be ready by the time I returned. I arrived home very late at night, tired but looking forward to seeing my newly painted wood.

As soon as I walked in the front door, I knew something was wrong. The soft gold color looked drab and dull, and had none of the gleaming shine of the sample. *Maybe I'm just too exhausted to evaluate it properly,* I thought. *I'll see what it looks like in the morning.* However, when I woke up and looked at the paint in the light, it appeared just as dull as it had the night before.

I called the person I'd hired to help me, and explained what was going on. "It's not right," I said. "It has no shine and looks muddy."

"That's impossible," he replied. "I was there myself while they put on the first and second coats of paint, and it looked exactly like the sample section we painted."

"What about the third coat?" I asked. "Did you see them paint it?"

"No," he admitted, "but they used the same paint, so I can't imagine what went wrong. Let me come over and take a look." He arrived at my home, and immediately saw what I was talking about. "You're right," he agreed. "It really is dull. All I can think is that it was a defective can of paint."

"I just know that the painters did something different for the third coat," I insisted. "I get feelings about these things, and I'm usually not wrong."

"I believe you," he said, "but it is a mystery to me. I even called the painters, and they absolutely insisted that they did three coats."

Suddenly, I had a thought. "Did the painters buy a new batch of paint at some point?"

"Yes, I believe the head of the crew told me they needed a few cans at the end to finish the job." He went to the garage and came back with a paint can. "Look," he said. "It's the same paint they used for the first two coats, and the same color."

"Let me see it." I took the paint can from him and read the label. It said METALLIC PAINT—CHAMPAGNE, which was correct. But just underneath, instead of SHIMMER, I saw the word MATTE.

"Kevin, do you see this? I knew I wasn't imagining it. They bought matte paint instead of shimmer. No wonder it looks dull."

Sure enough, when Kevin called the painter back, he admitted that he'd sent his younger brother to the store with the empty paint can so he could buy more. Obviously, the brother grabbed a can that looked just like the one he had with him, but neglected to read the label. Then the painters proceeded to go over all the wood with matte paint, covering the beautiful shimmer.

I'd solved the mystery, and of course the painters redid the wood with another coat of the correct paint. As I stood there on the day they left, admiring the gorgeous glow from the wood, I suddenly realized what a great wisdom lesson had emerged right before my eyes.

We are all from the same shimmering Source. We are light and glowing and radiant. We are meant to shimmer. As we'll see, however, our true shine becomes covered up with dullness. It's still there underneath, but we can't see it, and no one else can either. Sometimes if we work hard to dig down into a section, a little bit of the shimmer shines through, and in that moment, we get a glimpse of who we really are. Then we look at everything else about our self that still looks matted, and go back into forgetfulness.

There is nothing missing in you.
Your original shimmer simply got covered up,
but it is still there.

I am so grateful to whatever cosmic helpers orchestrated the painting "mistake" that was actually a great gift of wisdom. Every day I look at my glowing wood, and feel so blessed to be on this journey of uncovering my own soul's shimmer, and to have the privilege of teaching so many others how to uncover theirs.

TRANSFORMATION IS AN EXPERIENTIAL EVENT

"The search for wisdom is a great challenge:
to act on wisdom is an even greater challenge."
— Jagad Guru Siddhaswarupananda

How do we go from matte to shimmer?
How do we travel from forgetfulness back to remembrance?
How do we shift our identification?
How do we restore ourselves to wholeness?
The answer is contained in our next important Soul Shift, and it's the foundation for the rest of this book.

SOUL SHIFT

SHIFT FROM THINKING ABOUT TRANSFORMATION TO LIVING IT

Transformation is an experiential event—actually a long series of events. It's not a new way of looking at life. It's not a new collection of information. It's not a more enlightened way of behaving or living that you try to adopt, like changing your diet or deciding you're going to be nicer to people. Nothing is wrong with these intentions or choices, but they are not the same as transformation.

True transformation isn't something you understand. *You do it.*
It's not about feeling better. It's about *being* better.
It's about your consciousness actually shifting vibrationally.

It may sound so elementary to say this, *but your life actually has to change if you are going to transform.* You reach a certain point doing this work when it dawns on you *that you actually have to change.* You can't talk about it, or hope for it. You have to *do* it.

Remembrance is also an experiential event. It is not an intellectual concept or an attitude change. *I'm glad to know that at my core, I am divine and shimmering, so now I'm done. I am enlightened! This wasn't so hard.* That sounds delightful, except for one thing: You're still covered with matte paint.

Real transformation and authentic remembrance have to be vibrational shifts. When you make these shifts at your core, you'll be experiencing yourself differently, and experiencing everything else differently. You won't have to think about it—you'll be living it.

Looking as if we're changing and actually changing
are two very different things.
The real journey of remembrance must begin with
a sincere exploration into and discovery of
all of the ways our forgetfulness has insinuated itself
into every aspect of our lives.

The good news is that you've already begun that sincere exploration because you're reading this book. As we go forward, you'll learn much more about how you can make significant and permanent vibrational Soul Shifts.

From Shopping and Collecting to Transforming

I love to shop. When I can find the time, it is one of my favorite ways to relax from my very hectic and intense schedule. I enjoy looking for bargains and unique items, and finding gifts for people to save for their birthdays or other special occasions. I like seeing the abundance of creativity, color, and ingenuity that manifests into so many designs, objects, and works of art and beauty.

Spiritual shopping, however, is another story, and it's something I see all the time. There's a kind of "beginner spirituality" in which people often participate in the name of personal growth: "Oh yes, I'm on a spiritual path. I've read a few books. I bought some crystals. I have a chanting CD that I listen to sometimes in the car. Once I took a three-hour class on Reiki. For my last birthday, I had my astrological chart done. I recycle. I'm totally spiritual!"

I need to emphasize that *there's absolutely nothing wrong with any of these things, many of which I enjoy myself.* **However, they're not transformation—they are activities and acquisitions.** You might think of them as "spiritual appetizers." Perhaps they serve as the impetus to get us started on a path. The problem is that many people get stuck there, and don't go on to the main course—*doing the real experiential work of shifting all aspects of their lives to be living reflections of the Highest Consciousness.*

Another version of being a spiritual shopper is becoming a "spiritual collector," someone who collects spiritual information and mistakenly convinces themselves that the collecting is actually the transforming. I've met many spiritual collectors over the years. They attend trainings and seminars and have shelves of notebooks full of information that never becomes integrated into their behavior. When they talk to you, the conversation is crowded with spiritual platitudes and quotes, as if saying these things enough will make them real. It's like someone showing you a brochure and talking about how fantastic a place is, but they never actually took the trip.

**Saying something positive is not the same
as vibrating in a positive way.
Describing what something is like is not the same as living it.
You deserve to be an expanded being,
to live in a state of ripened, grounded spiritual attainment.
To become that, you have to shift yourself from the inside out.
And that takes work.**

We all start out in spiritual kindergarten. However, we need to under-stand that *authentic, lasting spiritual and emotional transformation requires attending spiritual graduate school.* That's what my life has been dedicated to, and it's hard work. It is not a series of fun activities. It's not "spiritual-ity light." It requires radical Soul Shifts, *shifts* being the operative word.

**Real spiritual transformation is not an activity or an attitude.
It is not only about having a series of practices we engage in,
or uplifting thoughts we cultivate,
or values we remind ourselves to remember.
It's a grounded, integrated, vibrational state of consciousness.**

Regular spiritual practices, inspirational tools, and conscious atti-tudes are all important. These things have been a part of my life for over 45 years. However, we need to go beyond just that and make choices that will shift not only our behavior, but also our consciousness.

Authentic spiritual transformation is not something you have to remind yourself to do. It's not like saying, "I know I am judgmental and don't give people a chance, so I'm going to try to be more loving," or "I know I'm controlling, so I'm going to try to count to ten and let other people talk first." That's a good beginning, but authentic transformation and lasting Soul Shifts require more: They call for healing whatever is there that necessitates the control, healing whatever is there that necessi-tates the judgment or the insecurity or whatever it is that needs to shift. *You're shifting from the inside out.*

Perhaps you're reading this and thinking, *Oh no, I think I've been a spiritual shopper! What do I do now?* First, you congratulate yourself on beginning your journey, which is more than most people will ever do. Then, you congratulate yourself on realizing that you are already trans-forming from a seeker into a seer. Then, with excitement and enthusi-asm, you continue reading and learning how to make real Soul Shifts.

"Everyone wants to be transformed,
but nobody wants to change."
— Frederica Mathewes-Green

At some point, we must be brutally honest with ourselves: *Have we actually transformed, or are we just talking as if we have? Have we changed our patterns, or have we just become an expert on them? Have we moved, or have we just rearranged the furniture?*

Collecting and rearranging revelations
is not transformation.
Sometimes it's just your ego trying to
look smarter about your suffering and your issues.

Remember: You don't want to just feel better.
You want to *be* better.
There is nothing wrong with rearranging the furniture,
but it isn't the same as moving into a new house.

You have many tools you've learned from your studies and from wonderful teachers, and hopefully you're acquiring many more in these pages. Use them to build a bridge to your freedom. Don't stare at them proudly and say, "Look at how many tools I've collected." That's being a collector, not a transformer.

This means getting everything out of your notebooks and journals and into your life. It means moving the information from your head into your very cells, moving it from your understanding into your living, your behavior, and your consciousness. This is the way we begin to transition from shoppers and collectors into transformers.

When you learn how to shift yourself vibrationally from the inside out, it's real and it's lasting. It must and will impact your life, your choices, your relationships, and everything about you. *As you shift, everything will shift.*

BAKING THE CAKE OF CONSCIOUSNESS

"Only the ideas that we actually live are of any value."
— Hermann Hesse

Imagine that you've decided to make an amazing cake, and you're going to get the best possible ingredients that exist anywhere in the world.

First, you visit a monastery where you purchase very expensive organic flour that's been hand ground by monks who chanted the entire time they were grinding the wheat. Then you fly to Hawaii, and hike up to a sacred waterfall to find special sugar that's only grown in this one place.

Next, you travel to South America to find rare chocolate that's harvested in the rain forest, and can only be purchased from an old man who lives in a hut hidden in the jungle. Then, on your way back home, you stop in Northern California and procure eggs from chickens who were given regular acupressure treatments, and had volunteers reading to them each day from ancient scriptures so that the eggs would be vibrating with divine and blessed energy.

Finally, you return to your house with all of these exotic ingredients. You lay them all out in your kitchen, and decide to invite some friends over. *"Hello, my dear ones,"* you say. *"I traveled all over the world so I could make an amazing cake for you. See this incredible chocolate? I remember sitting in the hut with the man who sold it to me. Look, here's a picture of us posing with the chocolate. I think he also gave me a healing.*

"Now, finding this sugar was really magical. Let me tell you about the day I spent at the waterfall. It was so hot, and we swam in a sacred pool to cool off. And these eggs—can you imagine eggs who have had the entire Bhagavad Gita and the Bible read to them? There was the most interesting guy there who gave me a past-life reading while we waited for the chickens to finish."

You're telling everybody stories about these ingredients and how exciting it was to get the ingredients, and how special the ingredients are. **There's only one problem: *Where's the cake?***

The cake is *not* the ingredients.

You have all of the ingredients, but there is still no cake. The cake needs to be baked. The cake isn't what it took to collect the ingredients. The cake is not the exciting trip to get the ingredients. The cake isn't the ingredients lined up on the counter with a picture of a finished dessert sitting next to it, nor is it an affirmation about how delicious the cake is going to be. **The cake is more than the ingredients. It is what happens when the ingredients are baked.** *You need to bake the cake.*

I created this metaphor several years ago, and love offering it to people because it illustrates **that all transformation has to be experiential, and not intellectual.** A lot of us collect the ingredients we think we need for transformation, such as teachings, wisdom, inspiration, tools, and techniques. But we don't do the actual baking and make the vibrational shifts necessary for the cake—our transformed self—to finally emerge.

What does it take to bake something? It takes *heat,* in this case, *the kind of inner spiritual heat that illuminates and melts away our emotional debris, and then forges all of our enlightened ingredients into a new, permanent form.* I'll be explaining how you can create that heat as we go forward, and give you foolproof baking instructions that have produced thousands of delicious "consciousness cakes."

All of us, including you, are baking. Perhaps you're at the beginning stages. Perhaps you've been doing it for a long time, and you can smell the delicious aroma of your attainment beginning to rise up. Maybe you've spent years baking and have some wonderful finished layers, but you're working on new ones in order to create a multitiered cake. Perhaps you've been getting impatient, doubting your entire baking process: *Why is this taking so long? Did I use the right ingredients? Why does this have to be so hard?*

We're standing together in the Soul Shifts kitchen. Is the oven hot? Absolutely. After all, it's the "oven of transformation." From its depths, the most delicious cakes of enlightenment emerge.

> **Don't take your cake of consciousness out of the oven.**
> **Keep baking.**
> **Baking seals the wisdom into your soul,**
> **so that once it's in, it can never be removed.**

When the cake is finished baking, a mysterious and miraculous alchemy will have occurred: *Everything you started with will have disappeared, and all that will remain will be wholeness.* When the cake is done, can you find the eggs? Can you find the sugar? Can you find the flour? Of course not. Why? The ingredients have been transmuted into something new and more amazing than their original form.

This is what spiritual baking does. It seals in your wisdom. It seals in your love. It seals in everything you've gained on your journey, so your attainment can't be removed or challenged by anything that happens to you. *Nothing can ever take away what has merged into you, and become you.*

I am here to tell you that I have been baked, and even though it is not always easy, *it's always worth it.* You're tasting the results of my baking right now, fresh out of my consciousness oven, made just for you.

We are here for remembrance.
Now you know that you aren't looking for anything
you won't be able to find,
because you've always had it.

There is nothing missing in you.
You just forgot that it was there.

You are a pulsation of Supreme Consciousness.
No matter what has covered you,
or painted over your radiance,
rest easy knowing that underneath the shadows,
you are shimmering.
You cannot be anything but shimmering . . .

🏵 4 🏵

Deep and Up:
Transforming Yourself from the Inside Out

"Who looks outside, dreams.
Who looks inside, awakens."
— Carl Jung

From a very young age, all I wanted was to be awakened. I didn't actually know that word yet or understand the concept—what I did know was that I wanted to live a life of love, service, and freedom. My plan was to somehow figure out everything that was wrong with me, work as hard as I could to fix each thing one by one, and eventually, I'd be a perfected human being.

But where to begin? *It seemed like a full-time job to watch everything I thought, everything I did, and everything I said.* By the time I was in my teens, I was already emotionally exhausted from micromanaging myself, and was still nowhere near "fixed." What was I going to do?

Fortunately, I had a cosmic appointment with my first spiritual teacher and was introduced to the principle that transformed my life:

To change what is on the surface,
find the source, and change things from there.
Go within, beneath the surface to the root,
and everything else will change.

I will never forget the first time I heard the simple but profound metaphor that Maharishi used to illustrate this principle: If you have a plant whose leaves are brown and withering, he explained, how do you fix it? Do you think, *The leaves are dry, so I'll water them*? The answer, of course, is no. **Instead, you go to the source of the problem, to the roots and the soil, and nourish the plant from there by providing it with water and other nutrients. Soon the leaves become healthy and green again.**

63

This made so much sense to me. Only someone who didn't understand that what nourished the plant was beneath the surface would attempt to make the plant healthy by watering the leaves and then wonder why the plant died. *Up until that moment, that person who didn't understand had been me!* I'd thought I was going to have to spend my life watching and watering every leaf. Now I realized that if I could tap into the source within me, I could achieve the freedom and fulfillment I was seeking.

Maharishi was talking about the practice of meditation when he taught this principle, and as I've shared, that is when I began my formal spiritual journey. As the years passed, I found that his message about the unseen source was not only described in the ancient Indian texts, but had always been present in religion and philosophy. Jesus taught that "the kingdom of Heaven is within." Buddha said, "The way is not in the sky. The way is in the heart."

The more I studied, the more I saw that all life really is structured from inside out. This is true even on the most basic cellular level. It's the healthy functioning of your cells that allows you as a being to function on the surface of your life. You're breathing because of cells deep within your lungs. You're thinking because of cells deep within your brain. *What is inside is controlling what happens on the surface.*

**It is the invisible that rules the visible world.
It is the invisible that allows the visible to work.
Therefore, when we contact the invisible within ourselves,
we contact the Great Source of everything.
From there, all authentic and lasting change can happen.**

This was the answer I'd been searching for, and it became the foundation for all of my work as a teacher. *The only way to make the permanent shifts we want to make on the outside of our life is to make them on the inside.* The more we connect with and enliven that infinite field of consciousness within, the more aligned we become with the qualities of that consciousness: expansion, intelligence, creativity, wisdom, and fullness.

SOUL SHIFT

SHIFT FROM TRYING TO CONTROL THE OUTSIDE TO SHIFTING YOURSELF FROM THE INSIDE OUT

**It's not rearranging things on the outside of your life
that is going to make a permanent impact.
It's rearranging things on the inside.
When you shift on the inside,
everything on the outside will shift.**

OPERATING FROM THE CONTROL ROOM OF CONSCIOUSNESS

Here is a Soul Shift contemplation:

What do you mean when you say "I want to change"?
You're hoping that your life will be different.

What is it that makes your life the way it is?
*Your outer life is a **product of choices you make in each
moment**—choices in behavior, choices in communication, and so on.
How your life looks is a reflection of those choices.*

What is it that creates those outer choices?
*Your outer choices are a reflection of **the quality and clarity of
your inner thoughts and emotions.***

**What is it that creates the quality and clarity of your inner
thoughts and emotions? Where do they come from?**
*Your thoughts and emotions come from **your inner state of consciousness. The quality and clarity of your thoughts and emotions
are a direct reflection of the quality of your consciousness.***

In our quest for fulfillment and happiness, we work on acquiring skills and setting goals, but we forget the most important ingredient in our recipe for mastery: *consciousness*. Every part of our outer and inner life—our behaviors, choices, feelings, and thoughts—is not only a direct reflection of the quality of our consciousness, *but from moment to moment, it is created and re-created by that consciousness.*

By definition, if your consciousness is at the source of all you think and feel and do, you can't permanently shift any of these things without first shifting your consciousness. You can try to adjust, monitor, control, and supervise your feelings, thoughts, and actions, but since they're sourced from your consciousness itself, they won't shift and remain shifted unless you shift at that most basic source level.

**To improve the quality of your life,
you must improve the quality of your choices.**

**To improve the quality of your choices,
you must improve the quality of your thoughts and emotions
that produce those choices.**

**To improve the quality of your thoughts and emotions,
you must improve the quality of your consciousness.
To shift everything, you must shift your consciousness.**

Just as the root is the control panel for the plant, consciousness is the control panel for everything in your life. Shifting things from the place of consciousness is like operating from a control room. You can try to control things one at a time, or you can find the control room that is in charge of everything. You already understand and practice this in many areas of your life. As modern technology has progressed, it has incorporated this principle of changing something at the source into so many advancements:

If you're old enough, you may remember that to close the windows in a car, you used to have to go to each window and turn the handle until the window closed. Now you push one button that is the source of the controls, and all the windows rise up automatically.

If you want to shut down your computer, you don't have to close each program one by one. You go to the source and ask the computer to shut everything down at once, and it does.

It used to be that if you wanted to write to a list of people, you'd have to send them something one by one. Now, you compose a message on your computer, and it can send what you want to everyone at once.

You go to the source and shift things from there.

FROM MANAGEMENT TO MASTERY

"Problems cannot be solved at the same level of awareness that created them."
— Albert Einstein

Our next Soul Shift is going to save you so much time and energy:

SOUL SHIFT

SHIFT FROM MANAGEMENT TO MASTERY

I meet many people whose idea of personal transformation is to manage themselves on a full-time basis. They start out with their list of rules: *I have to be confident today, especially at my interview. I have to make sure not to think any thoughts that aren't positive. I have to see the best in that person, no matter how terrible they are. I have to not get upset with the kids even if they're driving me crazy. I'm going to be patient with my secretary no matter how much she annoys me. I'm not going to be sarcastic when I talk to my brother; I have to not go into any judgment. I have to remember that I am a being of light, and everything is possible. I am going to stay centered, no matter what happens.*

Aren't you exhausted just reading this list? This is what happens when we "paint the leaves of our patterns green" rather than going to the root to heal the plant. We try to monitor and manage our thoughts, feelings, and actions, and hope for the best. It's like policing ourselves 24/7 without a break. *However, if and when that fails and we start to feel out of control, we resort to more extreme measures of suppression, repression, and denial.*

67

Have you ever been to an amusement park and seen the game "Whac-a-Mole"? It's a machine with a bunch of holes, and underneath each hole is a plastic mole that looks just like the subterranean mammal. When the game starts, the moles randomly pop up from their holes. The objective is to whack the moles back into their holes by hitting them on the head with a mallet. Of course once you whack one mole down, another pops up somewhere else, and you have to be really quick to hammer them all down and win a prize.

Many people spend a lot of time playing a game of emotional Whac-a-Mole, trying to control and get rid of every uncomfortable thought, feeling, and issue by pushing it down or away. We whack down an uncomfortable feeling here, but then it pops up over there. We push down a negative thought here, and just when we think we're in the clear and feeling centered, oh no—the fear pops up again somewhere else. We try to hammer down our insecurity, hoping no one sees it, and suddenly when we least expect it, it's back again. We attempt to stay positive and optimistic by knocking down our doubts and anxiety, but they stubbornly start popping up everywhere faster than we can catch them.

Emotional Whac-a-Mole is exhausting, time-consuming, and frustrating. It drains our energy and doesn't allow us to ever relax. Even when we successfully push down an emotion or control our thoughts, there's no satisfaction, because we know we haven't actually resolved it—*we've just temporarily scared it off.* We're already on the lookout for the next place that discomfort is going to emerge.

It would be like putting a Band-Aid on a terrible infection rather than finding out what's causing it and treating it at the source with antibiotics. No matter how attractive the Band-Aid may be, it's not going to solve the problem.

Watching every feeling, action, and choice
is not what personal growth is supposed to be about.
Constantly trying to control your thoughts and emotions
is not transformation, and it's certainly not mastery.

When you learn how to go deep into your consciousness,
you can transform your life by healing the source of your issues.
Otherwise, you just become a permanent babysitter
to yourself and your patterns.

Transforming from the inside out means that we do the work to discover the source of the behavior: *What's the source of my resistance? What's the source of my mistrust? What's the source of my fear of intimacy?* We go to the root, and shift it from there.

Of course, there's nothing wrong with working on making improvements on all levels of your life. Shifting at the source does *not* mean that you don't work on making shifts anywhere else. There are many essential changes we all can and need to implement in numerous areas, and I'll be offering you suggestions for doing this later on.

Sometimes, it's easy to convince (fool!) ourselves and others that we're masterful in our life because we look so busy and important, when the truth is we're actually running around trying to manage how out of control we really feel. Living with mastery is not the same thing as being successful. When you're not living from consciousness, you make poor decisions, ignore the obvious, get off track, and eventually spend a lot of time cleaning up after yourself. *Consciousness is actually the ultimate time-saver!*

Instead of just trying to manage situation by situation and control everything on the outside, you work on becoming more anchored on the inside, and cultivating your mastery from the inside out.

Save time. Be conscious.

Reassigning Your Spiritual Assets

I like to think of the shift from management to mastery as "reassigning your spiritual assets" from a focus on controlling the surface of your life to connecting with and operating from the depths.

**People think that mastery means successfully managing and controlling ourselves and others.
Nothing could be more untrue.**

**Real mastery transcends the need to manage.
When we are living in vibrational alignment with our Source,
we don't have to constantly micromanage the surface.**

The more Soul Shifts you experience, the more you will spontaneously make more enlightened choices, not because you're reminding yourself to, *but because they're a natural reflection of the shifts at the level of your consciousness.* You're no longer controlling your issues—you're dismantling them, and the energy that was being used to hold them together is now available to be used for expansion, creativity, and true power.

This is the added bonus to being more in mastery and less in management: When you're not spending as much time pushing down, controlling, judging, checking, double-checking, assessing, repressing, hiding, covering up, and comparing, you're actually free to be more conscious and present. This is a much better use of your spiritual assets.

A few years ago, I was the keynote speaker at a convention for financial planners. My presentation was about transformational leadership, and was very well received. At the luncheon afterward, a very serious-looking man approached me and introduced himself as the CEO of some big conglomerate.

"I have an important question for you," he began.

Assuming he was going to ask me about something in my talk, or for personal advice, I smiled and said, "Go ahead. That's what I'm here for."

He came even closer and, in a hushed voice, asked, *"What is the focus of your investments?"*

I stared at him for a moment, realizing that he somehow believed I was going to give him financial tips, which was laughable since I have a very nice team who does that for me. Seeing my hesitation, he tried again: "You know, is there an area of the market or an industry your investments focus on?"

"Yes, there is," I responded. **"Consciousness."**

"Excuse me, I must not have heard you correctly."

"Consciousness," I repeated. *"I have spent my life investing in my consciousness and enlightenment—with excellent returns, by the way!"*

You too will experience excellent returns and divine dividends as you reassign your spiritual assets and shift them from the Management Fund to the Mastery Fund.

Deep and Up

*"The further within myself I go,
the farther out to the world I can reach."*
— Chaiwat Thirapantu

I love trees. Trees are our tall, graceful, devoted, ancient guardians and protectors. We pass them by all the time, and forget that they aren't for decoration and visual delight—*they are keeping us alive.* Without trees, we would literally die. As human beings, we breathe in oxygen and breathe out carbon dioxide. The trees change the carbon dioxide back into oxygen for us, so that we can live. Without trees, we'd soon run out of the air we need to breathe. We are in the most intimate relationship possible with the trees and the plants around us. If you ever feel unsupported or alone, look at a tree, and know in that moment that it is serving you in the most profound way imaginable.

When we think of a tree, we think of the visible portion above the ground—the majestic redwood, the graceful palm, the mighty oak, the sturdy pine. But the most important part of the tree is not visible—the roots. *The root system of a tree spreads out approximately two to three times the width of the canopy of the branches.* As the roots grow, they look for nutrients and water in the soil, and reach out farther to find them. The farther and deeper the roots travel, the stronger they become, and the more steady and secure they can keep the tree.

Roots anchor a tree in the soil, keeping it stable and strong so that the harsh winds cannot knock the tree over. Without roots, a tree would wobble, and grow crooked. When roots aren't healthy, it's possible for a large tree to topple over easily even with very little wind or rain.

Trees are magnificent spiritual teachers, gurus, and guides, as they're continually revealing the secret of life to us. Nature illustrates a powerful Soul Shift principle in its beautiful offering of trees. This principle is the map I've followed on my own path and taught to those I serve:

SOUL SHIFT

SHIFT FROM FORWARD TO WITHIN, AND FROM FARTHER TO DEEPER

When we think of success, mastery, happiness, and accomplishment, most of us want to go forward and we want to go farther. We want to get more, do more, and be more. We want to move from where we are, so we look forward ahead of us. We want to have more, so we look farther in the distance because we think we don't have enough where we're standing.

Like the tree, which in going forward in its growth and farther up in the sky sends its roots deeper and within, so can we make this Soul Shift. *Instead of only focusing on going forward and farther, we learn to go within and go deeper.*

If I had to give you one key that articulates the Technology of Transformation, it would be:

DEEP AND UP

What does this mean? *It means that when we go deep, we can go up. It means that the higher we want to go, the deeper we need to dig.* My students use this a lot for vibrational recalibration, which we're about to explore. If you tune in to the vibration of this phrase, you'll find it will actually help you to go deep and feel higher. The word *deep* vibrates you into yourself, and the word *up* lifts you higher.

"Deep" means going as deep as you can on the inside, and rooting yourself to your most expanded consciousness. It means learning how to root yourself in wisdom, in vibrational authenticity, and in love. To go deep means digging deep for the truth by seeing what there is to see and feeling what there is to feel. It means locating your issues and blocks on the surface, but dismantling them at their source. It means allowing the roots of your own commitment to freedom to spread deep and wide so that when the winds of fear and challenge blow, you do not topple over on your journey.

"Up" means that the deeper we go within ourselves, the higher up we can climb. It means learning how to expand above our smallness and rise above our limitations. It means learning how to access our Highest and act from our Highest, not intellectually but vibrationally.

A tree is a magnificent example of deep and up. The deeper its roots spread in the soil, the higher the tree can grow. The same principle operates everywhere around us. If you want to build a one-story house, you don't need a deep foundation—you just need a slab. If you want to build a skyscraper, you need a much deeper foundation and must dig until you reach bedrock so that the building has stability.

What is the bedrock we need to find and connect to? It's consciousness. Consciousness is the foundation upon which you can build a truly expanded and masterful life. Rooted in consciousness, everything about you will flourish.

**Your greatest and only true foundation in life is your consciousness.
On the unshakable foundation of consciousness,
you can be anything, do anything, and build everything.
From the deepest place within you, you will be able to rise up.
This is how you can serve the world in a bigger way.**

All of the Soul Shifts concepts and practices contained in this book are designed to help you to go deep and go up, and to build a foundation of consciousness that will make you strong and steady from the inside out. **Consciousness is your ultimate backup team.**

Life is full of the unexpected. Haven't you had something challenging happen to you in the past few months that you couldn't possibly have predicted? We all have.

You can't specifically prepare for every single thing that you might have to encounter in your life—that would be impossible. It's this realization that drives many people crazy, and turns them into control freaks and chronic micromanagers. They live in a perpetual state of fear, knowing that they aren't prepared for the unknown, because they can't possibly know what exactly to prepare for.

For us, what's important to understand is that there is *linear preparation* and there is *global preparation*. Linear preparation means preparing for a specific event, goal, or challenge by gathering those skills necessary to successfully navigate through it: learning how to survive outdoors if you're planning to camp in a remote area; learning how to help your body heal if you're planning to have surgery; learning better study habits if you're planning to go to graduate school; learning how to care for an infant if you're planning to have a child.

Global preparation, on the other hand, means preparing for anything. How can that be possible? It is if you prepare your consciousness.

Transforming yourself from the inside out means
doing the inner work so that you are always in
a state of preparation.
You prepare yourself to be prepared
under whatever circumstance.
Preparing your consciousness is the best preparation
for everything.

You cultivate the qualities and abilities we'll be discussing: vision, intuitive wisdom, steadiness, compassion, and so many more.

This prepares you at the ground floor of your life so that whatever you're doing, you're bringing maximum consciousness to it. You're bringing stability, integration, wholeness, mastery, centeredness, and freedom from patterns that could sabotage you. That's true preparation.

Be prepared:
Expand your consciousness.

I feel very blessed to have somehow known I needed to go deep from such an early age. Before I worked on anything else, I worked on consciousness. Before I sought out success, I sought out consciousness. The tree of who I am has blossomed beautifully, and has been abundant with fruits of service and wisdom that I've offered to so many. None of this has occurred because I painted a lot of beautiful leaves. It's because I worked on watering those roots of consciousness. I went deep so that I could go up.

*"Why do you want to open the outside door
when there is an inside door?
Everything is within."*
— Satguru Siva Yogaswami

Since the first diamonds were mined in India over 3,000 years ago, the dazzling gem has been a symbol of eternity, of the mystical, of light, and of that which is indestructible. The word *diamond* comes from the ancient Greek *adamas,* which translates as "unbreakable, unalterable, unconquerable." (You can see the evolution of that root word into the modern English word *adamant.*) Perhaps you have a diamond ring, or bought one for your partner when you got married. Maybe you've inherited one from your mother or grandmother, as I did. If you're wearing it right now, you can gaze at it in wonder as you contemplate its miraculous origins.

Every diamond is between 990 million and 3.3 billion years old. Diamonds were formed by tremendous heat and crushing pressure around 100 miles below ground, in the mantle of the earth during its first few billion years of existence. Over time, volcanic eruptions carried the diamonds up closer to the surface. In the mining process, for every carat of pure diamond, half a million pounds of earth and rock must be moved and sifted.

Do you know why they're so sparkly? *Light normally travels at 186,000 miles per second, but a diamond is so dense that it slows light to less than half that speed.* The light enters the diamond and bounces around inside of it, refracting into all the colors of the rainbow and creating the exquisite brilliant sparkle.

To me, the diamond, like so many other gifts of nature, offers us a profound map to understanding our journey of transformation:

* It was born from unimaginable fire and pressure, out of which its brilliance and perfection emerged.

* It requires a tremendous amount of work—digging and dismantling—in order to be retrieved.

* Once you've found it, you have something precious and invaluable.

> Light, truth, and freedom are worth digging for.
> The diamonds of transformation are not scattered
> on the surface of your awareness.
> They are deep within you.
> They're worth all the hard work required to remove everything
> that's in the way of their retrieval.

This is the great journey we're on. *Journeying forward means journeying deeper.* When an archaeologist from a museum is searching for a great treasure or sacred object, they understand that at first, there will be more digging than discovering. They know the treasure is there, so they dig deep. And then they find one little chip of an ancient artifact, or one flake of a statue. It's just a chip, but they know that if there's a chip, the rest of the treasure can't be far behind. What was hard work now becomes exciting, and a new enthusiasm sets in.

Making Soul Shifts is like becoming a spiritual archaeologist, excavating your own light, love, wisdom, and wholeness. Each time you discover a piece of something, you conclude: *There must be a lot more in there, and if there is more in there, I'm not going to stop digging until I find it all.* Suddenly, you've shifted from feeling that you're trying to fix what's wrong with you to realizing with delight that you're on a great cosmic treasure hunt of the most divine nature.

DIGGING FOR THE SACRED

Not long ago I went on a personal pilgrimage to the Big Island of Hawaii, home to five volcanoes, three of which are active. Kilauea is the most active volcano in Hawaii, and one of the most active on Earth. Kilauea is somewhere between 300,000 to 600,000 years old; and according to Hawaiian mythology, it is the residence of the volcano goddess Pele, who's said to be living deep in the fire crater, which spews lava every day.

I always think of Hawaii as an island of the *fire that heals.* Whenever I'm there, I feel as if the volcano takes me inside of it, and Pele breathes her fire into me, purifying all that does not belong in my heart and soul.

During my most recent stay, I had the privilege of visiting an ashram founded to honor the work of a renowned and beloved female Indian saint, Sri Ma Anandamayi, for whom I've always had great reverence. Even though she's no longer in her earthly form, her presence was very strong everywhere I went on the beautifully landscaped property, and I felt honored to be there to receive the blessings that radiated from the land and her devotees.

As I was given a tour of the lush gardens, my eye was drawn to the top of a hill. My guide noticed my interest and said, "You must have spotted our Rudraksha tree."

"You have a Rudraksha tree?" I asked with great excitement.

"Yes," he replied. "You're welcome to hike up and see it. I think the seeds may have ripened and dropped onto the ground by now. You can take some with you if you like."

I thanked the kind man very enthusiastically, and immediately proceeded to begin climbing the hill. I've had a string of rare Rudraksha beads in the style of a necklace for many years, but the thought of seeing one seed that had just dropped off the tree, let alone many that I could gather myself, filled me with anticipation.

The Rudraksha tree is a very large evergreen that originated in the foothills of the Himalayas and other parts of Asia. It is uniquely mysterious in that its seeds are covered by an otherworldly cobalt-blue outer layer when ripe. Underneath the covering is a dark seed faceted with natural carvings in a mysterious geometric pattern of grooves that have particular significance depending on how many there are. *The truly miraculous thing about Rudrakshas is that most seeds come with a natural hole drilled in the center, as if the Divine intended us to use them as beads to form a chain, which is exactly how they are strung.*

Rudraksha beads have been used by Hindus, Buddhists, and Sikhs in *malas* (a set of prayer beads, similar to a rosary) for over a thousand years, as an aid during chanting or mantra recitation, and as a link between the earth and heaven. *Rudraksha* translates as "Shiva's tears," and refers to a story from the ancient text the Shiva Purana, which says that Lord Shiva went into meditation for the sake of all living creatures, and when he came out, he was moved to tears, and those tears became the Rudraksha seeds.

As I eagerly made my way up the hill, I couldn't help but witness myself in the moment and smile. *What an interesting creature you are, Barbara,* I thought. *Where someone else might get excited to go to a fancy restaurant or meet a famous movie star, here you are, giddy as if you've just won the lottery, trekking up a slippery ridge to dig in the mud for Rudraksha seeds.*

I finally reached the top of the slope and saw the exquisite and majestic Rudraksha tree. I walked up to its base, and when I looked very closely, there on the ground, half buried between the exposed roots, were some seeds. I knew that if I saw a few of them, there were hundreds more covered by the dirt. I felt like I was in heaven!

I got down on my hands and knees, and began to dig into the wet earth. The ground was littered with fronds, twigs, and rocks, and I had to move them aside to dig underneath and unearth the tiny, rare beads that were often hiding beneath a pile of mud and leaves freshly deposited from the last rainfall. As I reverently plucked each bead from the dirt, I brushed off the debris, and gratefully placed it in my pocket.

For a while, I worked in silence, and the only sounds were the wind blowing through trees, and the serenade of the tropical birds calling out in contented delight. I began to sing one of my favorite Sanskrit chants, honoring the great Supreme Consciousness that had led me to this extraordinary moment.

Suddenly, I was overcome with a sensation of blissful expansion, and my heart filled and thrilled with timeless knowingness.

This is how I have spent my whole life, I realized, ***joyfully digging for the sacred.***

There, at the foot of the holy Rudraksha tree, I saw the sincere and relentless seeker that I have always been—*on my knees, ignoring the discomfort and the debris, digging deep within myself for the seeds of the Divine that I knew had to be there; not caring what needed to be sacrificed, only knowing that I had to retrieve my wholeness; and then, carefully cleaning off and stringing together the beads of my attainment so that I could humbly offer them, with love and respect, as a necklace of wisdom to the world.*

I'm looking at the Rudraksha seeds right now. They're in a glass bowl on my office altar, here to remind me of what I am here to remind you:

Deep inside of you is everything.
Go deep.
Dig deep.
Root yourself deeply in the soil of remembrance.
Your own great consciousness is waiting there for you.

PART TWO

THE
TECHNOLOGY
OF
TRANSFORMATION

❀ 5 ❀

Your Cosmic Dance:
Spiritual Physics and the Secret of
Vibrational Transformation

"Science is not only compatible with spirituality;
it is a profound source of spirituality."
— Carl Sagan

Right now, you're probably sitting in a chair or lying in bed reading these words, feeling quite still and steady. Nothing could be further from the truth, though. *You're actually racing around the sun at 67,000 miles an hour!* That's the speed of Earth's orbit. If you're not dizzy yet, consider that our solar system—the sun and all of the planets, including your home on Earth—is an infinitesimal part of the enormous Milky Way galaxy. Our solar system itself is rotating around the galaxy's center at about 483,000 miles per hour! That means we're not only orbiting around the sun, but the sun in our solar system is taking us on a wild ride through space at about 137 miles per second! And we're not done: our galaxy is moving through the universe at about 1.3 million miles per hour.

What this means is that right now,
you are zooming through space at a speed of
millions of miles an hour.
In the minute it took you to read these two paragraphs,
you've moved 1,116 miles around the sun,
and 8,050 miles through the galaxy!

Tomorrow morning when you wake up, if you've been in bed for approximately eight hours, *you will have traveled almost 4 million miles in the galaxy and over 10 million miles in the universe while you slept!* No wonder that in spite of how much we rest, we often feel exhausted!

Perhaps what's even more amazing about these mind-boggling facts is that we don't even sense any of this motion. Everything feels perfectly stationary. Physics explains that this is because the speeds are constant. Nonetheless, isn't it outrageous that we have absolutely no awareness of what's actually happening?

As we contemplate this, we begin to open even more fully to the realization that **we are living in a mysterious, miraculous universe, and that we—you and I and all of us—are, by definition, a part of that miracle.** Yet it's only in the last 25 years with the creation of the Hubble Space Telescope and its ability to gaze far into the universe that astronomical theories have been proved to be realities. *What was invisible has now become visible.*

This is the way it has always been throughout the history of human civilization:

**As human beings, we assume that what we can see is the truth,
and that if we can't see or understand something,
it must not be true or even exist.**

Here are just a few examples:

* People were certain that the world was flat until it was proved to be round. Scientists and religious scholars believed that Earth was the center of the solar system and the sun and planets revolved around it, until they discovered that the sun was in fact at the center.

* In the 19th century, when Thomas Edison announced that he was working on the creation of an electric light, a British Parliamentary committee called the idea "unworthy of the attention of practical or scientific men."

* Up until the 1800s, no one, including the medical community, believed in the "germ theory" of disease and instead attributed the cause of sickness to "miasma," or bad air. Chemist Louis Pasteur was considered a quack for claiming that bacteria and germs caused disease, and suggesting that doctors wash their hands and sterilize their instruments to destroy the microbes that could kill their patients.

As someone who has always sought the truth beyond what was apparent, I love this quote from Arthur Schopenhauer, the 19th-century German philosopher:

All truth passes through three stages.
First, it is ridiculed.
Second, it is violently opposed.
Third, it is accepted as being self-evident.

What is the truth we're considering here on our Soul Shifts journey? It is this:

You are a vibrational being.
You are cosmic energy vibrating in a certain pattern
that makes up what you consider to be "you."
In order to transform yourself or your life,
you must transform yourself at the vibrational level.

SPIRITUAL PHYSICS 101

"If you want to find the secrets of the universe,
think in terms of energy, frequency, and vibration."
— Nikola Tesla

Think back on the last time you decided to listen to some music to uplift your mood. Maybe you were driving in your car, or working at home or the office, or doing some chores. You chose something you like listening to, and within just a few minutes, you felt calmer, or happier, or more cheerful. What if a friend had arrived moments later while you were still enjoying the music, and said, "You're in a good mood. Can you show me the thing that has shifted how you were feeling?"

You could point to your iPod or CD player, but that device wasn't what was affecting you so strongly—it was just the delivery system for the music. So where *was* the music? Could you touch or see it? **Of course not, because it wasn't a physical object that was having such a powerful impact on you—it was a *vibration*.**

The vibration of that particular piece of music was created by the artist to evoke a singular kind of vibration in you, the listener. That's why you specifically chose it over something else. If you wanted to feel romantic, for instance, you would choose a certain piece of music. If you wanted to feel reverent or inspired, you would choose another. If you wanted music to help you cry, you'd choose something else. Each song or piece of music would affect you in different ways not because of the title, or what you knew it meant to convey, but because the vibration of the music directly affected *your* vibration.

If you enjoy music, or the sound of birds chirping in the trees, or hearing waves washing up onto the shore, or the purring of your cat, or the voice of someone you treasure saying "I love you," then you already have direct experience with what we're about to explore: *the vibrational reality of life and its effect on you in each and every moment.*

Now for our lesson in what I call "spiritual physics."

Truth #1: Everything in the universe is vibrating energy.

This sums up the truth of life as we know it. Modern science confirms that everything in the universe—all sound, light, and matter, including you—is simply pure energy vibrating at different frequencies. *What we see as solid matter simply appears to be solid and unmoving through the lens of our senses, but when we look at that matter on a subatomic level and beyond, it isn't solid matter at all. Rather, it is pure energy vibrating at a particular rate of speed.*

Look around wherever you are right now. With your limited senses, it all appears solid and unmoving, but everything you see is in reality moving and vibrating, pulsating with energy. For instance, this book or tablet you're holding may appear solid, but it's actually made up of millions and millions of subatomic particles that are in constant motion. The tree outside of your window appears still, but it is vibrating and pulsating. *There is nothing that isn't always moving!*

When you gaze at yourself in the mirror, it appears that you're a solid form made of flesh and bones, correct? The truth is that you are in reality cosmic energy forming itself into neutrons, electrons, and protons that are vibrating in a particular pattern of vibration, a pattern we identify as a "human being."

Here is how Michio Kaku, an American theoretical physicist and futurist, and the co-founder of string field theory (which is one of the branches of string theory), defines reality:

"What is the universe? The universe is a symphony of vibrating strings. . . . So first of all, we are nothing but melodies. We are nothing but cosmic music played out on vibrating strings and membranes."

I love this description. Isn't it amazing to consider that there has never been a "melody" exactly like you, and there never will be again?

Truth #2: Everything in the universe is vibrating at a unique vibrational speed.

If everything in the universe is sourced from the same vibrating energy, why do you look different from a tree, or a cat, or a star? **The reason is that each particular thing has its own unique vibrational frequency or characteristic *based on how rapidly or slowly it is vibrating.*** You are vibrating at a different speed than the table, or a plant, or a cloud.

How does the speed of vibration determine the specific blueprint of an object?

When the vibrational frequency of matter slows down, the matter becomes more physically dense and solid.

When the vibrational frequency of matter increases or vibrates more rapidly, it becomes less and less dense, less and less solid until it eventually becomes etheric.

A simple example of this that you probably experience every day is water and its different forms. What we think of as water is actually the chemical compound H_2O: each molecule of water consists of two hydrogen atoms bonded to one atom of oxygen.

Physics tells us that cooling something slows down its vibration, and heating something speeds up the vibration. What happens when you put a liquid in the freezer? You're slowing down the vibration of that compound H_2O, and it solidifies into solid matter known as *ice.* If you do the opposite, and speed up the vibration of that H_2O by heating it, it changes form back from ice into a *liquid.* What if you decided to add even more heat and speed up the vibrational frequency of the H_2O now in liquid form by putting it into a pot on the stove and letting it boil indefinitely? The liquid turns into *steam,* and eventually appears to disappear!

The "slowed-down vibration" form of the H_2O—ice—appears very solid and dense. Imagine trying to put your hand through an icicle: you'd hurt yourself. However, the "sped-up vibration" form—steam—is a much less dense form of matter, so much so that you can't see it at all, and can easily put your hand through it, as if it isn't even there.

Has the H_2O disappeared? No—it still exists, but in a form so subtle that it is invisible to your eye. It's vibrating too quickly to appear solid and real, but it is there just the same. *The H_2O hasn't changed its essence—it's just changed its form.*

Truth #3: The Ultimate Source Energy never changes.

Let's sum up what we've concluded so far: All matter is vibrating energy, and that energy vibrates at different speeds and frequencies that make it either more dense, coarse, and manifest, or more subtle, refined, and invisible. However—and this is the big however—*even though this one source energy changes form, manifesting into everything that exists in creation, including you, it never changes its essence.* **It is always the same Ultimate Energy.**

Where Science and Spirituality Meet

It's only within the last hundred years or so that modern science has been able to observe and understand this phenomenon of matter as vibrating energy. Knowing that, you may be amazed to learn that over a thousand years ago, this same truth about the nature of reality was described in a sacred text known as the *Spanda Karikas*, or "The Doctrine of Vibration and Divine Pulsation." This collection of verses is one of the earliest texts of Kashmir Shaivism.

In Sanskrit, the word *spanda* translates as "throb or pulsation," and is a technical term for the *divine throb or vibration out of which, according to these verses, all matter arises and permeates everything in creation.* Long before the existence of modern physics, the Shaivite understanding, as presented in the *Spanda Karikas*, expressed what science now accepts as truth:

The *spanda* is the pulsation of
the Ultimate or Absolute Consciousness,
that primordial energy which is at the source of
everything in manifest creation.
When that pulsation or vibration "thickens,"
and condenses into slower and slower vibrations,
the formless becomes the form,
and eventually, individualized consciousness.

This understanding reveals that the vibratory energies that make up our body, our planet, and all of reality are "slowed-down expressions" of that same essential vibration or pulsation, in the same way that ice is the slowed-down vibration of water.

From this point of view, you and I are just very, very, very condensed forms of Supreme Consciousness!

I remember the first time I was introduced to and studied the *Spanda Karikas.* I'd been practicing meditation for over 25 years, and was already formulating my teaching about vibrational transformation, but had never heard of this ancient text. So when I read the translation of these verses, I was astonished to realize that in the 9th century, a great sage brought forth this profound wisdom about the truth of life that says exactly what science explains today.

Let's jump back from the 9th century to present time in the 21st century, and read the words of two renowned physicists as they describe the universe *using the same understanding as the Indian sages who lived 1,200 years ago.* First, Albert Einstein, thought to be the most influential physicist of the 20th century, is believed to have said:

> *"Concerning matter, we have been all wrong. What we have called matter is energy, whose vibration has been so lowered as to be perceptible to the senses. There is no matter."*

Theoretical physicist David Bohm, whom Albert Einstein called his intellectual successor, went on to actually describe reality in a way that even more closely mirrors the ancient mystics:

> *"Matter, as it were, is condensed or frozen light."*

I get chills when I read these quotes, and feel like I'm standing at cosmic, timeless crossroads where science meets self-realization. They are such marvelous and mind-blowing examples of the convergence between ancient spiritual knowledge and modern physics.

Fritjof Capra, an Austrian-born American physicist and author, eloquently described this convergence in his powerful book *The Tao of Physics:*

> *"The mystic and the physicist arrive at the same conclusion; one starting from the inner realm, the other from the outer world. The harmony between their views confirms the ancient Indian wisdom that Brahman, the ultimate reality without, is identical to Atman, the reality within."*

What an astounding time we're living in, when scientists have the most advanced tools and technology to see and prove what enlightened masters cognized in deep meditation and recorded by writing on palm leaves in the 9th century! Whether we understand ourselves from the teachings of ancient texts or prefer to see life through the eyes of modern science, *the unmistakable and spectacular truth is the same:*

**We are vibrational beings, and deep within us—
or, more accurately, at our subtlest, most refined level—
that same original essence of the Ultimate Source pulsates
in its unchanged form.**
**Not only is it there, it is "here" as well—
at the surface level of who we appear to be
as individual personalities.
Therefore, by definition,
we can't *not* be that Ultimate Supreme Pulsation,
which by definition *is* the All.**

You may believe that Ultimate Pulsation to be what you call God, Christ, Shiva, Buddha, Allah, the I Am Presence, or the Divine Light, or something else that has meaning to you. No matter what your belief, I hope this explanation fills you with the same experience of wonder and astonishment as it does for me every time I contemplate its significance.

It's astounding to realize that you and I are just a frozen, more condensed version of the Ultimate Energy and Source Vibration. I like to tell my students that we are all just **frozen consciousness popsicles!**

TRANSFORMING YOUR THOUGHTS BY
TRANSFORMING YOUR CONSCIOUSNESS

Now we come to the purpose of what has hopefully been a thought-provoking lesson in physics and metaphysics, and in fact the spiritual principle that is the foundation for my work and for this book:

**Most of us try to change ourselves on the level of our thoughts,
on the level of our feelings, or on the level of our behavior.
But this is control, not transformation.
True transformation must happen, and can *only* happen, at the level
of your vibration for it to be authentic and permanent.**

Doesn't this make sense? This is what I meant earlier when I introduced the idea of changing at the source, shifting from the inside out, and going beyond trying to manage yourself to mastering yourself.

**Transforming yourself is not about acquiring or learning
new information or concepts.
You're not just trying to think or behave differently.
You *are* different.
You're actually operating differently
from deep within your own consciousness.
You've transformed your vibration as a human being.**

One of my favorite childhood memories is of watching the 1954 TV production of *Peter Pan,* the musical adaptation of J. M. Barrie's wonderful novel and play. I vividly remember sitting on the floor in front of our small black-and-white TV (complete with rabbit-ears antenna), mesmerized by Peter and Tinkerbell coming in through the nursery window to take the children to Neverland. Peter sprinkles fairy dust on the family and instructs them to *"think lovely, wonderful, happy thoughts. And up you'll go!"* How I wished that I, too, could fly!

Wouldn't it be fantastic to always have positive, uplifting, expansive thoughts, and never be tormented by negative, limiting, frightened, or worrisome ones? We would all immediately experience more peace of mind, more confidence, and more joy. I think it's important to have the intention for our thoughts to be "lovely, happy, and wonderful," so lovely that they always lift us up. However, true and lasting transformation is not about simply trying to think differently, but actually *being* different. So how do we accomplish this?

Have you ever asked yourself where thoughts come from? *Your thoughts come from consciousness, that field of awareness beyond specific thoughts at a much subtler level of your being.* Your thoughts are only the final stage or the end product of your consciousness after the vibration of your consciousness passes through many filters, which we'll look at more deeply later in the book.

Imagine that consciousness is like a train beginning its journey at the main station, making numerous stops at many switching stations, until it reaches the end of the line. *That last stop on the route is called your mind.* From there, the "passengers"—your thoughts—disembark.

You can try all you want to control those "passengers," give them different, more attractive clothing, and hide them from sight, and you may even succeed for a few moments. But guess what? The next train is already pulling into the station from Consciousness Central, with a whole new load of thought-passengers. *Therefore, working on changing or controlling your thoughts once they have already arrived from your consciousness is a frustrating, exhausting, and useless endeavor. It's too late—you've already had the thought!*

**Just like a wave rises up from the ocean,
thoughts rise up from your own inner ocean of consciousness.
You cannot separate a wave from its source, the ocean.
And just as you cannot change the quality of the water
in a single wave without changing
the quality of the water of the ocean,
you can't transform the quality of your thoughts
and emotions *without transforming the consciousness
from which they arise.***

Here's another way to understand this:

Let's pretend you have a factory that uses green-colored wool to make many items of clothing. Everything coming out of the factory is going to be what color? Green, of course! You can tell yourself all you want that the clothing is red. You can visualize that this time when the wool is woven into a coat, it will manifest as red instead of green. You can put labels on the green clothing that state THIS IS ACTUALLY A RED SWEATER. But if the clothing was made with green wool, it is still going to be green.

The only solution would be to go to the source of the problem and change the raw material from which all the garments are made.

This is one of the most important and, I believe, life-changing shifts in understanding you can make—**that to truly transform your mind and the vibration of the thoughts it produces, you must go beyond the mind to its source, your consciousness, and transform at that foundational level.**

Beyond Positive Thinking to Positive Vibrating

Thinking positively is a wonderful practice. *But how do we go beyond simply trying to be a positive thinker and become a genuinely positive vibrational being?* This is the basis of the Soul Shift work I've done for many decades, and what I'll be explaining in the upcoming chapters. It's also one of the most important Soul Shifts you can make.

SOUL SHIFT

SHIFT FROM POSITIVE THINKING TO POSITIVE VIBRATING

You cannot permanently change your thinking without changing the *vibration of your consciousness.*

One of the ways our body/mind is designed is that it attempts to bring everything into harmony and balance. Therefore, even if we try to consciously control our mind and attitude from the outside, those efforts will inevitably fail if they're not built on a solid foundation from the inside—consciousness. It's true that you can force or overlay certain positive thoughts in your mind for a time, **but if those thoughts are not vibrating in alignment with the deepest vibration of your heart and your soul, you won't be able to sustain them.**

Your mind cannot sustain loving thoughts about yourself if deep within, you're vibrating with self-judgment.

Your mind cannot sustain thoughts about being abundant if deep within, you're vibrating with feelings of unworthiness.

Your mind cannot sustain thoughts about being capable and confident if deep within, you're vibrating with self-doubt and insecurity.

Your mind cannot sustain thoughts about wanting a fulfilling intimate relationship if deep within, you're vibrating with fear and mistrust.

For instance, you could try to hold a thought in your mind, such as *I deserve success and abundance,* but if that thought isn't vibrating in alignment with the truth deep within you, *those positive thoughts will be "vibrated out" and replaced by thoughts of a less harmonious vibration, such as those of fear, scarcity, and resentment.* No matter how sincere you are about seeing yourself or a situation in a positive light, you may find yourself frustrated, confused, or even feeling like you're somehow failing because you can't seem to "stop" armies of limiting thoughts from marching into your mind and taking over.

ARE YOU IN A VIBRATIONAL BATTLE WITH YOUR MIND?

Recently while I was at a speaking event, one of my assistants told me that a man had been waiting to talk to me for hours and seemed very distressed. "He's read all of your books and is a big fan of yours," she explained. "He seems really nice, but he says he's desperate to talk to you for five minutes." My presentation wasn't for a few hours, so I asked her to introduce me to him.

I liked Craig the minute I met him. He was a motivational speaker in the world of business and finance, and had a very sincere energy.

"I think something's wrong with me," he confessed, "and you're the only person I trust enough to share it with. I'm embarrassed to even talk about it."

"I'm honored that you feel that level of trust even though we haven't met before," I reassured him. "Tell me what's causing you so much agitation."

Craig looked around furtively to make sure no one was listening, and then with a very guilty look on his face, leaned forward and whispered, ***"No matter how hard I try, I don't always have positive thoughts."***

"I don't understand," I responded, slightly alarmed. "Do you mean you have bad thoughts that you can't control, and are afraid you will do something dangerous?"

"Oh no, nothing like that," he explained. "What I mean is, I've been working on myself for years, and I even get paid to teach others how to improve themselves and their business. I work hard to only think positive thoughts so that I'll attract good things into my life. But no matter how much I try, sometimes I still have scary thoughts about my career or angry thoughts about my girlfriend, and even if I attempt to drown the negative thoughts out with positive ones, they don't always go away. *I'm terrified that I'm failing at being a good person, and that something is terribly wrong with me."*

I reached out and took Craig's hands. "I want you to take in what I'm saying to you, because it comes from my heart," I said. "There's nothing wrong with you! You're not failing, and it's not your fault that you feel this way—you're just *missing some crucial information* that will help you understand yourself and your mind."

"Okay," he replied a bit shakily. "What do I do now?"

"I want you to make sure that you're on time for my lecture, and I want you to listen very carefully to everything I'll be explaining. Then find me at the next break, and we'll talk again."

During my session, I presented much of what I've been sharing here about vibrational transformation, and about recalibrating your consciousness so that the thoughts that arise from it are naturally vibrating with the Highest. I could see Craig sitting in the second row, furiously scribbling notes and enthusiastically nodding his head.

At the end of my book signing, Craig was waiting for me, and he looked like a different man: he was smiling and energized, and could barely contain his excitement. "Thank you, thank you, thank you!" he exclaimed. "Everything you said made so much sense. I feel like I just lost 1,000 pounds of anxiety. **During your lecture, it suddenly hit me that I've been at war with myself and my own thoughts. Could that be why I'm so exhausted all of the time?"**

"Yes, that's exactly what you've been doing, and it takes a lot of energy to be constantly fighting against your mind, rather than shifting from the inside out. I told you there was nothing wrong with you! There was just some missing understanding you needed. This is why I love teaching."

"And I love you!" he said with a grin.

I've met hundreds of "Craigs," sincere seekers who are beating themselves up or feeling that something is wrong with them because they can't seem to live up to the standards they've set for themselves. You may be surprised to learn, just as Craig was, that your sincere intentions to think more positively without *also* shifting your consciousness can often create a vibrational battle inside of you, one you don't even realize is taking place.

**The vibration of your conscious thoughts collides with
the vibration of your unconscious thoughts,
and the result is like a vibrational wrestling match!
Two parts of you are sparring for supremacy,
and your life and dreams are caught in the middle.**

Imagine your positive thoughts are being expressed by one part of you, and your unconscious contracted thoughts are being expressed by another part of you. Positive You says, *"I want to be a successful business owner!"* Contracted You answers, *"You don't deserve it. You always procrastinate, and you were a bad husband and father in your first marriage because you drank too much."* Positive You: *"Stop telling me I'm bad—I know I made mistakes, but I deserve abundance and fulfillment! I can be better this time."* Contracted You: *"Admit it—you feel guilty about all the ways you've been out of integrity. You've disappointed everyone! You aren't worthy of happiness. You'll blow it again."*

Now you're at war with yourself, a war between the unconscious emotional vibrations and the conscious thought vibrations.

What is the impact that these vibrational battles have on you?

1. Inner battles use up an enormous amount of energy.

I've worked with so many people who, like Craig, had no idea that their inner collisions were exhausting them.

**Often the vital energy we need to invest in our expansion, creativity,
and success becomes siphoned off by the effort
we constantly have to make, consciously or unconsciously,
trying to wrestle our fears, doubts, and insecurities to the ground.**

2. Inner battles create a chronic state of internal turmoil and anxiety.

Imagine that you're sitting between two people in the middle of a huge argument or fight that just goes on and on. How calm or centered can you feel? Not very! You're distracted by the chaos and drama, and even if you don't know or care about the people battling, you're still affected by their combative vibrations. This is what happens to us when we live in our own internal vibrational "war zone."

3. Inner battles give the universe—and everyone else—vibrational double messages.

"I deserve good things./I don't deserve good things."

"I want to succeed and lead, so give me responsibility./I don't trust myself to succeed and lead, so you shouldn't trust me either."

"Come here—I want love./Go away—I'm afraid of getting hurt."

"You can count on me to do a good job./I'm inconsistent and afraid I'll mess up and let you down."

Like a computer that gets frozen when you're giving it conflicting commands, your life can get stuck when you aren't vibrationally coherent, and you may not even be aware of what's happening. I've named this giving the universe/your loved ones/people you meet/your boss, colleagues, or potential clients "vibrational double messages."

I know many well-meaning people whose careers and finances have become casualties of those invisible vibrational wars. They had a positive dream, vision, or business goal, but unbeknownst to them, it wasn't in alignment with how they were emotionally vibrating deep inside their heart and consciousness. Some couldn't seem to get their project off the ground. Others did manifest success but then lost it, *because there were two separate sets of commands operating in their vibrational control room such as: "I deserve it./No, I don't deserve it."*

**Real transformation means
recalibrating yourself vibrationally—
"clearing out" old dissonant vibrational patterns
from your consciousness that are not serving you,
and "resetting" or shifting your vibration into one
that reflects higher frequencies of energy.**

When you shift vibrationally, what happens? As we saw earlier in our discussion on "Deep and Up," *you will naturally have more thoughts and emotions that are spontaneously and organically in alignment with the Highest truths and principles.* You show up in the world differently. People instantly feel it. Who you are on the inside and how you present yourself on the outside are coherent and in alignment.

This is exactly what happened to Craig. He decided to take some workshops with me in order to vibrationally recalibrate himself on the inside so that his inner reality matched his highest thoughts and visions for himself. He later sent me a delightful e-mail with an update on his progress. Here is an excerpt:

> *I'm writing you from London where I'm doing my first training for a huge international organization that I've been trying to hook up with for five years. How outrageous is that! They always liked me but said I wasn't the "right fit." After working with you, I realize that they somehow unconsciously sensed that, in spite of my bravado and show of confidence on the outside, inside I was much more shaky than I let on.*
>
> *Three weeks after my last seminar with you, I met with their board again, and this time, they couldn't hire me fast enough. I was blown away. I didn't do anything different or say anything different—but I sure was vibrating differently, thanks to this work. **I know you told me once I cleared up a lot of that internal dissonance and recalibrated my energy, people would sense it, and I can't believe how right you were.** I guess I wasn't giving them mixed energetic messages anymore, so I got the contract, and that's translated into doubling my company's profits for this coming year!*

Messages like this always make me happy that I'm a teacher. Craig made a huge Soul Shift when he realized that *he needed to do more than just think positively—he needed to be vibrating positively from the inside out.*

Does this concept of "recalibrating" ourselves sound complicated, mysterious, or impossible? It shouldn't. Remember: we are all vibrational beings, pulsations of that Ultimate Consciousness.

Everything that happens to us from without or within
is **simply a vibration that affects our vibration—**
what we think, what we do, what we feel, what we hear,
what we see, who we spend time with—
these all have a vibrational impact on us
that literally changes us moment by moment.

As we'll see, by learning what kinds of vibrational experiences create the highest frequency and the most beneficial impact, and then engaging in those experiences, we will be changing ourselves from our very source.

You can recalibrate or retune your vibration by beginning to create
powerful vibrational experiences **that will restore you**
to your highest vibrational frequency.

This is the exciting journey of Soul Shifts.

Everything Is Vibrating with Everything

"Every act, thought, and choice adds to the permanent mosaic:
Our decisions ripple through the universe of consciousness
to affect the lives of all.
Every act or decision made that supports life,
supports all life, including our own."
— David R. Hawkins, M.D., Ph.D.

In another lifetime within this lifetime, for a few years in the late 1960s and early 1970s, I was a bona fide flower child (not the drug-taking kind, but the meditating kind!). I hitchhiked up and down the coast of California, lived for weeks in a Volkswagen van cooking my brown rice on the side of the road, attended antiwar marches and handed out flowers to the rifle-wielding National Guardsmen, and danced under the moonlight at love festivals and Be-Ins (look it up if you're younger than 50!).

It was common then to carry signs that said: WE ARE ALL ONE. I wasn't sure what that saying meant, but I liked it. It resonated with something deep within me, the longing to somehow find a way to transcend the experience of separation and disconnection that had haunted me for as long as I could remember.

I had no idea back then, in my early days of being a formal seeker, that we really *are* all one!

**If you and I are made up of vibrating energy,
and everything around us is made up of
the same vibrating energy,
then *we are truly connected with everyone and everything.*
Even from the point of view of physics, if not metaphysics,
separation is not only an illusion—*it's an impossibility!***

We are all part of an infinite, vibrating sea of energy—the same, mysterious, outrageous field of energy. *That means you do not exist in a vacuum outside of that oneness. You cannot be separate from it, even if you insist that you are.*

As we contemplate what vibrational transformation means, our next Soul Shift points us in an important new direction.

SOUL SHIFT

SHIFT FROM THINKING OF YOURSELF AS AN EMOTIONAL/INTELLECTUAL BEING TO UNDERSTANDING THAT YOU ARE A VIBRATIONAL BEING

This is one of the most essential Soul Shifts I hope to offer you: *an invitation to begin understanding yourself not as an intellectual or emotional being, but as a vibrational being.*

**Even though you believe that you relate to things
intellectually or emotionally,
the primary way you relate to everything is *vibrationally.*
How you energetically vibrate with the world and with yourself
is what you identify with as "you."**

From the point of view of physics, you can think of the world as interacting fields of energy or vibration constantly vibrating with each other. We've seen that, at your essence, you are vibrating matter, Consciousness that has been "thickened" or condensed into a human being. *You are a walking vibrational field of energy in a perpetual dance with other vibrating fields of energy,* not just the energies you're aware of interacting with, such as people, but everything!

You're Always Making Waves

Let's tackle another lesson in spiritual physics, this time focusing on how your essential energy, or vibration, moves and interacts with the vibrational energy of the world.

Have you ever thrown a pebble into a body of water? If you have, you've seen physics in action, as the energy or vibration of the pebble interacting with the water traveled in circular waves and ripples out from the center. The pebble hit just one tiny spot in the pond or puddle, yet the impact of the vibration wasn't contained to that area, but rather went far beyond it. That's because of the nature of vibration: *physics tells us that all energy, or vibration, travels in waves.*

A wave is a pulsation or oscillation of energy traveling through space and through matter, such as air or water. Waves are the way energy, such as sound and light, gets transported and spreads out from its source. Some we can see, like those of physical energy that are created from the impact of the pebble on the water, or certain waves of light in the part of the spectrum visible to the naked eye. Others (such as microwaves, x-rays, radio waves, or electromagnetic waves) exist, but we can't perceive them. They're invisible to our eye and can only be measured with special instruments that can detect or "see" them.

We've all witnessed ocean waves crashing into each other, causing the water to splash and spray. This is an example of the vibrational "dance" between two fields of energy—in this case, water—but the interaction between energy waves is what actually makes up life as we know it.

**The dance of cosmic energy is always taking place all around us—
everything is vibrationally dancing with everything else,
from the smallest subatomic particles
to the gravitational pull of the stars and galaxies
and everything in between.
You are always dancing with everything!**

If everything is vibrating energy traveling through the universe in waves, *then we can imagine the universe as a huge cosmic ballroom filled with particles and waves dancing in billions of patterns and rhythms that form creation and everything in it!*

Let's shift back again from the cosmic to the personal, and the topic at hand: you and your particular unique vibrational "dance." Just as we've understood that all energy travels out in waves from its source, so do your vibrations or pulsations spread out in waves into the world around you from you as the source.

What makes up your personal vibrations? The most essential components are your thoughts and emotions. Thoughts and emotions are just electrical impulses in your brain with a certain content attached to them. *Every thought or emotion you experience forms waves of energy with a certain vibrational frequency.* An electroencephalogram (EEG) can record these voltage fluctuations or electrical activity in your brain.

Every thought you have creates a vibration or pulsation. Every emotion you experience creates a vibration. Every interaction, everything you see, everything you hear, and everything you experience creates a specific vibration. Just like all vibrations, these are comprised of energy.

Most of us realize that the thoughts we have and emotions we feel affect us—they uplift us or depress us; they inspire us or scare us; and so on. We often convince ourselves that if we don't tell others how we feel or what we think, they won't be aware of it or affected by it. However, we've seen that the nature of energy waves is to spread out, just as the energy of the pebble hitting the pond isn't contained in that one tiny area of water but travels outward in wave after wave. *Therefore, the impact of your thoughts and emotions is not just something you experience.*

Vibration affects vibration.
You are a vibration in constant action and reaction with everything.
Your thoughts and emotions are vibrationally broadcasting out
to the world all the time.
That means, as a walking vibrational being,
you're affecting everything all the time.
In fact, *it is impossible that you could <u>not</u> affect everything!*

Several months ago I was discussing this principle with a friend, and her 18-year-old son sat down to listen. "I like hearing you talk," Brent said, "and that's a very cool explanation. Of course, it doesn't apply to me."

"No? Why is that?" I asked.

"Because I always keep my thoughts and feelings to myself, so they don't get out. They stay in here where no one knows about them," he concluded proudly, tapping his head and his chest.

Smiling, I responded, "So, Brent, you're saying that your skin keeps all the vibrations from your thoughts and emotions locked in, right? The energy can't travel through your skin?"

Now he looked puzzled, as if he knew his logic was crumbling. "Hmm, I never thought of it that way," he confessed.

"Have you recently taken a picture on your phone and sent it to anyone?"

"Sure, this morning I sent my girlfriend a cute picture of my dog."

"That picture was changed into an electromagnetic wave that contained digital information and was sent through space to her," I explained. "Did she receive it?"

"Of course, immediately," Brent said.

"Did the phone or walls of your bedroom or all of the objects between you and your girlfriend stop the vibrational message from getting through?"

"Okay," he said, grinning sheepishly. "I get your point. *So believing that the vibrations of my thoughts and emotions stay locked inside of me and others don't feel them just because I don't talk about them is kind of stupid, right?"*

"Not stupid, dear—just unscientific!"

Why You're a Human Radio Station Broadcasting 24/7

Perhaps like my young friend Brent, you've believed that when you "hear" a thought inside your head, or feel a strong emotion, these vibrations aren't affecting anyone else and are secretly contained within your own system. Of course this is not true. *If you're experiencing thoughts or feelings that have a contracted vibration such as judgment, or a volatile vibration such as anger, or an agitated vibration such as fear, these energies are broadcasting out in waves. In the same way, if you're experiencing thoughts or feelings that have a more expanded vibration, such as love, compassion, or gratitude, these energies are also broadcasting out in waves.* Even the unconscious thoughts and emotions you aren't aware of are vibrating within you and radiating out, like a radio that's turned on but has the volume at a very low setting so you yourself can't even hear it.

Each thought, feeling, and internal reaction you have creates a vibrational wave of a certain frequency and quality, depending on the nature of the thought or emotion, and radiates, or broadcasts, that information out just like all waves do.

If you own a cell phone, you've probably used it in the last 24 hours, but have you ever considered how it works? When you talk into your phone, it converts the vibration of your voice into an electrical signal. Then it transmits that signal in the form of radio waves, an electromagnetic field vibrating at a certain frequency and traveling at the speed of light, 186,000 miles per second. Those waves are transmitted in all directions, and not in a straight line, just like the pebble thrown into the pond creates circular waves. A transmitter tower or cellular station calibrated to your phone number by your network picks up that specific frequency of radio waves, and sends or broadcasts them to your friend's phone, where they are changed back into electrical signals and then into the sound of your voice.

You can't see the radio waves traveling through space carrying the sound of your voice, but they are there, easily passing through substances like glass and wood on their journey. *Therefore, why would you think that the waves of your thoughts and emotions would be limited by the edges of your body and that nobody would feel or sense them?*

**You are a vibrational being,
and you're not just living in the world—
you are *impacting* the world, broadcasting and transmitting
the vibrations of your thoughts, emotions, and consciousness
in the same way that a radio station broadcasts a signal
out into the atmosphere
so it can be picked up by a radio, phone, or computer.**

Unlike a radio station, however, you don't get to decide when you transmit. You're *always* transmitting, just like one of those 24-hours-a-day stations that never goes off the air: "All you, all the time!"

The next question to ask yourself, then, is, "What *am* I broadcasting?" The answer is thought provoking to say the least: ***You are broadcasting everything*—everything that is vibrating in you as you.**

Each of us has a "vibrational recipe," which is the sum total of all of our thoughts, emotions, decisions, beliefs, and attitudes. These vibrational ingredients combine together in a particular way to make up what we can think of as our unique "orchestra," with its own "sound" or impact. It's as if all of the parts of you are like individual instruments playing separately, but when those instruments join together, they form a "vibrational symphony." That vibrational symphony is what people "hear," or feel, when they are near you, or even when they think of you. They tune in to your particular broadcast channel, and whatever's playing is what they experience.

By the way, whether you're conscious of it or not, the first person receiving the broadcast is you! *You're the first recipient of all of your vibrational waves.* So, for instance, that angry thought you have about someone else has to reverberate through your own system on its way out. The waves of vibrational energy pass through your mind and body before they radiate farther out beyond you to the world.

When you're upset with someone, it's not as if the negative thoughts or feelings you have about that person are like arrows that your mind "shoots" at them, and the vibration is no longer inside of you. On the contrary, the vibration still resonates within you, as the source of the "signal." Understanding this is a good incentive for doing the work of shifting and healing your vibrations from the inside out.

VIBRATIONAL FLASHBACKS:
HOW YOUR VIBRATIONAL PRESETS TRANSCEND SPACE AND TIME

We've seen that vibrational energy transcends space, but it also transcends time:

Your unconscious thoughts and emotions, both from the present and the past, are always broadcasting out to the world, even if you're totally unaware that they exist. They are "preset" channels in your consciousness.

It's not just your conscious thoughts that are always broadcasting. It's the thoughts you're not conscious of—what you can think of as your *emotional and mental programming*. We'll talk much more about your brain's programming later on, but basically, **it's the vibrational sum total of all thoughts you've been thinking and emotions you've been feeling, not just consciously, and not just recently, but for years and years throughout your whole life. I call these your broadcast "presets," vibrational channels that you tune in to automatically and unconsciously.**

Have you ever accidentally left your TV or music player on when you were sure you'd turned it off, or thought you'd hung up after a phone call but discovered that you hadn't pushed the "off button" firmly enough and were still connected? Now imagine that you have old vibrational broadcasts from experiences that happened decades ago, and they're still playing over and over, on preset channels, sending out vibrational messages that are no longer accurate or what you want to communicate.

Maybe that "program" consists of thoughts and feelings that combine to vibrate the message, *Love hurts. I don't want to let anyone get close to me.* You're single and doing everything you can to find a partner, yet can't understand why people seem to stay away from you. Perhaps you have another old program that contains mental and emotional content that combines to vibrate the message, *Something's wrong with me. No matter what I do, I'll never be good enough.* On the surface, you have confidence in your abilities, but you just can't seem to attract enough new clients.

This is a way to understand what happens when you believe that you're done with an issue or event from the past, but the vibrational impact of it is still reverberating inside of you and broadcasting those vibrations out.

Remember our discussion about "inner battles," different thoughts colliding within you? Now it may be easier to understand **why simply focusing on consciously sending out positive thoughts or vibrations isn't enough unless those vibrations are** *in alignment with what you are unconsciously broadcasting.*

If you have old vibrational experiences still pulsating inside of you, you may think that they're just memories, but they're much more. *They're not memories if they still have an emotional charge with them.* They're alive and broadcasting in present time.

> **Memories can carry an emotional vibration.**
> **Sometimes when we think we've finished with**
> **a challenge or issue, we've dealt with it behaviorally**
> **but haven't resolved it vibrationally.**
> **We think we're living in the present,**
> **but we're vibrationally stuck in the past.**

We're usually not even aware that we have "old vibrational programs" broadcasting. We might just have the experience of being disturbed by stray thoughts or emotions that seem to come out of nowhere, and whose origin we can't place. It's like when you hear a beep or buzzer go off in your house, and start looking around for its source, but can't figure out where it's coming from. *Did I set an alarm? Is that my smoke detector?* Hearing it but not knowing how to turn it off drives you crazy. You want to know what's causing the disturbance.

Your mind works in this same way. Its nature is to want to line everything up to make sense. It often will take your old vibrational broadcasts and look for evidence that their source is in present time.

> **When there's an old vibration broadcasting from inside of you,**
> **such as fear, mistrust, shame, anger, and so on,**
> **and your mind doesn't know where the energetic vibration**
> **is coming from,** *it will look for something to pin it on*
> *in your present-day reality.*
> **Your mind won't register it as an**
> **"old or outdated" vibrational message.**
> **It will feel like it's happening in present time,**
> **and from a vibrational point of view, it is.**

Most of us experience "vibrational flashbacks" all the time:

Your husband does something that is slightly annoying, but you find yourself feeling furious and unloved.

Your boss gives you some constructive criticism, and you suddenly feel rejected and swallowed up by feelings of unworthiness.

Someone you don't know well passes away, and you are overwhelmed by unexplained emotions of depression and grief.

A friend forgets to remind you about a party, and you feel betrayed and plagued by feelings of mistrust.

This process is called "projection." You're projecting your inner vibrational experience onto whoever or whatever is around you. *You're experiencing present-time reality through the filters of old vibrational realities.*

The problem, of course, is that you don't realize you're projecting, and you truly believe that what you're feeling is really happening. Your husband really doesn't love you. Your boss really thinks you're worthless. You really are horribly depressed. It's really true that you can't trust your friends. Of course, not all of your emotions and reactions arise from vibrational flashbacks, but you see the world through the lenses of old vibrational glasses more than you realize.

Another way to say this is:

We see things through the eyes of our issues!

If we wore glasses that were tinted blue, everything we saw through those lenses would appear to be blue. If our glasses were yellow, things would have a yellow tinge to them. Our minds are like those glasses: *The lens of our preset programming "tints" reality.*

The concept that our thoughts or our mind isn't a reliable compass for our journey has its roots in ancient teachings. Eastern spiritual traditions define ignorance as when we don't realize or have forgotten that we have glasses on that are coloring and altering our perception of what's real, and believe what we're seeing as blue is really blue, or what we're seeing as yellow is really yellow. *The Sanskrit word for this illusion of our perception is <u>Maya.</u>*

Maya is a term originating thousands of years ago in the Vedic literature of India, and can be translated to mean "illusion" or "delusion."

Maya is the illusion created when our true, great Self becomes identified with a limited physical and mental reality. It's the phenomenon we've discussed as the "freezing" or contracting of our Great Consciousness into the dense physical forms we identify with. It's our big sleep, our forgetting. It's why reality looks solid to us, when it's actually vibrating particles. It's why we think "we" are this physical body walking around, instead of understanding that we are the Supreme temporarily living in a body.

More simply put, *Maya means that we're seeing things, but not as they really are.* By now, you probably accept this at least theoretically from the Soul Shifts journey we've taken. However, here we're looking at it in a much more personal way—how, in our everyday life, our own mind creates illusions and delusions that we consider to be real.

We've all had this experience of Maya in very practical ways. Think back to somebody you were crazy about many years ago, perhaps your first crush or first partner, someone you thought was just wonderful. You were so happy and in love with them. When you remember this now, you may say to yourself, *What was I thinking? I didn't even know the person. He was on the football team, so I decided he was perfect. It was all a delusion.* Or, *I was so blind. I didn't realize she didn't have the capacity to love me or anyone.* Your mind saw what it wanted to see. One day, the veil of Maya lifted, and you saw the person for who they are, and actually always were. *How could I have not seen the truth?* you wondered. The answer is: Maya!

Every time I explain this to my audiences or students, I delight in watching their eyes get wider and wider with revelation. They suddenly understand why, in spite of their sincere efforts, they feel like who they truly are hasn't been expressing itself fully to people and to the world in general, or why they feel stuck in emotional energies from the past.

Isn't it amazing to see the world through "vibrational glasses"? This is what's so exciting about what we'll be learning in our upcoming Soul Shifts: *How to recalibrate your old vibrational patterns from the past so you're not unconsciously vibrating out old energies that don't reflect who you are today.* With this new understanding, you'll be able to radically transform the way you interact with everything and everyone, and discover the key to your authentic and lasting transformation.

"Smaller than the smallest particle,
greater and more expansive than the largest existing reality,
the very Self lies hidden and concealed
in the cave of the Heart of all living creatures."
— Katha Upanishad 2.20, 6th century B.C.

"Our planet, our society, and we ourselves are built of star stuff."
— Carl Sagan, *Cosmos,* 20th century

We began this chapter contemplating the miraculous—that we are all space travelers, hurtling through the universe at millions of miles an hour. So, too, we end with the miraculous: The same mysterious and awe-inspiring Cosmic Intelligence that has designed this incomprehensible and extraordinary dance of suns and planets and galaxies has also designed the remarkable blueprint of your own existence. Every single atom in your body originated 13 billion years ago from an exploding star. All of the chemical elements in the universe and in you are star-born.

There is only one truth, whether it is cognized by
ancient sages or measured by modern physics:
The smallest space within you is one with
the greatest space without.
Seen from the eyes of either the mystic or the scientist,
you are light vibrating with light.

In this moment, you are dancing.
Nothing that is you is still.
Your consciousness is pulsating.
Everything within you is vibrating in shimmering waves of light.
You are a miraculous vibrational masterpiece, a star child,
and you are not dancing alone.
You have billions and billions of vibrational partners—
people, animals, trees, clouds, dust, galaxies, everything.
You're dancing with everything and everyone.
They are cosmic relatives, after all.
You are never alone.
You are always already home.

❀ 6 ❀

How Are You Vibrating?
Ascending from Performance into Presence

*"Your every thought, feeling, perception, spoken word,
and performed action reverberates into the universe."*
— Swami Muktananda

One of my favorite TV programs when I was a teenager was the classic *Star Trek* series that became one of the most popular science-fiction shows of all time. It followed the adventures of the starship USS *Enterprise* and its crew, who were exploring the Milky Way galaxy in the 23rd century. As part of its mission, the *Enterprise* was always looking for "Class M planets," where the atmosphere had enough nitrogen and oxygen to be breathable and feasible for humanoid colonization.

Before the ship would approach a new planet and attempt to land a craft or "beam" a team down for exploration, it had to encounter and assess the atmosphere. The crew would check their instruments to see if the field around the planet had dangerous debris, volatile forces, or other conditions that would destroy the starship if it attempted to enter the atmosphere, or toxic gases that would kill the crew once they arrived.

Why am I reminiscing about *Star Trek,* and what does planetary atmosphere have to do with *Soul Shifts*? We know that a planet is a mass of matter with an atmospheric field around it. So, in essence, you are a "planet"—matter with an atmosphere. You're the "Planet Rebecca" or the "Planet Steven" or the "Planet Shannon," as I'm the "Planet Barbara." Just like a planet in our solar system, you too have a vibrational, electromagnetic field around you!

There's a beautiful line in one of Walt Whitman's poems from *Leaves of Grass,* written in 1855: "I sing the body electric." Even though the poem was written many decades before our present-day scientific advances, the phrase was accurate: **From the scientific point of view, you are basically an electrical being and your body actually *is* electric!**

Right now, for example, you're alive because once every second, cells in your heart produce an electrical pulse that keeps it beating. When that electrical pulse stops, the heart can't function, and your body dies. Your nervous system itself is a huge network of nerve cells transmitting information to one another through electrical signals in a process called *neurotransmission*. It's estimated that your brain has as many as 86 billion neurons, all operating at once. *Every time you have a thought or experience an emotion, it's because millions of neurons have been sending electrical impulses back and forth.*

Electricity produces magnetism. **Therefore, as an electrical system, you generate a vibrational, magnetic "atmosphere" around you that is not as dense as the physical matter of your body, and is invisible to the eye yet very real.** Your body is constantly sending out signals of particular frequencies and strengths. Remember that we talked about how your vibration travels out in waves and affects everything? This is what we can call your "vibrational climate," or atmosphere.

The vibrational atmosphere around you contains the most concentrated form of your vibrational broadcasts: your mental energy, emotional energy, and spiritual energy.

Long before modern science understood and measured our electromagnetic reality, many traditions—including Buddhism, Sufism, Taoism, Hinduism, the Kabbalah, Theosophy, and others—spoke of the subtler body that surrounded the physical body. It has been referred to as "the etheric body," "the rainbow body," "the auric field," "the spirit body," or as the "body of light" that is a part of you, but is not the flesh and blood you consider to be "you."

Let's try an experiment:

Take both of your hands, palms facing in toward one another about 12 inches apart, as if you were about to clap. Very slowly, begin to move your hands toward each other, but keep them from actually touching so that they're just about two to three inches apart. Notice if you feel the energy between your hands getting "thicker" as they get closer together.

Now keep your hands just a few inches apart, and move them in and out several times. Can you feel any sensation in your hands as you move them? Does it feel like something tangible is between your hands? Perhaps the energy feels dense, like Jell-O.

What you're feeling is your actual vibrational energy field! If you can, try this experiment with someone else, and see how close you need to move your hands toward one another before you feel "something," regardless of the fact that this "something" is invisible. Even if you feel nothing, those energy fields do exist, and are interacting long before you get physically close.

For the purpose of our galactic metaphor, we're calling this your "atmosphere." Just as a space traveler would have to enter a planet's atmosphere before landing on the physical planet, you are always "entering" the vibrational field around people in the same way that they're entering yours.

**When you meet someone, see them,
or stand close to them—
even before the person speaks—
you enter their "planetary atmosphere."
Of course, at the same time, they enter yours.
You move into each other's vibrational energy fields.**

As soon as you're in someone's "vibrational atmosphere," you definitely feel something. *What's vibrating around them impacts you vibrationally.* This actually isn't a new concept to you. Even though you may not have thought about it before from a vibrational point of view, you experience this invisible energy around people all the time:

* You meet someone, and instantly there is a change in the vibration of how you're feeling. You feel drawn to them or repelled, relaxed or agitated, safe or wary, uplifted or uncomfortable. The person puts you at ease and makes you want to engage with them, or gives you a bad feeling and makes you want to leave.

* You enter someone's home and instantly notice that the energy is warm and inviting, or that you can't wait to get out of there.

* A new person arrives at your workplace, and you immediately feel drawn to them and want to get to know them, or feel an instant dislike for them and decide to avoid them at all costs.

Sometimes these reactions are subtle and you aren't even aware you're having them; sometimes they're very intense. Yet almost always, you can't find a logical explanation for your reactions, since they're not based on facts or reason, but just what you call a "feeling":

I don't know what it is about that person, but I just don't feel comfortable around her.

The second I saw our new account manager, I knew I could trust him before he even introduced himself.

He's a perfectly pleasant guy, but something about him always bugs me.

Every time I go to my cousin's house, I feel so agitated and angry, even though nothing specific happens that upsets me.

I immediately liked my son's new teacher when I saw her and could tell she had a kind heart.

How is it possible that you had such specific and strong responses? **You were "in orbit" around their "planet," and "checked their atmosphere"!**

Your vibrational field tunes in to someone's vibrational field, and you assess them vibrationally before you even have enough information to assess them intellectually or emotionally— and they do the same to you.

This is what we mean when we use the phrase "I checked them out." *Whether you're aware of it or not, you are, indeed, always taking vibrational readings on everyone, just as they're taking vibrational readings on you.*

In our last chapter I introduced the Soul Shift from thinking of yourself as an emotional or intellectual being to understanding that you're a vibrational being. Now our next Soul Shift is going to help you understand your relationships with everyone.

SOUL SHIFT

SHIFT FROM THINKING OF YOUR RELATIONSHIPS AND INTERACTIONS WITH PEOPLE AS EMOTIONAL TO UNDERSTANDING THAT ALL OF YOUR INTERACTIONS ARE PRIMARILY *VIBRATIONAL*

If, as we've seen, you are primarily a vibrational being, it follows that all of your relationships and interactions with others are not just emotional, but are actually and primarily vibrational. *You are a walking vortex of vibrational energy.*

When you encounter someone, no matter who it is, their vibration has a particular impact on yours. **You can't *not* be affected by people, and they can't *not* be affected by you.** It has nothing to do with what they say. It has to do with how they—and you—are vibrating.

It follows, therefore, that everyone is always assessing you vibrationally. They're not consciously thinking, *Now I'll assess this person's vibration,* but they are, indeed, energetically assessing you, and you are assessing their vibration as well. You are in a constant mutual process of vibrational assessment.

You're always being assessed vibrationally by others.
Long before you say anything or do anything, you are being felt.
Your vibration is your most powerful form of communication.

I repeatedly remind my students that *"We're always communicating, whether or not our mouth is open."* You're communicating vibrationally, unconsciously broadcasting out energetic "messages" from your planet, as well as receiving messages from the people around you. This explains why it takes just a few seconds for you to get a sense of someone when you meet them. The research of psychologist Albert Mehrabian suggests that only 7 percent of someone's first impression of you is based on what you say, while the remaining 93 percent of how you impact someone is attributed to body language and tone of voice. I believe these are really ways the research is measuring what we've been calling *vibration*.

VIBRATIONAL INTERFERENCE AND YOUR VIBRATIONAL ASTEROID BELT

Have you ever had someone say, "You just totally misinterpreted what I expressed. I was complimenting you, but you heard it as a criticism"?

Have you ever had someone tell you that you sounded angry with them, even though you merely asked a simple question in a way you thought was neutral and innocuous?

Have you ever tried to share your enthusiasm or admiration with someone you wanted to impress, only to have your words "come out all wrong"?

These are experiences of what I call *"vibrational interference"—your true message or intention meets interference on the way out as it passes through your vibrational field, and the other person's message meets interference as it enters your field before you receive it.*

Everything from inside of you must pass through your vibrational field on its way out to others, and everything from the outside must also pass through your vibrational field on its way into you.

Your vibrational field is the filter through which everything must pass going in both directions. You couldn't bypass it even if you wanted to. You might have the greatest information you hope to share, the most inspiring concept you're attempting to explain, or the most sincere emotion you're intending to express, but they all must travel from inside out through your energy field, your vibrational atmosphere. In the same way, everything that comes to you from others—love, information, feedback—must pass through your atmospheric energy field before it "lands" on your planet.

What is that interference? **Think of it as a sort of "vibrational asteroid belt."** Asteroids are chunks of rock and metal that orbit around a star, mostly in a "belt" between the planets. Scientists believe that they're pieces of planets that broke up, along with leftover material from the creation of a solar system that never formed into planets. In science-fiction novels or movies, spaceships are always in danger of being hit if they try to pass through an asteroid belt on the way to a planet (even though in real life, scientists say asteroids are too spread out for collisions to occur).

I like this metaphor because **it's helpful to think of your highest intentions, thoughts, and communications leaving your "planet of consciousness" and colliding with your vibrational asteroids—broken pieces of old patterns and emotional programs still "floating" around your atmosphere.** In the same way, other people's energy from their "planets" tries to connect with yours, but collides with your vibrational asteroids.

Remember our discussion about your "vibrational broadcast presets," certain frequencies of emotional energy that have been automatically and unconsciously vibrating and sending out vibrational messages? When we add this to our metaphor about your planetary atmosphere, you can get a clear picture of these vibrational collisions:

Your old vibrational programming is part of what makes up the energetic field around you.

People enter your field and sense or receive your vibrational messages, even though you haven't communicated those messages with words and perhaps don't intend to.

These people have collided with your vibrational asteroid belt.

Imagine that you got all dressed up to attend a special event, but on the way to the gathering place, you had to walk through rain, mud, and piles of garbage. These circumstances would "interfere" with your pristine appearance and alter it so that by the time you arrived at your destination, you wouldn't look anything like you did when you started out.

This is a simple metaphor to describe the phenomenon of "vibrational interference," something you experience every day without realizing it. **What you eventually say, or how you eventually act, or what choices you eventually make—in other words, the "you" others experience—is the end product of the trip from your consciousness (or planet) through your own atmospheric interference.**

Just like the rain, mud, and garbage would alter your appearance if you had to walk through them on the way to a party, so your vibrational interference alters your energy, distorting it from your highest vibration or intention. By the time you pass through your own atmosphere and put your thoughts or feelings into speech, or even just are in someone's presence, the "you" who shows up may not be the "you" that you hope will show up.

**On the journey from within your consciousness out to the world,
your pure messages, thoughts, or emotions bump into
vibrational energies and patterns
pulsating or "orbiting" in your atmosphere,
and end up getting "muddied" or vibrationally altered.**

This is why we feel things like *I didn't mean to sound so harsh,* or *I didn't mean to come off as so insecure,* or *I didn't mean to say things that scared him.* We believe that we're sending out one communication or intention, but by the time it travels through our vibrational field and "arrives" at its destination, it's been tampered with.

Hopefully, you're beginning to see how essential it is to understand yourself vibrationally, and not just psychologically or intellectually. Of course, even though we're exploring this concept of vibration using the analogy of planets and atmospheric fields in order to make it easier to comprehend, it's important to remember that *you're not exactly like a planet!* As we saw earlier, your vibrational "atmosphere" doesn't start at the edge of your skin, in the way that a planet's atmosphere begins above the surface. It's not as if you have actual self-contained energies like satellites floating around your head!

**Your vibrational field isn't *outside* of your body:
It's broadcasting out from deep within the control room of your
consciousness, affecting your own body as well as
creating an energetic field in and around you.**

With that said, let's go back to our metaphor.

Look Out! It's Your Emotional Space Junk

Once I watched a fascinating show on the Discovery Channel about the massive amount of "space junk" floating around in Earth's atmosphere. When we look up at the night sky, we imagine that between us and the moon and distant planets it's all just empty space, but this isn't true. I was surprised to learn that there are millions of pieces of human-made debris zooming around our atmosphere. Right now there are discarded and broken booster rockets, nonfunctional satellites, lost equipment, random pieces of metal, solar panels, and other "space waste" all hurtling around Earth at speeds up to 17,500 miles per hour, making this very dangerous and deadly debris.

There's even what we might think of as an official "outer-space cemetery" called the "graveyard orbit." It's a corridor 22,000 miles above our planet where nonfunctional spacecraft are left when they're no longer needed or operational. I was fascinated by this idea of debris that's no longer functional, but is still traveling around with "us"—Earth—in our trip around the sun and the galaxy.

Most of us, as we've seen, have our own vibrational equivalent of space junk—not physical objects, but old vibrational energies that, like ancient satellites, are still broadcasting energetic messages about things that happened a long time ago. These unresolved emotions from the past are part of what makes up that Asteroid Belt of Emotional Debris around us.

Just like old booster rockets and antiquated satellites, our vibrational space junk is not functional, but it's still there.

Imagine that, years ago, you experienced a painful breakup with someone who hurt and perhaps even betrayed you. Those intense emotions became a vibrational broadcast orbiting around your consciousness. You can picture them like a vibrational satellite, sending out messages like *My boyfriend was a jerk. I hate him. I will never forgive him. Men are disgusting.* (Guys, please change the gender to fit your own past circumstances!) Those vibrational messages play over and over, traveling around in your vibrational field.

Time passes; you grow older and haven't been able to find a partner. *I can't understand why no one has come into my life,* you complain. The problem could be your space junk—old emotional debris that's cluttering up your vibrational field. It's not functional, but it's still there.

You may read this and think, *But I haven't seen that person in 15 years,* or *Those things happened to me a long time ago. I'm over it. How could the feelings about them still be floating around in my emotional atmosphere?* **Unless you've consciously switched off the broadcast and transmuted the energy, they're still there, and could still be transmitting without your even realizing it.**

Even if you're in a relationship, your emotional space junk can negatively impact you and your partner. Remember that everything coming toward you and from within you has to pass through that vibrational atmosphere. You may not be aware that the vibration from your old Anger Satellite or Mistrust Satellite is coloring how you act or sound, but this happens all the time.

Part of the work I'll be offering you in this book will be to recalibrate yourself by *vibrating out* all that is no longer in alignment with who you are today. Isn't it time to get rid of your vibrational space junk? You can begin by asking yourself these questions:

Soul Shift Recalibration Questions

What kind of vibrational and emotional space junk might be orbiting around me?

What caused it? How long has it been there?

What emotional collisions has this vibrational debris created between myself and others?

Remember that what you can see, you can shift.

WHAT PLANET ARE YOU FROM?
UNDERSTANDING YOUR VIBRATIONAL INHERITANCE

Have you ever met someone who you concluded was very strange, and found yourself somewhat sarcastically saying or thinking, *What planet is he from?* This is actually a legitimate question for us.

If, as we've seen, you're a vibrational being, then what kind of planet *are* you from? How did the vibrational field around the "Planet You" get created? What is the condition of your vibrational atmosphere, and what's the source of any "emotional asteroids" like anger, agitation, and fear that are floating around?

To find the answers, first we have to go back to your "vibrational origins." You and I and everyone else grew up on our own "vibrational planet" with its own unique atmosphere. This planet was called your family and your household. It had a particular energetic climate and frequency that affected you and vibrationally programmed you in profound ways.

I call this your *"vibrational inheritance,"* as our next Soul Shift explains.

SOUL SHIFT

SHIFT FROM SEEING YOUR PAST AS A SERIES OF EMOTIONAL EVENTS TO UNDERSTANDING THEM AS *VIBRATIONAL* EVENTS THAT HAD A *VIBRATIONAL IMPACT* ON YOU

We've all done some contemplation on how the emotional events of our past have affected our personality, our habits, and our choices. This important Soul Shift says that to really understand yourself—to see what there is to see about yourself and then shift—it's essential to realize not just *what* happened to you, but the *vibrational impact events and circumstances have had on you.*

Most of us experienced love and caring growing up, but often there were other energetic realities as well, even if they were never put into words. *In your home, were there vibrations of fear or anxiety? Were there vibrations of shame or scarcity? Were there vibrations of sadness? Anger? Perfectionism and control? Vibrations that the world isn't fair? That you need to hide your success because people will become jealous?*

We've seen that vibration affects vibration, and everything is always vibrating with everything. Children are like vibrational sponges. When you were young, you didn't have the language skills to articulate your experiences, but you certainly felt the emotional and mental vibrations in your home and couldn't help but be impacted by them, even if you don't remember this happening. Those vibrational frequencies were broadcasting 24/7 from your parents and extended family and were your vibrational inheritance.

Your parents were your first *vibrational teachers*.
In the same way that you probably learned
to speak your native language with the exact accent
your parents used, or acquired the same behavioral habits,
all without consciously being aware that this was taking place,
you learned to vibrate at similar frequencies
to those you experienced every day while growing up.

Another way of saying this is that *we can't help but begin to vibrate like the energies with which we come into contact. That's because our nature as human beings is to harmonize with what and who are around us.* We adjust our behavior and communication to fit in with our environment. If everyone's applauding enthusiastically at a concert, it's difficult not to applaud. If everyone's walking quickly in a crowd, it's difficult not to keep that same pace. If everyone's laughing watching a play or show, it's difficult not to laugh.

Have you ever sat next to someone who was singing or humming the same song over and over? Have you ever had to listen to one of your kids incessantly practicing a song for a play at school? Eventually, you'll find yourself humming that tune even if you can't stand it. "I cannot get that song out of my head," you complain. You began to vibrate with it without even realizing this is taking place.

These aren't conscious decisions. We don't think, *Everyone's laughing, so I will laugh also,* or *The crowd seems excited about the touchdown and has jumped to their feet, so I suppose I will join them,* or *Since this stranger is humming, I might as well hum along.* Spontaneously, we find ourselves laughing; we find ourselves leaping to our feet; we find we can't get the song out of our head. Whether we realize it or not, we're actually being vibrationally drawn into what's taking place.

Our nature as human beings is to naturally and intuitively
"tune" ourselves to vibrate at the same frequencies as those around us
in order to achieve a sense of harmony.
I call this "vibrational resonance."

THE MYSTERIOUS POWER OF VIBRATIONAL RESONANCE

One day in 1964, during a junior-high-school science class, my teacher announced that he was going to give us a demonstration of how energy interacted with energy—in this case, sound energy. He set up two tuning forks, each mounted on a sound box on the lab table, and struck one of them with a rubber mallet. The tuning fork began to vibrate at a certain frequency, and so did the air inside of the box, producing a distinct sound we could all hear. Then my teacher put his hand on the fork to stop its vibration, but we could still hear the sound. To our astonishment, it was coming from the second tuning fork. Even though no one had touched it, the second fork had begun to vibrate all on its own as if by magic, and produced the same sound as the first.

How did this occur? The two tuning forks were connected by the surrounding air particles, which transmitted the energy of the sound waves. **The vibration of the first tuning fork "forced" the second tuning fork to vibrate at the same frequency.** My science teacher explained that this was called *"resonance"*:

**Resonance is when an object that is interconnected
with another like it
forces the second object into vibrational motion.**

Even at the time, I was fascinated with this demonstration. I sensed that it was significant way beyond the lesson being presented to our class of 14-year-olds, and I was right: *Just as the second tuning fork resonated with the first after being impacted by its vibration, we as human beings unconsciously adjust ourselves vibrationally to match the vibrations of those around us.*

When you begin to understand vibrational resonance, you'll find it explains so many life experiences:

* Vibrational resonance explains why we become so affected by other people's moods, energy, or vibrations even when we try everything we can to not let that happen.

* Vibrational resonance explains why we may find ourselves thinking or behaving in ways that aren't our usual self when we're with groups of people—family, old school friends, crowds—who create a significant vibrational impact on us.

* Vibrational resonance explains why we actually become like the people with whom we spend the most time.

* Vibrational resonance explains why we have a vibrational inheritance from the circumstances of our childhood, even if no one ever instructed us to be a certain way.

This is why we often do or feel things that are emotional or behavioral habits we can't seem to break, habits we can see are part of our vibrational inheritance. These emotions or behaviors are like the song you can't get out of your head because you heard it over and over again.

**Many of our mental and emotional patterns
are like familiar "songs" we've heard our whole life,
songs that we unconsciously "sing"
and vibrationally resonate with,
whether we want to or not.**

I've seen countless examples of vibrational resonance in my students, and whenever I explain this concept, people are flooded with revelations that explain so much about their personality and patterns. Here's a true story that illustrates the power of our vibrational inheritance.

Sabrina is a beautiful, intelligent, sensitive, and very successful woman. All of her life, however, she's been plagued by fear, anxiety, and chronic suspicion of the world and everyone in it. These emotional patterns kept her from letting others get too close, even her own husband and children, and no matter how hard she tried, she had difficulty trusting and could never relax. Sabrina lived as if she was always in danger of calamity. She hated being pinned down or committing to anything, because, in her words, it made her feel "cornered and trapped."

"I don't understand where I am blocked," she confessed to me. *"I realize that every day I feel and act as if I'm living in a war zone, but I've never been able to figure out why.* I didn't have a traumatic childhood or experience any trauma, but I'm always terrified, to the point of making myself sick with anxiety."

"What about your parents' childhood?" I asked.

"My parents? What does that have to do with me?"

"If you didn't grow up with any reason to not trust," I explained, "you've probably inherited vibrational patterns from them. This means that when they were younger, they must have had reasons to feel all the same things you feel every day."

For a moment, Sabrina got very quiet. Suddenly, her eyes filled with tears, her face turned white, and she began to shake.

"Oh my Lord," she said in a trembling voice. "I feel like a huge explosion just went off inside of my brain. You're absolutely right. *My mother and her whole family escaped from Eastern Europe. All my life I've heard terrifying stories about how in the years before they left, they couldn't trust anyone, had to lie and hide to avoid imprisonment or worse. Many of their friends and neighbors disappeared never to be seen again. They lived like this day and night, preparing to sneak out, ready to flee at a moment's notice, not knowing if they would make it in time. I can't believe I never saw this.*"

"This was your vibrational inheritance, your vibrational lineage," I offered. "**Your mother grew up with the vibrations of suspicion, constant anxiety and fear of being destroyed, the need to cover up the truth and not get too close or attached to anyone or anything, and always looking for the opportunity to escape. This was how she was programmed.**"

"But I was born in Boston, so how is it possible that I've felt all of those things and never experienced them?"

I shared this information about vibrational resonance and all we've been learning here, helping Sabrina understand how she learned to vibrate with these same emotional frequencies of fear and mistrust because that's what was vibrating around her, even from the time she was in her mother's womb.

"This explains everything down to the smallest details!" Sabrina exclaimed. "Do you want to hear something eerie? I will only park right next to the exit in parking lots, including enormous ones that are almost empty, even if it means walking 15 minutes through the lot to the store. And I won't park in parking structures where I can't find a spot close to the exit booth. I'll just go home. My husband gets so exasperated with me, and I get very angry with him, as if he doesn't understand how crucial it is—even though I don't either. I never could figure out why I did that, and thought maybe I had some kind of mental problem."

"No, my dear," I reassured her. *"You were just being prepared in case you had to escape."*

Sabrina began to weep as she realized how, even though her mother had fled terror and tyranny in her homeland, she'd brought the vibrational habits with her, and unknowingly passed them along to her daughter, not verbally but vibrationally.

"I always judged my mother as being backward and unsophisticated for being so cautious in her adult life, and keeping to herself," she confessed. *"For the first time, I understand why she was the way she was, and why I've been the way I am."*

Understanding her vibrational inheritance changed every aspect of Sabrina's life. She worked hard to see what there was to see and locate all of the habits she thought were just her "personality," but were actually vibrational flashbacks to a place far away where she'd never been, and to circumstances she'd never had to actually face. Day by day, she began to vibrationally recalibrate herself using the techniques you'll be learning. She started having moments of true intimacy and trust with her loved ones. Most of all, she had a new vibrational experience, one she'd never had before: *the sense of being safe and at peace.*

Exploring Your Vibrational Inheritance

Your vibrational inheritance isn't the only thing contributing to your makeup as a vibrational being, as we'll see moving forward, but it is a large part of it. Once you spend some time contemplating the concept of vibrational inheritance and how it may have played out in your own life, you'll begin to see connections that will first shock you, then amaze you, and, eventually, relieve you.

I often have my students explore this topic by making a list of sentences that begin with:

No wonder I ____.

Here are some of Sabrina's:

No wonder I hate making plans and telling people where I'll be, under the guise of being spontaneous.

No wonder I haven't fully unpacked the boxes since we moved into our new apartment three years ago, as if we'll have to leave soon.

No wonder when someone knocks on my door and I'm not expecting anyone, I start to panic.

No wonder when people ask me questions about anything, even people I love, I feel interrogated and like I can't breathe.

No wonder I hate to talk about myself unless I know someone really well.

No wonder I try to blend into the background and be the "invisible CEO" in my own company, claiming that I'm just modest.

No wonder I get furious at my daughter when she talks about our family on her Facebook page, and even more furious when she puts photos of me up.

Can you see how all of Sabrina's "preferences" or "personality traits" are the responses of someone who feels as if she has to keep a low profile, not get too comfortable, and protect herself from the "enemy"?

I suggest you make your own *No wonder I ___* list. This isn't what will ultimately change these patterns, but by identifying them, you'll begin to dismantle them.

You can also begin to explore your vibrational inheritance by working with these other Soul Shift questions:

What was the energy behind the communication and words—not the actual words—in my family?

What was the vibrational atmosphere in my house—not the events, but the vibrational frequency?

What vibrational "tunes" do I think I learned to resonate with, and have been "singing" ever since?

If you look at your household and family from a vibrational point of view, with no judgment but just with assessment, you will begin to see the roots of your "vibrational inheritance."

Maybe in order to harmonize with the vibration of anxiety, you became cautious and hypervigilant.

Maybe in order to harmonize with the vibration of negativity and judgment, you became arrogant and critical.

Maybe in order to harmonize with the vibration of not making waves and keeping a low profile, you became introverted and protective.

Maybe in order to harmonize with the vibration of mistrust of others and the world, you became reclusive and guarded.

Now for the really good news: Your vibrational inheritance and your subsequent vibrational habits and broadcasts are just how you've been programmed. They aren't *you!*

Your habits and patterns *aren't* who you are.
They're *how you've been vibrationally calibrated or "tuned."*
Much of what you think of as your "personality" are simply
leftover vibrational echoes,
vibrational habits you've unconsciously adopted,
never realizing that they've run much of your life.

Relationships: Understanding Vibrational Proximity

What makes vibrational resonance work?

Why do we become so influenced by the people in our environment and those we love?

The answer to both of these questions is the same: I call it *"vibrational proximity."*

Vibrational proximity means that
two people/objects/vibrational systems have to be
close enough for resonance between them to take place.

Right now, in this very moment, you're experiencing the effects of vibrational proximity between two huge masses that are in enough proximity to affect one another: Earth and the moon. You probably know that the gravitational pull of the moon's atmosphere creates tides here on Earth. Even more significant, the moon's gravity slows down our rotation, acting like a sort of enormous braking system. If the moon didn't exist, we'd be rotating much faster, and a day on Earth would be radically shorter, lasting only about six to eight hours!

The Earth also profoundly affects the moon. Our gravitational field keeps the moon in orbit, which is why it rotates around us. Without Earth nearby, the moon would soon drift away to orbit the sun on its own, or wander around until it got pulled into another gravitational field, abandoning us for another planet!

Even though there are other enormous planets in our solar system, they don't impact Earth like the nearby moon because they're not in vibrational proximity to us. **In the same way, even though we've seen that everything vibrates with everything, some things vibrate more powerfully with other things when they're in vibrational proximity.** In my junior-high-school science experiment, the tuning forks could resonate because they were in vibrational proximity. Your vibrational inheritance could take place because you were in vibrational proximity to your family.

If you're a vibrational being or "planet" with an atmosphere, and you're in regular, very close proximity to another person or "planet" with its own atmosphere, very powerful resonance takes place, and you have profound vibrational effects on one another. *This is called a "relationship"!*

An intimate relationship is actually a sort of vibrational duet. *When you're with another person for an extended period of time, an energetic synchronization takes place.* You tune yourself to each other's vibrations and, for better or for worse, start to continually vibrate together in innumerable ways.

When you're intimately involved with someone, such as a partner, spending time with them, or living with and sleeping with them, your energy field and theirs are in vibrational proximity.
You will begin to vibrationally resonate together, tuning your vibration to theirs.

We all know that people who've been married for a long time somehow look alike in a way we can't pinpoint. They may walk and talk alike, and even if they don't get along, they seem to be operating from the same vibrational channel. They've been in vibrational proximity for so long that they are in a constant state of resonance.

Have you ever had the experience of spending a lot of time with someone—a friend, a partner, a work colleague—and noticed that their "energy" is affecting you negatively? To your dismay, you find yourself thinking like them, communicating like them, and behaving like them.

"He is not having a good effect on me," you confess to a friend, or *"She brings out the worst in me,"* you admit to yourself. **You aren't consciously changing—the vibrational proximity has set up resonance between you, and your system is attempting to harmonize with the other person, whether you want it to or not.**

As you learn to understand all of your relationships as vibrational, you'll begin having many revelations about the vibrational dances that have taken place between you and people in your past, as well as those taking place now. You're probably already seeing your relationships through the lens of your new "vibrational glasses," and making important and eye-opening connections that explain a lot, and perhaps help you see yourself and others with more compassion.

Later we'll be looking more closely at how your vibrations affect other people, and how theirs affect yours, as we introduce the idea of making good "vibrational choices" for yourself.

Your Vibration Is the Medium Through Which Your Message Must Pass

"Who you are speaks so loudly I can't hear what you're saying."
— Ralph Waldo Emerson

When I was 18 and began studying for my undergraduate degree in communications, I was fascinated with the brilliant work of Marshall McLuhan, the Canadian philosopher of communication and media theory who, 30 years before its creation, predicted the World Wide Web. Professor McLuhan is known for coining the phrase *The medium is the message,* and really pioneered the study of the interrelationship between the individual and the means by which humans communicate with one another. His focus was on the mediums we used at that time (such as the telephone, typewriter, and television), and how they altered and therefore became part of our message.

In this same way, you are the medium through which your message—or vibration—must pass:

You have to vibrate your truth from your whole being.
You can't just speak it or think it.
Your words and actions on the outside
need to be *backed up by your vibration on the inside.*

Now that you're beginning to see yourself as a vibrational being, your understanding of how you communicate is going to change. Instead of just asking yourself: "What should I say?" you might want to add the question: *"How am I vibrating?"*

SOUL SHIFT

SHIFT FROM ONLY SPEAKING YOUR TRUTH TO VIBRATING YOUR TRUTH

We think our words are like attractive wrapping paper that covers up our vibrations, but the truth is that our vibrations are the wrapping paper for our words.

Your words are always wrapped in your vibrations. They can't sneak out of your house of consciousness without them, or leave your planet of consciousness without having to pass through your atmosphere. Remember our Soul Shift that you are primarily a vibrational being. *So your words are a combination of the verbal content you've decided to convey, delivered in a particular vibrational package.*

You can't fake your vibration. You can't hide your vibration. You can't camouflage it with words. You can't hide it behind actions, or try to manage its appearance. People will feel your vibration, even if they don't register that this is what they're feeling.

If you're saying, "Trust me—I know what I'm doing," but your communication is unconsciously delivered in the wrapping paper of anxiety and fear, people will feel it. If you're saying, "No, I'm not mad about what you did to me," but your communication is wrapped in an angry vibrational covering, people will pick it up. If you're smiling and saying sweet things, but your message is covered in judgmental wrapping paper, people will sense it. You could be the most eloquent and charming communicator in the world, *but your words will never speak more loudly than your vibration.*

129

*"However many holy words you read, however many you speak,
what good will they do you if you do not act upon them?"*
— The Buddha

What does it feel like when someone is vibrating their truth, when what they're saying on the outside is in total alignment with their inner reality? *I've been in the presence of great saints who did not have to speak a word, and yet I could not stop weeping just being in the high vibration of their energy field.* I remember the exact moment when I met each of my spiritual teachers: Maharishi Mahesh Yogi in 1970, and Gurumayi Chidvilasananda in 1995. In both situations, I was about 30 to 40 feet away when I saw them, and yet my immediate reaction was that my eyes filled with tears without even understanding why. My heart felt like it had just exploded with joy.

Recently, I was blessed with a similar experience when I was privileged to meet His Holiness the 14th Dalai Lama during a conference at which we were both speaking. His Holiness saw me in a crowd and walked through the people toward me to place a scarf around my neck and take my hands in his. We stood there for one minute, our eyes locked, and it was as if an eternity passed. He said very few words to me, but they were charged with ancient recognition, and contained vibrational libraries of infinite wisdom and messages for my heart and soul. It was an eternal moment during which so much more occurred than what appeared to be taking place on the surface.

What happened when I met each of these great beings? *It was as if I'd walked into a vibrational ocean of pulsating divine love—and I had.* These masters vibrated from the core of their beings with the frequencies of wisdom, compassion, and grace. **Their words were secondary—verbal containers for the powerful healing vibrations that the teachers embodied. They didn't have to say anything, and because they were vibrating at these high frequencies, people were moved just to be near them.**

This morning, while finalizing this chapter, I read a beautiful passage by Marshall McLuhan in which he is speaking about Jesus, and describing this same phenomenon of the message and the messenger vibrating as one:

> *In Jesus Christ, there is no distance or separation between the medium and the message: it is the one case where we can say that the medium and the message are fully one and the same.*

This is a more modern yet beautiful description of this Soul Shift concept: that when we are vibrating as our Highest truth, our words, and indeed our entire being, will pulsate with that truth—and we will be a walking, breathing example of wholeness.

**No amount of impressive behavioral or verbal
wrapping paper can camouflage your vibration.
Your vibration will always speak more loudly
than your words ever could,
and will broadcast itself even if you don't say anything.
There's no substitute for doing the real work
of vibrational transformation.**

FROM PERFORMANCE TO PRESENCE:
BECOMING A VIBRATIONAL MASTERPIECE

I hope by now you realize that *your vibration is always making a difference,* and that you're beginning to understand the fascinating mechanics of how that takes place. It doesn't matter how you want people to see you or what you say—they will feel everything that you vibrationally bring into that moment.

The only question left is: **What *do* people feel in your presence? *When you show up, who shows up?***

SOUL SHIFT

**SHIFT FROM ASKING YOURSELF "ARE PEOPLE LIKING ME?"
TO "HOW AM I VIBRATING?"**

Making this Soul Shift moves your awareness from trying to manage people on the outside to tuning in to yourself on the inside. You'll be learning a lot about assessing your vibration and recalibrating it as we go forward—this is just the beginning of our exploration.

Until then, here are some Soul Shifts questions for you to begin courageously contemplating:

Soul Shift Recalibration Questions

When I show up, who shows up?

What vibrations or energies do people feel in my presence?

What energetic messages do people pick up from me beyond the words I say?

When people enter the atmosphere of my planet, what do they feel?

What is my vibrational impact on the people in my life? How do my vibrations affect others, especially the people closest to me?

Am I a vibrational asset to others?

There's another word for the quality of your vibration, and that is *presence*. What is presence?

Your presence is the way your vibration is perceived by others.

Your presence is the sum total of every thought, feeling, and experience you've had in your life.

Your presence is your unique vibrational recipe of energetic frequencies that change from moment to moment.

Your presence is the one-of-a-kind song your vibrational orchestra plays.

Your presence is the energy pulsating beneath your words, the silent, invisible reality of who you are that radiates out from you in wave after wave.

**Your presence is the vibrational product
of every moment of your life.
It's the vibrational signature of your consciousness.
Ultimately, it's what will move, uplift, and inspire people.**

We live in a world where we are conditioned to focus not on presence, but on performance. When we think of achieving success, influencing people and contributing to the world, the first thing we ask ourselves is: *How can I perform better?*

Our final Soul Shift for this chapter is really the central purpose of this book.

SOUL SHIFT

SHIFT FROM MASTERING YOUR PERFORMANCE TO MASTERING YOUR PRESENCE

True mastery is about presence. You can't fake presence if it's not there. This is what the rest of our Soul Shifts journey will be about: *learning how to vibrate from the highest possible place,* which ironically, is the key to performing better in every area of your life.

**Asking yourself, "How can I impress people?" is the wrong question.
Ask yourself, "How can I recalibrate and raise my vibration
to the highest possible frequency?"
Then you don't have to try to impress anybody.
You will *be* impressive.**

"People should not worry as much about what they do
but rather about what they are. . . .
We should not think that holiness is based on what we do
but rather on what we are, for it is not our works which sanctify us
but we who sanctify our works."
— Meister Eckhart

I love this profound quote from Meister Eckhart, the 13th-century German mystic, theologian, and philosopher, because it echoes all that we've been exploring. *Who we are—our presence, our vibrational reality, and not what we do—sanctifies and raises up everything else in our life.* This is the truth. Now, we go one step beyond this to perhaps an even more significant truth:

The best way to serve the world
is to raise the quality of your vibration.

Ultimately, this is the essence of this journey and the work we are doing—learning how to recalibrate your vibration so that you're vibrating at the most harmonious, uplifting frequency possible.

This is your destiny:
To become a vibrational masterpiece.

To become the most exquisite song,
The most haunting, healing melody,
The most intoxicating, delightful dancing waves of energy and light,

So that people cannot help but run to be near you
just as we joyfully run to greet the sparkling sea,
so that people cannot help but turn toward you
just as we gratefully turn our face toward the radiance of the Sun,

So that people can thank God that you are alive, here and now,
because, just by thinking of you, they feel absolutely certain
that they are on the right planet.

In this way, you will sanctify the world
with your very presence.

❈ 7 ❈

Everything Counts:
Cultivating Vibrational Credibility

"Happiness is when what you think, what you say,
and what you do are in harmony."
— Mahatma Gandhi

Many years ago, when I was just beginning to experience some success in my career, I decided to treat myself to a vacation at a well-known beach resort in Mexico as a reward for finishing my first book. I wasn't a very experienced traveler at that time, but I'd heard all about this tropical paradise from friends, read the colorful, enticing brochure (pre-Internet!), and could hardly wait to experience the warm weather, turquoise sea, and sunshine. Mother Nature, however, had other ideas, and the moment I arrived at the hotel, an enormous storm also arrived and lasted for the entire five days I was there. I'd expected a delightful, relaxing experience, but instead I got cold, unrelenting rain, flooded rooms, leaking restaurants, and no power for much of the time. All I wanted to do was take the first plane home, but every flight was sold out so I was trapped in soggy, disappointing misery.

On my last drenched day, I was speaking with one of the waiters I'd befriended, and sharing how disappointed I was to have had such bad luck during my stay.

"Well, señorita," he replied, "I'm sure you will have better luck if you come back when it's not the rainy season."

"Rainy season?" I responded with shock. "Are you saying this is the rainy season? But the brochure didn't mention anything about that. In fact, I remember it specifically advertising that this was one of the sunniest spots in Mexico, especially in the summer."

"Sí, it is most of the time," he answered cautiously. "When it's sunny, it is very sunny, very hot, and so beautiful. But this is July. It rains. I'm sorry that you came for sun and got the storms."

This story illustrates something we've all experienced—that when we're told we will get one thing and instead get another, some part of us feels disappointed, misled, and ripped off. What upset me at the time was that *the advertisement of the pleasant conditions I thought awaited me didn't match the actual conditions I experienced.*

Each of us is like that brochure I read years ago: We "advertise" a certain vibrational message, hoping to invite people to interact with us/ hire us/love us—in other words, to visit our "resort." **The problem arises when we intentionally present ourselves in one way, yet what people experience is very different. The "resort" of our personality looks wonderful in the brochure, but when people arrive, they find themselves dealing with conditions they didn't expect.**

I call this giving "mixed vibrational messages." We are "advertising" one vibration, but consciously or unconsciously, we're covering up another that is often more authentic. For instance:

If you're trying to act very controlled on the outside, but you're feeling out of control on the inside, you're giving a mixed vibrational message.

If you're trying to appear calm and confident on the outside, but are frightened and agitated on the inside, you're giving a mixed vibrational message.

If you're saying loving and uplifting things, but inside you're feeling judgmental and angry, you're giving a mixed vibrational message.

If you're trying to appear detached and independent on the outside, but are feeling insecure and needy on the inside, you're giving a mixed vibrational message.

If you're trying to sound powerful and authoritative, but inside you're full of self-doubt and confusion, you're giving a mixed vibrational message.

Mixed vibrational messages aren't always comprised of a more positive outer projection hiding a more shaky inner feeling. Sometimes they're the opposite: **you're broadcasting a vibrational message that lowers**

people's expectations of who you are. This would be like the hotel in Mexico advertising a modest facility with run-down shacks, only to have the guests arrive and find it was actually a luxurious five-star resort. By downplaying people's expectations, no one could be disappointed!

Here are some examples:

If you're trying to act cold and indifferent on the outside in order to protect yourself, but you're actually a warm and deeply caring person, you're giving a mixed vibrational message.

If you present yourself as meek, insecure, and apologetic so that you don't appear threatening, but are actually powerful, knowledgeable, and wise, you're giving a mixed vibrational message.

If you try to appear like you have nothing to offer and are less competent than others, but you actually have much to give and long to make a difference, you're giving a mixed vibrational message.

What is the impact of these mixed vibrational messages? We project what I call a lack of *"vibrational coherence."* As we've discussed, human beings feel comfortable when things are harmonized and in tune, when there is a consistent relationship between our expectation and our experiences. We order a turkey sandwich, and don't expect to be served a tuna sandwich. We take our children to a movie titled *Happy Family,* and don't expect to see a horror film. We call a dear friend we've known for many years, and don't expect her to act like she doesn't care about us.

These are simple examples to help illustrate that it is indeed very disconcerting and disturbing to expect one thing and then receive something entirely different—there is a lack of vibrational coherence. *In the same way, when you aren't aware of your own lack of vibrational coherence, it has a less than positive effect on those around you.*

**When your words and vibration don't match,
you're broadcasting a lack of vibrational coherence.
Each time you present yourself one way on the surface
yet people sense a different vibrational reality underneath,
these mixed vibrational messages create agitation and confusion.**

None of us like getting mixed vibrational messages from others. An important part of Soul Shifts is courageously looking at how we, ourselves, have also been broadcasting mixed vibrational message without realizing it.

What Is the Soundtrack of Your Life?

Right now, think about a movie you've seen in a theater or on TV, one of your favorite films of all time. Choose a movie that was very touching, emotional, or compelling in some way. Remember how you felt watching it—moved, exhilarated, frightened, excited, uplifted, sad, outraged, or inspired. The film was so well done that it was impossible to not be affected by it. Perhaps you can even remember some of the music playing in the background of a famous scene, and how even now, if you hear that melody or song again, it brings you right back to the movie.

Imagine that same movie, but this time with no soundtrack, no music, just dialogue. Really think about it.

For instance, you're watching a fantastic, passionate, emotional film—*Avatar, Titanic, Star Wars, Jaws, The Notebook, The Godfather, Ghost, The Hunger Games, Spider-Man, The Matrix, E.T., Rocky*—except there's no music. There are people looking scared on a boat, or running through a jungle, or in a boxing ring, or saying a heartfelt good-bye, or expressing deep emotion to each other. *No sound. No music. Boring, right?* If you've ever seen a documentary about the making of a movie, and they show a scene before the soundtrack was put in, it looks really odd, and does very little to impress you.

Why is this? The soundtrack is the vibrational message and content of the film. *It's what makes the movie come to life and creates emotion in the viewer. The music makes the dramatic moments and the dialogue more meaningful. That particular vibration tells us whether to be frightened, whether to expect something amusing to happen, whether to feel sad, whether to feel joyful, or whether to feel hopeful.* The soundtrack is communicating a vibrational message to our brain that resonates with certain emotional frequencies, and suddenly, we're crying, or our heart is pounding, or we are afraid—all because of what we're hearing.

Now remember that same movie you loved, but this time, instead of imagining it with no soundtrack, *pretend that the music playing in the background doesn't match the dialogue or action.*

For instance, a romantic kiss between two lovers has frantic chase-scene music playing behind it. A terrifying scene where aliens are attacking the world has romantic, uplifting music playing. A tragic scene of someone saying good-bye to his dying child has happy circus music in the background. If you were watching a film like this, you'd sit in the theater or in front of your TV and think, *This is really bizarre—the soundtrack doesn't match the script. I can't tell what I'm supposed to be feeling. It's giving me the creeps!*

A composer creating a musical score for a film or TV show tries to write music that is *vibrationally coherent with the story and dialogue.* They wouldn't compose cheerful background music for what is supposed to be a sad, poignant scene; or suspenseful music for what is supposed to be a joyful, delightful moment. If they did, they'd be fired! A masterful composer hopes that the vibration of the music will blend harmoniously with the dialogue and cinematography so that the viewer doesn't even notice the sound—it just seems to go perfectly and organically with the visual.

By now you've probably guessed that this metaphor is leading somewhere, and it is: **You have your own personal soundtrack! If your life is a movie, and your words and actions are the script, then the soundtrack is the energy vibrating inside of you that's "playing"—or transmitting—nonstop.**

Your soundtrack is just another term for your vibrational field. It's the next step in understanding the metaphors we've already used: *your vibrational broadcast, your vibrational wrapping paper,* or *your planetary atmosphere.* Every thought, every feeling, everything that has happened to you makes up your soundtrack, like a *vibrational orchestra of energy.* It's not something people hear with their ears, but as we've seen, they definitely register it vibrationally.

> **You have your own vibrational orchestra.**
> **It is the soundtrack of your consciousness,**
> **playing behind your words and actions,**
> **and broadcasting its vibrational message out to the world.**

Remember the Soul Shifts question: "How am I vibrating?" One way to answer that is to ask yourself:

"What is the soundtrack that's playing in my life?"

What emotional message does your vibration communicate to others? When people are in your presence, what do they feel? *How people feel in your presence may be very different from what you're trying to get them to feel.*

Here are some common vibrational soundtracks:

* You present yourself as upbeat and cheerful, but your vibrational soundtrack is sad, haunting, melancholy music like you'd hear in a tragic movie.

* You try to appear cool and confident, but your vibrational soundtrack is scary music appropriate for a horror film, where something awful is always about to happen.

* On the surface, you try to come off as strong and authoritative, but your vibrational soundtrack is children's music like you'd hear in a nursery-school playroom.

* You appear cooperative and harmonious, but your vibrational soundtrack is menacing, threatening music like you'd hear in a violent movie.

You've seen how you're always sensing the vibrational messages people are giving you before they even say a word. Now you can be even more specific as you understand that you're not just sensing vague energies—**you're "hearing," or picking up, a specific vibrational soundtrack that's communicating a particular emotional message.** If you think about it, you've experienced this so many times in your life. Someone is saying all the right things, but the whole time you're thinking to yourself, *What's wrong with me? Why don't I feel comfortable with this person?* or *She's always so sweet and cooperative, yet why do I always get the feeling that she's angry?*

You are constantly receiving vibrational messages from people that have nothing to do with what they're saying, just as they're receiving vibrational messages from you that have nothing to do with what you intend to communicate.

Of course, you don't just have one soundtrack playing no matter what you're doing or whom you're with. You have a multiplex, with dozens

140

of movies—your work and career movie, your relationship movie, and many more! Each "movie" or life situation elicits different vibrational re-actions from within you, and a different soundtrack. For instance, maybe in your personal relationships you tend to act cool or independent, even with those you love, but your soundtrack is actually very dramatic and emotional. Perhaps in professional situations, you present yourself as co-operative and harmonious, but your soundtrack is aggressive and scary.

Are You Giving Out Vibrational Mixed Messages?

When you imagined the movie with a soundtrack that didn't match the script, it was as if the film was giving you mixed messages. The vibra-tion of the music may have said, "You are supposed to feel sad," but the dialogue and action said, "You're supposed to be excited and uplifted." This is an example of lack of vibrational coherence, and what I call *"vi-brational dissonance."*

**Vibrational dissonance occurs when
you're saying or doing one thing, and vibrating another.
The lack of coherence or resonance between the two
creates tension in yourself and those around you.**

The dictionary defines *dissonance* as a "tension or clash resulting from the combination of two disharmonious or unsuitable elements." This is exactly what vibrational dissonance is: **an energetic agitation or clash that results from the parts of you that are not integrated, or that are disharmonious.**

Your vibrational dissonance has an enormous impact on every aspect of your life. When you begin to contemplate this principle, and discov-er what vibrational soundtracks have been playing behind your words and actions, you'll suddenly understand why certain relationships didn't work out or why people have responded to you in ways you've never understood.

**Often we feel things that have happened to us don't make sense,
because we're only referencing the "dialogue and action portion of
our life movie"—what we said and did—
and not the vibrational broadcast, or soundtrack, behind it all.**

A few years ago, a very sweet man named Ashok came to me for help because, in spite of his wonderful credentials in the tech field, he was having a very difficult time getting a job. He'd been at the same company for several years, and when they downsized, he began looking for a comparable position elsewhere. His résumé was impressive; he'd received an excellent education; and he had no trouble being confident, charming, and poised during his interviews. However, he'd always receive calls politely telling him the same thing: although they had liked him very much, they'd hired someone else.

After sitting with Ashok for a few minutes, I could feel his vibrational dissonance. He was like a walking war zone with a perpetual battle between the vibration he tried to project—of confidence, skill, and steadiness—and how insecure he actually felt on the inside. His outer presentation said, *"I'm trustworthy. I'm going to do a great job. You can count on me."* However, I could sense another part of him on the inside that was very shaky.

I explained this to him, and he looked puzzled. "But I'm not saying anything that doesn't sound sincere, and I've been told I have a very self-assured demeanor."

"You do," I agreed. "That makes it even more disconcerting to people. You're there saying, *'Here are all of my accomplishments. I'm a totally reliable person, and you'd be smart to hire me.'* That sounds impressive, and your credentials are impeccable. Now, imagine that you have a twin brother who comes to the interviews with you. As you sit in the chair calmly radiating ease and intelligence, your twin stands behind you screaming, *'Don't trust me! I'm never in integrity; I'm just a fraud! I know I'm going to screw things up!'*

"Obviously, you're not saying those things out loud," I continued, "but they are the vibrational soundtrack of some old, unresolved emotional energy broadcasting out from within you. **People can sense your vibrational dissonance, even if they don't know what that means.** Something just doesn't click for them, and they pass on hiring you."

Ashok looked at me, his eyes wide with revelation. "You just explained my entire life," he confessed. "That's exactly what I'm feeling deep inside whenever I'm under pressure or think I'm being evaluated—which is all the time, even when I meet women. I can almost sense 'Ashok #2' behind me about to fall apart, and I have to use so much energy to shut him up.

"What's even more uncanny is that the words you used to describe what my vibration is saying are so close to exactly what my father used to tell me—that I was always messing up, that people would judge me for coming from a family of Indian immigrants, and therefore I was somehow less than others."

"And that's your vibrational soundtrack," I agreed. "The words and actions of your movie belong to a story about a successful Stanford graduate making it big in the tech world, but the soundtrack playing behind you is more like *Slumdog Millionaire*. **That's why people experience the vibrational dissonance. You've been giving out mixed messages: your self-deprecating vibration doesn't match your marvelous credentials and accomplishments.**"

What happened to Ashok in the next few months was inspiring. He used some of the recalibration techniques I'll be teaching you, and began to "vibrate out" his old programming about being a fraud. He continued his job search, and you can guess what happened next: he was hired by one of the biggest firms in his industry and given a senior management position that was way more than he'd hoped for. When he called to tell me the good news, he shared that the best part was that the CEO of the company told Ashok that he hired him because he felt "solid and dependable, like the kind of man who knows who he is, where he's from, and where he's going."

"There was no trace of *Slumdog Millionaire* to be found!" Ashok said with a laugh. "I think I've officially changed my soundtrack to the one from *Top Gun*."

WHAT'S THAT NOISE? YOUR VIBRATIONAL COMMOTION

Have you ever gone to someone's house for a quiet adult supper, and the whole time you're there you can hear their young kids running around wildly in the back hallways and bedrooms? You thought that the idea was to get together for a calm evening and are doing your best to enjoy yourself, but all the while there's nonstop commotion in the background—yelling, banging, crying, shrieking—pure bedlam. Even though the children aren't physically in the dining room with you, it's hard to relax because you can feel the energetic disturbance right around the corner.

Just like this, when we have vibrational dissonance between what we try to present to the world and what's going on in the background of our consciousness—it creates what I call *"vibrational commotion." People can't see what's happening inside of us, but they can sense our disturbances.*

Imagine the part of you that greets people in the front room of your personality is *"the front person"*—the "you" that you want to project to others, the wrapping paper on the outside of who you are. However, in the back room are all of the other parts of you banging around like kids who've been told they can't come out. *People can't see those parts of you, but they can feel the vibrational commotion they cause in your consciousness.*

This was what originally happened with Ashok. He seemed so peaceful and steady on the outside, but his interviewers could feel very loud vibrational commotion coming from the back room of his personality, commotion that unconsciously disturbed them enough to conclude he wasn't the right man to hire.

Think of someone you've recently been with, and in whose presence you felt tense. On the surface they were very pleasant, but something didn't feel right. It's possible that you were feeling their vibrational commotion.

**We are always unconsciously sensing
other people's vibrational commotion,
and they are sensing ours.**

"Vibrational commotion" is another principle that helps to explain what we've been discussing so far in this book. If you have a lot of vibrational commotion, people will feel it. *It's very distracting because it's also emotional commotion, and no one likes to be around that.*

When you begin using this work to create inner harmony between all of the dissonant parts of you, the "kids" in your back room will settle down! There will be less and less vibrational commotion, and in your presence, people will feel calmer, safer, and more uplifted. *You'll become more vibrationally appealing.*

**When you resolve your vibrational commotion,
your energy will feel vibrationally coherent.
The more vibrationally coherent you are,
the more people want to be around you and in your energy field.
People want coherence. They want harmony.
They are attracted to the energy of wholeness.**

We all want to experience peace. So the less commotion that's present in your energy field, the more peaceful you'll feel to yourself and others. How will this affect your life? In every possible way!

WHERE ARE YOU WOBBLY?

"Perhaps the surest test of an individual's integrity is his refusal to do or say anything that would damage his self-respect."
— Thomas S. Monson

Imagine that you owned a really precious object, maybe something you'd inherited from one of your parents, such as a beautiful crystal vase, or a statue, or an irreplaceable family heirloom, and you wanted to display it on a table. If you noticed that the table was shaky because the legs weren't even, or one of them was cracked or broken, would you feel confident placing the valuable item on it? The answer, of course, is no. You wouldn't want to risk the rickety table collapsing or tilting over, and thereby breaking your treasured possession. *I don't trust that table,* you'd conclude, *because it's too wobbly.*

**When we aren't living with vibrational coherence,
we become what I call vibrationally "wobbly."
Something about our energy doesn't feel solid or reliable to others,
because they're sensing our energetic dissonance and commotion.**

When I began teaching about Soul Shifts, I wanted to find a way to explain the impact of our vibrational dissonance and commotion to my students, and I came up with *wobbly. How do we feel around things that are wobbly? They make us anxious.* We've all had the experience of sitting at a table in a restaurant, and discovering that one of its legs is shorter than the others. It's difficult to relax when the table is always shifting, and we try to get the waiter to fix it or we move to another table so that we can enjoy our meal.

To understand how people feel in your presence when you're wobbly, visualize yourself in a conversation with a friend whose arms are completely overloaded with packages. They're trying to balance the bags and boxes but there are too many for them to carry, and it looks like, at any minute, they'll all go tumbling to the ground. You're making an effort to talk to your friend, but they're very distracted because they're trying hard not to drop anything, and therefore don't seem to be paying much attention to what you're saying. You feel tense just looking at the other person because you're feeling their tension: *Their energy is wobbly.*

Our vibrational dissonance makes us seem energetically wobbly to others. Just like the uneven table at the restaurant, we don't appear steady and solid. There's a precariousness to us. It's as if we're trying to talk, interact, and make decisions while standing on a rocky boat being tossed around by stormy ocean waves. What we're saying may sound good, but we don't look very substantial and reliable.

When we're energetically wobbly, we vibrate unsteadiness to others. We seem unbalanced, and therefore it's more difficult for people to trust us, believe in us, and feel safe with us.

Many years ago, on a trip to Bali, a guide took me on a trek through lush and beautiful landscapes, and we came to a wide river. Spanning the river was a very old footbridge made of broken, cracked wood and ancient-looking ropes. *"You can cross, missus,"* he gestured with a wide smile. Staring at the bridge, I was filled with trepidation. Why? Because it looked wobbly, and I wasn't certain that it would not collapse under my weight and drop me into the dark river.

Sensing my skepticism and hesitation, the guide gingerly walked out across the bridge and then trotted back, to demonstrate that it was safe. Again, he said, *"You can cross, missus. Okay to cross."*

Clutching his hand, I crept slowly, step by treacherous step, across the now-swaying bridge, trying to avoid the portions that looked like they were about to give way at any second, gritting my teeth at the sound of the creaking and cracking. Eventually, I arrived safely on the other side.

My compassionate guide beamed at me with great pride, and he bowed and congratulated me as if I'd just climbed Mt. Everest rather than practically crawling along the bridge: *"Very good crossing, Missus! Very good crossing!"* Then he did something that so beautifully reflected the pure-hearted sweetness and reverence of the Balinese people—he turned back toward the bridge and bowed to it, saying, *"Very good bridge. Very good bridge."*

All of us are, in a way, vibrational bridges that we invite people to stand on or cross over. *"Trust me,"* we say. *"Believe in me. Invest in me. Hire me. Love me."* What we're promising is that we won't collapse, that we can be counted on, that we are solid and sturdy and safe. We're hoping to be a "very good bridge."

As seekers, we have an obligation to find out
where we are wobbly and where there is
a lack of vibrational coherence within us,
so that when we say to people, "You can cross,"
we are confident that
the bridge of our character and consciousness will hold.

My experience crossing the Balinese bridge has always stayed with me as a great teaching moment. I confess, however, that I've always wondered if my delightful guide was honoring the bridge for being "very good" as a ritual he regularly practiced once on the other side, or if he was thanking it for being a "very good" bridge because it didn't collapse under this very anxious tourist!

EVERYTHING COUNTS

"We are what we repeatedly do.
Excellence, then, is not an act but a habit."
— Attributed to Aristotle

Almost every day in the news, we see yet another story of the destructive effect of wobbliness. We read about someone who seemed so masterful in one area of life, but came crashing down in another. They had strong financial steadiness but no emotional steadiness, or they had great business mastery but were not living in integrity. Some legs of their "table"—or life—were very sturdy, but others had been neglected and caused the whole table to collapse.

Why was this the case? **They decided that having high standards only counted in one area of their life, but not in others.**

Perhaps it's a renowned athlete always striving for excellence and preparing himself impeccably in his sport, who decides that in the area of personal relationships, the same standard of integrity doesn't count.

Maybe it's someone who lives with tremendous consciousness and compassion in her family life, but chooses to conveniently go unconscious about business dealings that are not totally legal.

It might be someone who is known for being a famous, one-of-a-kind entrepreneur and business owner who never compromises his values regarding his product, but won't invest the same quality of time and care in his failing marriage.

These are all examples of *selective consciousness*—when someone chooses to be conscious about some things, but not about others.

**The decision to be very conscious sometimes
and not so conscious at other times
is the source of so much of our suffering,
and certainly one of the most significant causes of our wobbliness.**

How do we heal our wobbliness, and cultivate vibrational credibility? We need to remember that everything counts.

SOUL SHIFT

SHIFT FROM PICKING AND CHOOSING WHEN TO BE CONSCIOUS TO REMEMBERING THAT EVERYTHING COUNTS

This is a profound Soul Shift, and one that is at the foundation of so many other Soul Shifts we've been discussing. *It invites you to shift from being selectively conscious to becoming unconditionally conscious—not just some of the time, but all of the time.* When you've made that commitment to remain conscious, you're committed to "seeing what there is to see" as we saw in our Soul Shifts Mantra. **The more you're willing to see, the more you can shift, and the less wobbly you'll be.**

One of the saddest things for me as a teacher and a seeker is to see how people decide what counts and what doesn't count, as if certain days of their life are expendable. *Today, I'll go unconscious and make choices that aren't from my Highest. Today, I'll be stubborn and in resistance. Today, I'll shut down emotionally because I'm angry at the person I love. Today, I'll take out my frustration on my children. Today, I will do a sloppy job at my workplace, or hand in a less than excellent report.*

Most of us don't consciously make these decisions, but when we choose to indulge in less than conscious behaviors, we're saying, in essence, that the day, or hour, or moment doesn't count, isn't precious to us, and isn't worth our Highest.

**How many days of life do you have left:
Six thousand days? Nine thousand days? Eleven thousand days?
How many of those are you willing to write off
by saying that they don't count?**

What if I gave you the assignment to look at a calendar and mark which days for the rest of your life aren't important to you—which days are expendable and don't count? Of course you couldn't do that. You *wouldn't* do that. Yet isn't this how so many of us live, as if some days don't deserve our best?

What if the Universe, God, Spirit, or whatever name you have for the Supreme came to you and said, *"I've decided that from now on, some days will not be important anymore. So I'm announcing that every fourth day there will be breathable air. However, for the other unimportant days, you're going to get a toxic mixture to breathe. Sorry, but I can't be expected to be at my best every day."* You may think this is a farfetched metaphor, but how different is it from the decision you make to not support yourself equally every day by being fully conscious? Don't you deserve the best every day?

Would you say to your own children, *"I'm going to be a good mother every other day"*? Or, *"One week I'll be conscious and in my Highest, but the next week I'll be angry and harsh, because you don't deserve it every week"*? You would be horrified to hear somebody talk that way about their children—and yet, **this is how we treat ourselves when we negotiate with consciousness.**

There are people who are going to die by the end of today. There are people who would give anything to have just one more day with someone they love. There are people who would gladly take every day someone else decides doesn't count and add it to their life span. The truth is that every day is precious, and every day counts.

**What would it look like if you actually decided
to not just be fully awake some days of your life,
but every day of your life?**

Soul Shift Recalibration Technique

Try saying these statements out loud, or adapting them to your own less than conscious choices, and see how it feels:

"It's okay if today, I indulge in my anger, because today doesn't count."

"It's okay if today, I shut down and shut off emotionally, because today doesn't count."

"It's okay if today, I don't honor what I know is true and make decisions that are totally out of integrity, because today doesn't count."

"It's okay if today, I take a vacation from my values, and treat others disrespectfully, because today doesn't count."

"It's okay if today, I [fill in your own example here], **because today doesn't count.**"

This is meant to be a very uncomfortable and difficult exercise, but it's one that can jar us into wakefulness and out of denial.

My students often use a variation of this Recalibration Technique to snap themselves out of unconsciousness when they find themselves about to engage in or already engaged in less than conscious behavior. You say the phrase "Right now, it's okay if I ____, because today doesn't count," and you fill in whatever it is you're contemplating doing, or have already started doing.

For instance, you feel like yelling at your partner and telling them everything that's wrong with them. Instead, you can take a moment by yourself and say out loud: "Right now, it's okay if I *say cruel, hurtful things and make my partner feel terrible,* because today doesn't count."

Here are some other examples:

"Right now, it's okay if I *don't apologize to my kids for losing my temper,* because today doesn't count."

"Right now, it's okay if I *drink too much and am unclear for my presentation tomorrow,* because today doesn't count."

"Right now, it's okay if I *lie to my boss about the project she asked me to do,* because today doesn't count."

Naturally, saying these things out loud and hearing your own words creates the opportunity for a powerful and instantaneous shift back to your Highest.

EVERYTHING IS EVERYTHING

How do you decide what does and doesn't count? How do you determine whether today is the day you're going to do things halfway, or whether this is the month that you're not going to pay attention to your commitments? How do you choose in which moments you are going to show up with integrity, and in which moments it's okay for you to not honor your Highest Self?

SOUL SHIFT

SHIFT FROM "ALL OR NOTHING" THINKING TO UNDERSTANDING THAT EVERYTHING IS EVERYTHING

One of the biggest traps into which people often fall is "all or nothing" thinking, and this is one of the main causes for our habit of making things not count:

We decide that certain things are important and others aren't.

We believe that how we behave in one area won't affect another area.

We commit to doing something 100 percent and giving it our all, and then conclude that other things aren't really "anything," so it's okay to not bring ourselves fully to them.

Now that we've understood the vibrational interrelationship between ourselves and all things in existence, we have to conclude that *everything is everything.*

Everything is everything.
Everything affects every moment.
Every choice affects another choice.

Every way you show up today affects how you will feel tomorrow.
Every way in which you go unconscious or stay awake in your life affects your ability to be more or less conscious tomorrow.
Everything counts.

This moment, or any moment, can only be the culmination of all the moments that went before. You can't rise up to 100 percent in this moment if you have been giving 25 percent in every moment before.

How do we allow ourselves to make things not count? *We engage in an unconscious process of constantly bargaining with ourselves:*

"I'll do this task that I want to do and apply 100 percent of my abilities, but I won't give my best to this other task I don't really want to do."

"I'll work with excellence when my boss is around watching me, but I'll slack off when she's out of town."

"I'll be honest with the people I love, but I don't have to be honest with everyone."

"I'll choose to rise to my Highest on Sundays, because that's the day I go to church, but I'll realize that I'm just human the rest of the week, and indulge in the parts of me I'm not proud of."

These are very dangerous decisions, the kind that make us vibrationally wobbly—we deliberately choose to not be consistent. **People who bargain with themselves lose in life, because everything counts.**

Here are a few symptoms that emerge when we live as if everything doesn't count:

* We find ourselves making a lot of excuses about why we didn't do something.

People who decide to discount the importance of certain things never like to admit that this is the case. It sounds harsh to say, "I decided it wasn't important to call you back/get my work in on time/do a good job," or "I just didn't feel like doing it, so I made your request or need unimportant." Instead, they make excuses: "I lost your number; I was doing more research; I didn't think you really needed it by then," and on and on.

* We start to feel a strange false sense of victory giving less than 100 percent, as if we got away with something, and as if doing less than our best without getting caught is some kind of accomplishment.

I see so many people living their lives this way. *I know I didn't give it everything. I didn't care enough to make it count. So, if I don't do well, that will be why.* What does this cover up? The fear of facing our own inadequacies or admitting our own insecurities, rather than mastering these. You fear that if you try your best, you're still going to fail, so ahead of time you decide that it doesn't really matter or count that much.

SMALL THINGS MAKE A BIG DIFFERENCE

"The happiness of most people we know is not ruined by great catastrophes or fatal errors, but by the repetition of slowly destructive little things."
— Ernest Dimnet

At this point, you may be thinking to yourself, *I know that everything counts. I'd never deliberately decide to be wobbly.* For most of us, though, it doesn't happen that way.

**We don't decide to live unconsciously—
we choose one small moment of unconsciousness.**

**We don't decide that we don't care, and things don't count—
we choose to make one small thing not count.
However, these small moments of unconsciousness, small choices,
and small decisions add up and create big consequences.**

There is no such thing as a small thing. *In fact, it is the little things in life that are often the most deadly.* All it takes is one tiny screw that's loose or one wire not correctly connected to cause a plane to crash. All it takes is one small spark to start a wildfire that can destroy hundreds of homes and cause millions of dollars of damage. All it takes is one small particle of bacteria that can cause a deadly plague such as the Black Death, which wiped out a third of the population of Europe 700 years ago. All it takes is a driver taking their attention away from the road for one second as they check their texts to cause a fatal accident.

**One moment of unconsciousness can change our lives
and the lives of others forever.
Your spiritual obligation to the world
is to do everything you can to live with consistent consciousness.**

How do we begin? *We need to understand that we don't just suddenly go unconscious.* We don't just suddenly feel wobbly. We don't just suddenly decide that things don't count. **There is always a sequence of downwardly spiraling moments. We start out in the first moment moving one inch off from our integrity, and then two inches off—and before you know it, we're really off.**

Have you ever been swimming in the ocean, which looked deceptively calm from the shore but in which there was actually a very strong tide? All of a sudden, you notice that you've quickly drifted far from where you entered the water. The same strong undertow that had made you drift so rapidly now makes swimming against it exhausting.

**So often in life, we don't realize that
we're being pulled along by some kind of energetic tide
or vibrational undertow—
from a person, from a situation,
from something we're doing that influences us,
or from unconscious, unhealed parts of ourselves.
Before we know it, we've drifted.
And as you know, when you drift and are trying to
get back against the pull of the tide, it's not so easy.**

Small things make a big difference. When we don't pay attention to where we are or what forces are pulling on us, we can easily drift off course—in our relationships, our business, our health, and even our integrity. We've all had this experience, whether it's been drifting off financially, drifting off emotionally, or drifting off spiritually.

What does this drifting look like? It's the small equivocation, the minor adjustment in our usual values, the bargaining with our self in which we insist, *"It's not that bad,"* or *"It's just this once"*—except that then we do it again and again. We don't realize that these small driftings add up, and become a huge drift from which it's very difficult to return.

When we don't pay attention, we can drift off without knowing it.
We ignore small things,
because we choose unconsciousness over consciousness.
Then we suddenly find ourselves somewhere we don't want to be,
and maybe somewhere from which we don't know how to return.

What is the antidote for all of this? *Consciousness. There's no substitute for consciousness.* There's no substitute for paying attention. There's no substitute for seeing what there is to see.

The amount of time we spend in our lives trying to get back from wherever it is we've drifted to, or trying to convince ourselves and others that we haven't drifted, or cleaning up our emotional messes created by drifting takes far more than what it would have taken to be—and remain—conscious in the first place.

CULTIVATING VIBRATIONAL CREDIBILITY

"If you have integrity, nothing else matters.
If you don't have integrity, nothing else matters."
— Alan K. Simpson

From as far back as I can remember, I've always made everything count. I didn't tell myself when I was in junior high and high school, *This is just school, not the real world. I'm not going to know these teachers after I graduate, so why should I do well? School doesn't count.* I made every test count, every project count, every day in class count. It had to be as good as it could be, and no less. It was the same in my relationships. No matter who I was with, even if I sensed that I wasn't going to end up with that person forever, I did my best to be present in the relationship with a totally open heart, total devotion, and total commitment.

When I began my career as a meditation teacher at the age of 20, I brought this same attitude to everything I did. I vividly remember setting up and giving my first public lectures, which were held on Thursday evenings at the local public library. I made posters (handwritten; no computers yet!) and put them up on bulletin boards around town, inviting people to come learn about meditation and spiritual freedom. This was in 1971, when no one had even heard of meditation, let alone considered practicing it. I'd get dressed up and arrive at the library with my notes and portable chalkboard, waiting to offer this priceless information to the seekers of truth.

Most of the time, one person would show up—*one person* sitting alone in the large library classroom, staring expectantly at this 20-year-old girl with long dark hair! Did I think to myself, *Darn—I don't want to speak to only one person. I'll just do a really quick version, 10 or 15 minutes, and then get out of here?* No. **I'd give the complete 90-minute presentation to that one person with as much excellence, enthusiasm, and devotion as if there were 10,000 people in the room.**

Lecture by lecture, poster by poster, hundreds of tiny radio shows and living-room seminars and local TV shows later, I arrived at a level of success and notoriety I never could have imagined attaining, one I hadn't even desired. All I had wanted to do was to be a teacher and do my part to uplift the world.

What do you think happened then? By the time I did speak before 10,000 people, by the time I was on television talking to millions of people at once, by the time I did everything else that my destiny had in store for me, I was ready. Why? **It was because *I made everything count from the beginning.* That mastery was not something I scrambled to put together at the last minute. It was something that I'd been practicing in every minute of my life, for my entire life, whether or not anyone was looking.**

I knew I'd always done my best and made the most sincere, 100 percent effort I could make. That knowledge is what created a solid foundation of mastery. *I wasn't just talking about mastery—I'd been choosing to live it each day, long before anyone knew who I was.* So, when the universe wanted to "put something valuable on me," I was absolutely *not* wobbly.

What had I been doing for all those years that prepared me to have the opportunity to serve humanity in so many big ways? **I'd been cultivating "vibrational credibility."** I created this phrase to describe a very important Soul Shift: *You could have the best credentials in the world, but they'll mean nothing if you don't have vibrational credibility.*

My intention for the past few chapters has been to help you understand the mechanics of what creates a state of vibrational credibility: *When people feel you, that vibration matches and is coherent with what you are saying or how you represent yourself. You're not giving mixed vibrational messages. Your vibrational soundtrack on the inside matches how you show up in the world on the outside.*

SOUL SHIFT

SHIFT FROM TRYING TO LOOK GOOD TO CULTIVATING VIBRATIONAL CREDIBILITY

Most people want to achieve material credibility: a prestigious job, or financial status, or a long and impressive résumé, or millions of Facebook "likes," or tons of Twitter followers. All of these things make them look good to others, and of course, to themselves. Nothing is wrong with this. **However, vibrational credibility isn't about just looking good, but rather living with wholeness, so that what people see and feel are the same thing.**

How do you know if you possess vibrational credibility? Ask yourself these questions:

Soul Shift Recalibration Questions

"Do I trust myself to show up in my Highest, most integrated, authentic self, not just when it's necessary, but all of the time?"

"Do I trust myself to notice when I'm not in my Highest, and to know how to shift back?"

Don't worry if your answers to these questions are things like "Sometimes," or "Not as much as I should," or "Yes, except when I'm around my family," or "Help! What do you mean by my Highest?!" The rest of our journey is going to introduce many new Soul Shifts that will help you learn not just what needs to shift, but *how* to shift.

I don't know what life has in store for me tomorrow—none of us do. *What I do know is that at all times, I will absolutely show up as my Highest, most consistent self, no matter what the circumstances, no matter how horribly I'm treated, no matter how frightening or difficult the situation is.* Why am I so certain about this? Simple: **It's just not an option for me to do anything less than that.**

One of the most important things I can offer you, then, is another Soul Shift that will transform your understanding about what it means to live with mastery.

SOUL SHIFT

SHIFT FROM THINKING OF MASTERY AS AN ATTITUDE AND AN INTENTION TO BE EXCELLENT TO MAKING MASTERY AN ACTUAL PRACTICE AND A HABIT

True mastery is not an idealistic attitude. It is a habit and a practice. It's a skill that you can only learn by practicing mastery, practicing commitment, and practicing doing things 100 percent, so that it becomes second nature. *When living in anything less than that mastery has been removed as an option, you will have made a profound Soul Shift.*

You can't suddenly decide to be masterful
once you get your ideal job,
or once you find your dream relationship,
or once you're handed an amazing opportunity.
You can't decide to be masterful because suddenly,
it counts, and expect excellence to surge forth.
You have to have been in the everyday habit
of being masterful and making everything count.

Imagine that you want to run a marathon. You can't simply decide in the last two weeks before the race that you're going to start training. What's going to happen if you do this? You'll have no stamina. You won't be able to finish or survive the race without injury because your lungs and muscles need training, and that training can't be rushed or made up. You can't take shortcuts.

This is how life is as well. *There are no shortcuts to mastery.* I have a saying:

**Everything counts,
and shortcuts show.**

When we try to cover up our lack of vibrational credibility, we look energetically and vibrationally out of breath, as if we just rushed into a room at the last minute right before an exam or meeting started, hoping no one will notice. But they do.

The Universe Is Anxious to Build Upon You

"Use me, God. Show me how to take who I am, who I want to be, and what I can do, and use it for a purpose greater than myself."
— Oprah Winfrey

My grandmother Esther used to knit colorful, lovely afghans for her grandchildren. I treasured my afghans just as I treasured my Nana, and even years after she passed away, I held on to the last remaining one, in spite of its shredded and worn condition, until one day it finally fell apart.

I remember when I was young, watching her create each knitted square with its own special pattern. By themselves, the afghan squares were beautiful, but when she was done collecting them all in a basket, she would perform her final magic—sewing them together so that they'd become a beautiful blanket that would wrap me in her love.

We each have many pieces of ourselves. *Just like the afghan, for you to be whole means that all of your pieces need to be connected, stitched together to form one integrated, coherent, harmonious "you."*

There is a beautiful word in Tibetan, *wangthang,* which means "authentic presence." The literal translation of *wangthang* is "field of power." What brings about this authentic presence, according to the renowned Tibetan Buddhist teacher and scholar Chögyam Trungpa, is "emptying out and letting go."

I love this word and its significance, because I believe it aligns closely to my own spiritual experience and unfolding wisdom, as well as to all we've been examining: **Authentic presence, authentic mastery, isn't created by the adding of actions or qualities to make us more impressive, but rather by the opposite—the releasing and letting go and recalibrating of all that is not authentic within us.**

What will be left, then, will be our wholeness, the true vibrational masterpiece that we already are.

This is the Soul Shift work we are doing.
The more whole you are,
the more holiness will work as you and through you.

One day many years ago, while I was deep in the vibrant stillness of meditation, I heard the sacred whisper of a voice offer these words to me:

"The universe is anxious to build upon you."

This was such a simple message, yet its powerful truth took my breath away. The universe was anxious to build upon me. I needed to prepare myself to be a steady foundation for whatever it was that I was meant to do.

Now it's time for this chapter's final Soul Shift.

SOUL SHIFT

SHIFT FROM LOOKING FOR GREATNESS TO PREPARING YOURSELF FOR GREATNESS

Isn't this a beautiful contemplation? The universe is anxious to build upon *you!* What, then, is your job? It's just what we've been seeing—to prepare yourself for greatness by making the foundation of your consciousness so strong and so steady that you are the opposite of wobbly. You become the most reliable of bridges across which wisdom, love, creativity, and service can travel through you and out to the waiting world.

To help you remember why you are doing this work, here's a prayer I wrote for you:

⌒⌣ PREPARING FOR GREATNESS PRAYER ⌒⌣

The universe is anxious to build something great upon me.
May I stop looking for greatness, and prepare for it.

May I not run after importance,
but make myself such a steady foundation
that I naturally become a platform
on which something important can be supported.

May I become a "very good bridge"!

PART THREE

SOUL SHIFTS
FOR
PRACTICAL
SPIRITUALITY

❈ 8 ❈

Taking a Stand for Awakening: From Contraction to Expansion

"No matter what your spiritual condition is,
no matter where you find yourself in the universe,
your choice is always the same: to expand your awareness or contract it."
— Thaddeus Golas

It's time to introduce a universal principle that's going to be your map for transformation, so you can actually start making Soul Shifts. Understanding this cosmic law will help you put the concepts of the first part of the book into practice. This simple but profound principle is the foundation of all development and all growth. In fact, it's operating right now in your body, and all around you in our physical universe. It is:

The principle of expansion and contraction.

During our spiritual physics lesson, we learned that energy, or consciousness, is always vibrating at particular frequencies. It is always moving and never static. **However, it's not just moving randomly. It's unfolding in one of two directions: expansion or contraction.**

Contraction occurs when energy slows down. The slower the pulsation of energy or vibrational frequency, the thicker and more condensed the energy gets, until it becomes rigid, solid matter. This is what happens when water freezes into ice. The molecules of the liquid are cooled and are forced to move closer together, becoming solid and contracted.

Expansion occurs when energy speeds up. When atoms or molecules are heated, they become energized and vibrate more vigorously. This allows them to have greater freedom to move away from each other, and this creates more volume or expansion. The more rapid the vibration of energy, the more expanded and less condensed or contracted it becomes, as in when ice melts into water.

**The principles of expansion and contraction
are essential to our universe
and, therefore, are essential to you as part of that universe.
You are also always expanding and contracting.**

The two forces of expansion and contraction are operating in you all the time. There is a current of energy in you and your life that's expansive, or what we'll call "life-enhancing," and a current of energy in you that's contractive, or what we'll call "life-diminishing."

**Life-enhancing energy = expansive.
Life-diminishing energy = contractive.**

The polarity between the life-enhancing currents or expansive energy and the life-diminishing current or contractive energy is a constant. Your own body is alive and functioning because of these two forces.

Right now as you read these words, you're alive because you're expanding and contracting. Your heart is beating 60 to 100 times a minute, expanding and contracting to pump five or six quarts of life-giving blood through your body every 60 seconds. Your lungs are expanding to take in the air you breathe, and contracting to expel the waste product, carbon dioxide. Your very existence began with a miraculous expansion of the embryo into a fully formed human being, the expansion of your mother's womb to make space for your expansion, followed by the contractions that forced you out of that womb and into the world.

Perhaps even more important for our exploration isn't what's happening in your body, but what's happening from moment to moment in your consciousness:

**Every experience you have either expands you or contracts you.
Every thought you have either expands you or contracts you.
Every relationship, conversation, or interaction with another person
either expands you or contracts you.
Everything you see, watch, read, and feel creates either
a life-enhancing vibration or a life-diminishing vibration.**

You experience expansion and contraction all the time without realizing it. If you're feeling frightened or anxious, for instance, what happens to your body? Your stomach contracts into knots, your throat tightens, your muscles clench up, and your breathing becomes shallow.

Your physical body is just reflecting a contraction that's taking place in your emotional/spiritual body. On the other hand, when you're happy and feeling safe and appreciated, your muscles loosen up, your breathing slows down, and your whole body relaxes.

Let's do a quick experiment:

Take a moment right now to imagine yourself doing something that makes you really happy. Perhaps you're with the person you love, or participating in an activity you really enjoy, or somewhere beautiful out in nature, or playing with your kids, or cuddling with your animal companion. See yourself in that situation, and visualize how it would look and feel how it would feel. Linger in that feeling for a few more seconds with your eyes closed if you wish.

Now bring your awareness back from whatever you were imagining, and notice how you're feeling right now. You're probably feeling more expanded.

Take a deep breath, and erase that experience from your mind.

Now this time, I'd like you to imagine doing something you can't stand, something you really don't want to do. Perhaps it's an activity that scares you, or a conversation you're afraid to have with someone. Perhaps it would be seeing someone who's hurt or betrayed you. Maybe it's something that you've been putting off doing, but know you should do.

See yourself in that situation, visualizing how it would look and feeling how it would make you feel. Hold that image for a few more seconds. Okay, now take a deep breath and let that thought go.

Now bring your awareness back from whatever you were imagining, and notice how you're feeling right now. You're probably feeling much more contracted, and maybe even irritated that I made you do that exercise!

Just so I don't leave you feeling this way, take one more moment and imagine being embraced by someone you love—a partner, a family member, a friend you haven't seen in a long while, even someone who's passed from this earth. Allow yourself to feel the love enfolding you, the deep connection that transcends time and space, and just linger in that for a moment. Okay, you should be feeling more expanded again!

Even during this brief exercise, you probably noticed the difference between the experience of expansion and contraction. *Expansion is more like that melted ice that becomes water: we feel open, spacious, and able to move and flow. Contraction is more like the water that froze and became ice: we feel dense, hard, limited, and unmoving.*

Expansive energy creates freedom. Expansive energy creates healing. Expansive energy creates forward movement. Expansive energy creates space for the gifts of the universe—love, abundance, wisdom, and creativity—to flow into your life. **This is why the vibration of expansion is life-enhancing, and why it's necessary to help shift you, recalibrate you, and transform you.**

The opposite of this is contractive energy. Contractive energy creates stagnation. Contractive energy creates bondage. Contractive energy creates suffering. Contractive energy creates barriers and blocks that prevent you from receiving what the universe has to offer. **This is why the vibration of contraction is life-diminishing, and why it makes it difficult for you to grow.**

It seems obvious, then, what path to follow:

**To heal, to open, to be free, to grow,
to unblock ourselves and break down our barriers to receiving,
to create the space for the fullness of
Universal Grace and Goodness to flow into us,
and to experience the inherent expansiveness of our soul,
*we need to strengthen the current that's life-enhancing
and eliminate the current that's life-diminishing.***

SOUL SHIFT

SHIFT FROM CONTRACTION TO EXPANSION
BY CULTIVATING EXPANSION
AND ELIMINATING CONTRACTION

This Soul Shift is one of the most important and fundamental keys to transforming ourselves. It invites us to take inner and outer actions that will be life-enhancing and allow us to vibrate with expansive energies. **Rather than merely trying to focus on each individual place in our lives where we feel knotted, stuck, congested, or blocked, we cultivate as much expansion as possible, and eliminate as much contraction as possible.** This shift from contraction to expansion will create the optimal conditions for us to recalibrate to the Highest Consciousness, which of course is the definition of the ultimate expansion.

Un-crunching Your Magnificence

*"If you bring forth what is within you, what you bring forth will save you.
If you do not bring forth what is within you,
what you do not bring forth will destroy you."*
— Gospel of Thomas

When I was little, I used to love magic animal-growing capsules. Perhaps you remember these, or have given them to your own children. Little pieces of sponge are cut into animal shapes and then squashed into pill-like capsules. When the pill is placed in water, the gel covering slowly dissolves, and the sponge soaks up the water, expanding and expanding until the full shape reveals itself as some kind of colorful animal—a giraffe, or a dog, or a lobster, or an elephant. I was fascinated by the expansion process, and would watch carefully as each tiny corner of the sponge unfolded. My favorites were the jumbo capsules, because it took longer for the animal to open.

I decided to create a sponge-animal zoo, and would watch with great anticipation each time I dropped a new capsule into the tub during my bath time to see what animal would emerge. For some reason, certain animals weren't manufactured as often as others, and I recall waiting a long time to get an orange monkey to join his fellow sponge brothers and sisters on my shelf. What always frustrated me, however, was that I couldn't watch the expansion process over and over again. Even though I tried squeezing the animal back into the capsule, it wouldn't crunch down again. *Once the sponge animals were expanded, it was permanent.*

Many years later when I began to teach about this principle of expansion and contraction, I suddenly remembered my sponge animals and understood why, at the time, I was so mesmerized by watching them grow:

We are like those crunched sponge animals—
we get condensed, contracted, and vibrationally squeezed
into small spaces of limitation,
encapsulated by our patterns and our forgetfulness.

We can't completely see who we are or
how we're supposed to be
at our full, expanded potential.
Perhaps some of us has unfolded,
but we just know that there's more.

What crunches us down? We explored how our very first "crunch" is the movement of our Supreme Consciousness into the "capsule" of our physical body, where our true nature gets disguised and our feeling of disconnection from Spirit sets in. *Then, our life circumstances and programming often squeeze us—and freeze us—resulting in our remaining small. We make our thinking small. We make our power small. We make our love small.*

The problem with crunching ourselves down is that we get used to it, and adapt to the contracted state of being. *After a while, it doesn't feel small—it just feels normal.*

It's easy for us to become comfortable with and adapt to contraction. We get used to our contracted ability to feel, our contracted freedom to express ourselves in a relationship, our contracted way of making decisions or handling problems, our contracted behavior around family members or friends in whose presence we don't feel we can be ourselves, and our contracted thinking. **We learn to tolerate and numb ourselves to the *discomfort of diminishment.***

This is how many of us live, trying to squeeze ourselves into a small personality, or a small heart, or a small, not fully shaped life. Yet, like the sponge animal, we're so much bigger—if only we could be set free.

Living in small spaces inside of ourselves is excruciating.
We pretend that we're in a mansion, but secretly,
we feel we've somehow gotten stuffed into a closet.

Just like the sponge animals are ready and waiting
to unfold and expand to their natural forms,
so we are ready to free ourselves of our prisons of limitation
and expand to our full, magnificent shape.

The sponge animals need water to expand. What is our "water" in this metaphor? What is going to expand us, and where can we find it?

The answer is so simple. *It's the expansive, life-enhancing energies that are all around us, and already inside of us. It's the energies of love, of joy, of intimacy, of connection, of beauty, of wisdom, of spirit and grace.* We don't need to wait until some magical force picks us up and puts us into a cosmic pool of water. We're already living in that cosmic pool! We just need to dip in, and just like the sponge animals, once we expand, we won't ever fit back into our contracted limitations again.

This Soul Shift understanding is something I live by. It's been one of my most powerful practices for grounding my awakening, and has been a crucial light on the path for my students: **Cultivate expansion and eliminate contraction. Expand things that expand you. Contract things that contract you.**

Let's try another experiment:

Take one of your hands and squeeze it into a tight fist. Keep it clenched. Don't stop squeezing, and while you're doing that, notice how the rest of your body feels. You've probably tensed up; your breathing has gotten choppy; you may be holding your breath; your heart rate may even have sped up. Okay, now you can unclench your fist.

You may have just been surprised when your fingers didn't unclench fully or instantly. That's because they were in the habit of being contracted, even though it was only for 15 seconds. You may also have been surprised to realize how much maintaining that clenching and contraction in one small part of your body immediately and powerfully affected the rest of your nervous system.

This was a very physical way to demonstrate another important understanding about expansion and contraction.

**Contraction uses up a lot of energy.
It takes a lot of energy to maintain a contractive action
or a contractive emotional or mental state,
even if we aren't aware of it at the time.
When we're using our energy to sustain contraction,
we have less available for expansion.**

When I have my audiences participate in this little experiment, I add a second part to it: I ask them to continue to squeeze their hand, and turn to the person next to them and attempt to have a pleasant conversation. If you have someone near you now, you could both try it. Trust me—it's not easy. *The contractive energy you're vibrating on the inside will make it difficult for you to not look, sound, and feel contracted on the outside.*

This can explain how you've felt in some of your relationships. Imagine two people vibrating with a lot of inner contraction, as if they're both clenched up inside, and yet trying to be loving, caring, open, and considerate on the outside. I get tense just thinking about it!

**It's difficult to love in an expansive way on the outside
when you're very contracted on the inside.
There's a vibrational clash between how you're feeling
and how you're trying to communicate or behave.**

When you have a lot of vibrational contraction in your system, you'll be broadcasting that contraction out to the people in your life, as well as to the rest of the world. Remember my metaphor of trying to talk to someone who's balancing a lot of packages and appears wobbly? They're distracted by what they're carrying. This takes that concept one step further, as we understand that our wobbliness doesn't just come from being out of balance inside of ourselves, *but from the internal distraction we experience from our contractions.*

THE HEALING POWER OF EXPANSION

We've discussed the Soul Shift principle of removing internal conditions that prevent us from experiencing ourselves at our Highest—"vibrating out" energetic patterns and unresolved emotional energies that are blocking the flow of the life force into us and through us. How does that removal take place? What conditions do we need in order to create a vibrational shift? Here is a new Soul Shift Practice:

ᥫᩚ When you want something removed or extracted ᥫᩚ create a condition of expansion.

If you get a splinter in your hand, what do you do to make removing it less difficult? *You create a condition of expansion.* You soak your hand in hot water so that the splinter comes out more easily. You don't ice your hand, contracting the skin so that it holds the splinter in more tightly. You expand it.

If you want to open a jar that's stuck, you create a condition of expansion by running the top of the jar under hot water. Then it can turn more easily. You don't hold the jar under cold water in order to loosen the lid.

If you have an infection in your toe, your doctor will advise you to soak it in hot water to draw the pus up to the surface and out. He won't tell you to dunk your foot in ice, which would cause the skin to tighten around the infection. The heat creates a condition of expansion.

Conditions of expansion produce opportunities for things to vibrationally move and shift.
Just as heat allows the molecules of ice to vibrate more rapidly and move apart so that the solidity of the ice melts into water, just as the hot water allows the splinter to dislodge, so vibrationally expansive conditions create space for what's been stuck or rigid in you to begin dissolving.

I was very excited when I figured out the correlation between expansion and healing. I'd experienced it in my own process and with thousands of students, but I had never completely taken apart the mechanics—*that when we create conditions of internal vibrational expansion, old energies that have been stuck inside of us can naturally start to unwind and dissipate.*

In the simplest of examples, imagine that your child or someone you love has hurt themselves, and the contractive energy of fear and anxiety has been stirred up inside of them by their accident or injury. Instinctively, you embrace them, saying sweet and soothing things. You are creating a condition of expansive energy with your love, which is the most expansive force in the universe.

Your expansive vibration acts like a "melter" of their contracted vibration of fear and shock, and within a few minutes, your loved one begins to calm down and feel better. The expansive energy or vibration literally recalibrated the contracted vibration they were feeling, and helped it to dissolve.

SOUL SHIFT

*

SHIFT FROM TRYING TO RESIST OR REMOVE EMOTIONS, PATTERNS, OR UNDESIRABLE ENERGIES TO CREATING CONDITIONS OF EXPANSION SO THAT THESE ENERGIES CAN VIBRATIONALLY UNWIND AND DISSOLVE

This Soul Shift offers us a vision of how transformation takes place. Rather than battling against emotions, patterns, and habits, **we create conditions of expansion so that the energy that's holding the vibrational structure of those patterns tightly together begins to recalibrate.**

You might want to think of conditions of expansion like an *emotional or spiritual ultrasound.* Doctors and physical therapists use ultrasound treatments to warm up the muscles around an area of tightness or spasm. The sound waves cause the muscle fibers to expand so that they stop contracting around the spasm and thus hold it in place, like uncurling your fingers that have been tightly grasping an object. In this way, the expansion of the surrounding muscles creates space so that the knot can begin to unravel.

Now that we understand more about the life-enhancing energy of expansion, we need to look more deeply into the life-diminishing energy of contraction. *Contractive energies work in the exact opposite way than expansive energies: they tighten, rather than loosen; they create less space, not more; they inhibit, rather than promote, movement.*

Think of water contracting and eventually freezing around an object. The object is tightly trapped in the ice, and there's no space for it to move. **The more contracted something is, the less likely the possibility of it shifting.**

Unfortunately, it's human nature to contract around our pain, problems, or issues. Instead of opening, we close. Instead of exposing ourselves to love, we isolate. Instead of moving the energy out by talking about whatever's bothering us, we crunch our feelings down. We choose contraction instead of expansion, and by doing so we prevent the very healing and liberation from suffering we so desperately want.

We all have old remnants of ancient wounds, disappointments, heartbreaks, and betrayals buried within us. They're the shards of innocence, hope, and faith left over from battles with those we loved or tried to love, battles with those we trusted or wanted to be trustworthy to, and perhaps lost battles with our own integrity and self-respect.

We cover these wounds with the hard calluses of contraction, thinking that we're protecting ourselves from more pain, **but our protections become our prisons, holding our love and our life force captive.**

What instrument should we use to pierce through the tough covering of our false protections? We use wisdom.

Wisdom pierces the outer layer of our callousness and contraction and brings light to what we had hidden in darkness.
We locate those knots, those shards, those energetic thorns, and once we find them, we melt them with vibrational expanders—with compassion, with courage, and with love.

TAKING A STAND FOR AWAKENING: YOUR INNER BATTLE BETWEEN EXPANSION AND CONTRACTION

The life-enhancing and life-diminishing currents aren't energies that merely sit dormant within you, waiting for you to jump into one river or the other. They're not passive. They pull and push on you like all forces of nature. A force is defined as an energy of pulling or pushing that changes an object's state of motion or shape. You could say that expansion and contraction are always fighting each other for supremacy inside of you.

The battle between expansive energies and contractive energies is going on all of the time in your life, and my experience is that *this battle will intensify when you commit to transforming yourself.* Make no mistake—growing, shifting, and awakening isn't simply an ascension into bliss. *It's a series of vibrational battles.*

The sooner you accept the fact that these vibrational battles exist, the more relaxed, steady, and successful your process of transformation is going to be. If you pretend that there's no such thing as inner battles, you're going to be caught off guard again and again.

It's almost certain that you've experienced this in some way. Perhaps you've been on a diet and experienced the battle between the part of you that wants to be disciplined and successful, and the part that wants to indulge. Maybe you decided to give up smoking or another addiction and had to experience the battle between the part of you wanting to be healthy and free from your compulsion, and the part that didn't want to give up the crutch. If someone badly hurt you in the past, you may have found yourself in a battle between the part of you that wanted to love again, and the part that didn't trust and wouldn't let anyone get close.

On the Soul Shifts journey, the battle is between the expansive part of you that's trying to free you from all limitations, and the contractive part of you that's trying to keep things controlled and contained. Another way to think of these battles is that they're collisions between the two opposing forces of expansion and contraction, and in any given moment, one side or the other is going to win.

**All personal and spiritual transformation
is a series of vibrational battles and collisions:
Collisions between the part of you that wants to expand
and the part of you that wants to remain contracted;
Between your truth and your untruth;
between your vision and your fear;
Between your commitment to your awakening
and the temptation to go back to sleep;
Between your Highest Self that's trying to emerge
and the limited you from which it's breaking free.**

In your process of rebirthing yourself, there will inevitably be inner collisions, and collisions invariably create discomfort. Here is where your Soul Shifts wisdom will be invaluable. Whenever you're experiencing discomfort, instead of asking, *"How can I get rid of this discomfort?"* a more expansive question would be:

"What's colliding with what inside of me right now?"

For instance:

My excitement about a new project is colliding with my fear of failure.

My desire for intimacy is colliding with my fear of trusting and getting hurt again.

My desire to start my own business is colliding with my lack of confidence in myself.

My happiness for my friend who's getting married is colliding with my jealousy that she found her perfect partner and I haven't.

My compassion for my sister's unhappiness is colliding with my anger at her drinking and indulgent lifestyle.

Collision means that there are two forces working within us at the same time, and as you can see from these examples, they're pulling in different directions—battling for control. So, instead of saying, "I feel depressed, I feel sad, I'm uncomfortable today," ask yourself, "What's colliding with what right now?" *Go beyond the emotional disturbance, and look for the source of your agitation.* Most of the time, you'll find that you're caught in the middle of a vibrational battle—*your* vibrational battle. **Once you understand what emotion or intention is colliding with another, you'll be able to make the important decision of which side you're rooting for.**

GO TEAM EXPANSION!

"Conviction . . . is worthless till it converts itself into conduct."
— Thomas Carlyle

This summer, I caught a bit of one of the World Cup soccer matches on TV. The stadium was exploding with excitement and intensity, filled to capacity with 70,000 screaming fans. Even though I don't follow soccer and didn't know much about who was playing whom, it was easy to understand what was happening because the fans for each team were completely identifiable. They were dressed in team colors; their faces were painted in team colors; they wore wigs and waved flags in team colors.

The camera would pan over one section of the crowd, and I'd see thousands of people decorated in yellow and red. On the other side of the stadium, everyone was in blue and white. There didn't seem to be one neutral person there. Toward the end of the match people either looked elated and on the verge of manic joy, or as crushed and heartbroken as if they'd just witnessed a terrible tragedy.

When the program was over, the station switched back to a local reporter in the United States who'd been watching the match with a group of college kids hanging out at their local bar. "Who have you been rooting for?" the interviewer asked.

"Our team was eliminated a while ago," one young man explained, *"so we wait to see who's matched up, and then we pick a team to cheer on."*

I loved this response: Once we see what the sides are, we can decide which side we're on. This is such a wonderful metaphor for this point on your transformational journey. *You have to decide which side you're on.*

There are always going to be two vibrational teams within you, each wanting to be victorious. One team is the Expansion Team, and the other is the Contraction Team. **Which side will you choose? You'll want to root for the team that's expanding, because it is the only victory that ever matters.**

SOUL SHIFT

SHIFT FROM WAITING PASSIVELY TO SEE WHICH PART OF YOU WILL TRIUMPH TO SIDING WITH AND CHEERING ON YOUR EXPANSION TEAM

Unlike the championship matches or games in a sport,
your inner battles don't take place just once a year
or every few years.
They are going on all day, every day.

Instead of passively watching the forces of expansion
and the forces of contraction pulling you in
one direction or another,
you decide which side you're rooting for,
which energy you want to be triumphant.

You say "I'm on the side of my Highest, of my freedom."
You take a stand, and you show up
to cheer your Expansion Team on to victory.

Do you want to be on the side of resistance, fear, and contraction, the team that's going to lose? No, you want to be on the winning side.

Ultimately, consciousness will triumph. Wisdom will win. So you take a stand and show up in your life cheering for the right team. You don't wake up each day and say, *"I wonder who's going to win today. I wonder if I will spend the day in contraction or expansion."* You choose expansion—and by the way, *you are* the team.

For instance, you're experiencing a collision between the part of you that wants to go ahead with a project, and the part of you that's tired, frustrated, and grumpy about all the time it's taking. Every day, you feel the vibrational battle playing out inside of you between your Expansion Team and your Contraction Team.

Here's a typical day: You're just starting your work. Your Expansion Team gets excited about a new contact you made who might be able to help you or refer you to someone valuable. *Score one point for Expansion!* Your Contraction Team attacks back with negative thoughts about why you can't trust anyone, and reminds you of the last person who said they'd do a favor for you and never followed through. You feel deflated. *Score one point for Team Contraction.*

Your Expansion Team experiences a sudden upset and loss of stamina because a phone call you were waiting for never came through. When the Contraction Team attacks with more doubts about the viability of the project, the Expansion Team is getting too tired to push back. Sensing your weakness, the Contraction Team rallies and runs you over with self-criticism for how poor your idea was in the first place, and how you'll probably never get it off the ground. *Score another point for Contraction.*

Now it's time for bed, and that day the score is 2–1 in favor of the Contraction Team. *How do you feel? Depressed, tense, and defeated.*

Have you figured out what's missing in this scenario? *You are*— **your Highest Self, your vision, your mastery, and your consciousness. Who are you rooting for? How can you support that team and cheer them on to victory? What can you do to strengthen the Expansion Team?**

The next day, you're revitalized, armed with your Soul Shifts wisdom and ready for battle. You start out by spending 15 minutes meditating, and reading a few passages from one of your favorite motivational books or the Bible, or listening to a few minutes of an uplifting audio lecture or piece of music. *It's an early-morning score for the Expansion Team.*

You make sure to eat a good, healthy breakfast (expansion food), rather than grabbing a doughnut (contraction food) on the way to your office. *You're honoring your body = another Expansion Team point.* The score is now 2–0, with Expansion in the lead. You call a good friend to experience some love and connection, and to offer them some support for a crisis they're going through. *Love and compassion = one more point for the Expansion Team.*

So far, the day's been fantastic. Then, a challenge: someone you were hoping would be available to meet with you about your project calls to say they aren't interested. This is a crucial moment in the battle—who will gain the advantage? *The Contraction Team tries to push forward, offering their same old story about how no one is ever there for you, but this time you're ready. The Expansion Team pushes back with a long list of people who have indeed been reliable and supportive over the past few months, and already has several individuals in mind whom you're going to call next. The Contraction Team slinks back to their side of the field in defeat! Score! And victory!*

This is an entertaining but really accurate way to understand how your inner battles play out, thought by thought, choice by choice, moment by moment.

Your day doesn't just unfold.
It's a constant encounter between
expansion and contraction.

Mastering your life doesn't mean sitting on the sidelines and
passively watching to see who is going to triumph each day.
It means *taking a stand for the Highest*,
and using all of your resources
to strengthen the expansive energies so that
they can be victorious.

You wouldn't send your child on a class camping trip without supplies, would you? You'd want them to be comfortable and prepared for anything. You'd make sure they had enough warm clothing, extra snacks in case they got hungry, mosquito repellant, a first-aid kit in case of emergency, flashlights and extra batteries, and so on. You would think ahead to what might happen, and then plan accordingly.

This is how you need to show up on your transformational journey, prepared and planning accordingly for the very predictable tactics of the

Contraction Team, armed with expansive artillery and loyal to your Expansion Team.

BEYOND GOOD OR BAD:
SEEING EVERYTHING THROUGH VIBRATIONAL GLASSES

"And here is the test of truth: anything that makes you weak
physically, intellectually, and spiritually,
reject it as poison; there is no life in it, it cannot be true."
— Swami Vivekananda

At the beginning of this book, we explored the importance of seeing yourself as a vibrational being and seeing your relationships as vibrational interactions with others. You were invited to shift from thinking of your past as a series of emotional events to understanding them as *vibrational events* that had a *vibrational impact* on you. Now we're ready to get practical, and bring this wisdom into your life today.

Everything that happens to you affects your vibration. Moment by moment, you're vibrationally interacting with and being affected by every experience you have, every person with whom you interact, and everything you hear and see. *What vibrational impact are all of these things having on you?*

SOUL SHIFT

SHIFT FROM JUDGING SITUATIONS AND EVENTS AS GOOD OR BAD TO ASSESSING THEIR VIBRATIONAL IMPACT ON YOU

Our usual way of evaluating a relationship or situation is to render a sort of judgment on it, concluding that "It's good" or "It's bad." "He has a good effect on me" or "She has a bad effect on me." "I had a good time" or "I had a bad time."

Remember what I offered at the beginning of this chapter:

Every experience you have either expands you or contracts you.
Every thought you have either expands you or contracts you.
Every relationship, conversation, or interaction with another person
either expands you or contracts you.
Everything you see, watch, read, and feel creates either
a life-enhancing vibration or a life-diminishing vibration.

When you understand the principle of expansion and contraction, you become empowered to no longer passively experience what happens to you and judge it after the fact as positive or negative, pleasing or not pleasing. **Instead, you assess how people and situations affect you vibrationally, so you can make better choices. Is their impact *life-enhancing* or *life-diminishing*?**

No encounter with a person or experience is ever neutral. Each time you interact with someone or something, it shifts or tunes your vibration slightly in one way or another, like loosening or tightening a string on an instrument. Some people and circumstances recalibrate you in a life-enhancing way, creating more resonance and tuning you to your Highest vibration because of their particular vibration, like tuning an instrument to its perfect pitch. Other people and situations recalibrate you to a life-diminishing vibration, creating more dissonance and imbalance, like adjusting an instrument so that it's out of tune.

This new Soul Shift moves us out of a right-wrong/good-bad paradigm (which in itself can cause us to contract), and instead poses some important questions.

Soul Shift Recalibration Questions

**How does this person/situation/environment/activity
/TV show/conversation/relationship/food
impact me vibrationally?**

**Does it help me vibrate in a more expansive way,
or a more contracted way?**

How is it serving me?

You can begin asking yourself these questions about everyone and everything in your life, looking at the situation or person through what I call your "vibrational glasses." Here are some hypothetical examples:

* You're invited to an evening pool party given by someone at work.

You always feel tense around this gentleman, but normally you'd show up at his event without even contemplating it, because you love parties and he has a fantastic house and excellent food. You put on your vibrational glasses, ask yourself the Soul Shift questions, and are surprised by your answers:

The way this man impacts you is negatively. In his presence, you feel anxious, judged, and agitated. He always has a contractive effect on you when you spend time with him. His energy is aggressive and negative, and he's always gossiping about your co-workers. The last time you attended one of his parties, he got completely drunk and began insulting his wife right in front of her. You left and felt unsettled for an entire day.

The verdict: Going to the party doesn't serve you at all.

* You're very busy with work and family projects, and haven't taken much time lately for yourself. A friend calls asking if you'd like to meet her for a walk in the park.

You are slightly annoyed just thinking about it, because you feel like you can't spare even a minute. In addition, you've been feeling overweight, and the idea of putting on exercise clothing stresses you out. You put on your vibrational glasses, ask yourself the Soul Shift questions, and are surprised by your answers:

The way the walk would impact you vibrationally would be very uplifting. You always feel better when you're out in nature. The park and your friend would definitely help you vibrate in a more expansive way, and probably serve you to be more relaxed when you returned home. Even though you might initially feel uncomfortable exercising, it will definitely serve your highest goals for yourself.

The verdict: Meeting your friend for the walk will be a life-enhancing experience.

You can see that, in each of these scenarios, the question of *whether or not you liked or didn't like the situation was not the issue*—the important consideration was *how each of the circumstances would impact you vibrationally—expanding you or contracting you.* For instance, you like parties but don't like your co-worker's parties and how they contract you. You don't like exercising and adding one more thing to your list for the day, but you feel expanded when you see your friend and finally get your body moving.

Hopefully you're beginning to appreciate how invaluable this Soul Shift is.

When you assess your life from a vibrational point of view,
and not from the point of view of the ego or even your personality,
you can make much more expansive, uplifting,
and life-enhancing choices for yourself.
You'll experience less confusion and inner turmoil because
you're asking the right questions, and not the wrong ones.

Instead of "Do I like this?" or "Does this feel good?" you ask,
"How is this going to affect my consciousness?"

A word of caution: *It's important not to allow your old patterns to trick you into believing that something expands you because it feels good.* That's not what we mean by expansion, and it's why I explained expansion as life-enhancing. It doesn't just temporarily make you *feel* expanded. It actually expands the power of your vibrational field.

Once someone tried to convince me that doing indulgent things expanded him. "When I go to a party and have five drinks, I let loose and start laughing and screaming. I feel so free! It's a blast! I'm having fun, so that expands me, right?"

"Nice try," I replied. "I hate to inform you that *this isn't expansion— it's intoxication.* It isn't life-enhancing to go unconscious and temporarily poison yourself, to be unaware of how you're affecting other people, and to not remember much of what happened."

How free are you if you need to depend on something
***to make you* feel free?**
True freedom is not only *freedom to do* certain things,
but *freedom from* those things, inside and outside,
that don't serve your Highest.

SURROUNDING YOURSELF WITH EXPANSION

*"The key is to keep company only with people who uplift you,
whose presence calls forth your best."*
— Epictetus

There's a great saying from one of my favorite Indian devotional poets, Mirabai, who lived in the 16th century: *"Give up bad company and keep company of those who love God instead."* What she meant by bad company is company in which the energy is not focused on the Highest, company that is not life-enhancing but life-diminishing, company in whose presence you feel contracted. It's very important for you to think about the company you are keeping, *not from the point of view of judgment, but rather from an attitude of assessment.*

**We always unconsciously recalibrate our vibration
when we're around other people.
It's automatic. We can't help it.
It's the nature of energy to shift its vibration
when it interacts with other forces of energy.**

Imagine pouring water into three different containers: a drinking glass, a square metal box, and a thin vase. The water will interact differently with the shape of each object by adjusting its own form. It will appear to be square in the box, like a cylinder in the glass, and like a skinny tube in the vase. The quality of the water remains the same, but its appearance changes.

This is what happens to us in our relationships and interactions with others, which is why contemplating the company we keep is a wise thing to do. A word that will help you in this endeavor is *discrimination*.

How are you using your discrimination? For example, is it being a good friend to someone to listen to their constant complaints, gossip, and negativity? Is this really loyalty, even though when you see their name pop up on your phone, your stomach contracts into knots, and each time after your conversations end, you're drained and depressed? How does this affect your consciousness and your own integrity?

I call these kinds of associations based on negativity "indulging in emotional junk food," as *contractive conversations and behaviors often taste good at first. You may get an instant ego high for a moment after binging on sarcasm and judgment, but soon you feel sick.*

**What we consume is not just what we put into our body,
but what we put into our heart and our consciousness.
Eat wisely.**

Some people are "expanders." Their vibrational presence will naturally have an expansive impact on yours. It's not because they do things for you or compliment you, but because of how they are vibrating. Take a moment right now and recall someone you know who is an expander. Just thinking about them should immediately expand you.

Then there are people who are "contractors." Their vibrational presence will naturally have a contractive impact on yours because of how they are vibrating. These may even be people you like or love, but they are still having a life-diminishing effect on you. Take a moment and think of someone you know who is a contractor—but not for too long!

Basically, your job is to find and hang out with the expanders and avoid the contractors. It really is that simple.

I'm not saying that expanders never experience moments of contraction, or that contractors never rise up to a moment of expansion. I'm certainly not saying that contractors aren't lovable or deserving of all good things. However, as you'll see once you begin looking around through your vibrational glasses, at any given point in our life we do fall into one of those two categories. Of course our status can change at any moment!

The question is, which one of these are you: Are you primarily an expander or a contractor? When people see you, do they expand? Do they contract? Are you like the sun, which heats up someone's vibration with radiant warmth and causes them to expand, or are you like an ice storm that freezes them and causes them to contract?

This is the work you're doing—recalibrating your vibrational presence so that you become an expansive presence on the planet. The more you become an expander, the more your vibration will have an expansive impact on others, thus helping them also to become expanders.

Expanders aren't just people. Spirit and Cosmic Intelligence has provided us with an innumerable selection of miraculous expanders. Here are just some of them:

The moon	Fresh fruit
The stars	Sunlight
Trees	Oceans, lakes, and rivers
Flowers	Birds
Animals	Colors
Music	Hugs and kisses
The sound of the wind	Sunrises and sunsets
Laughter	

All of these are life-enhancing energies. Just a few seconds experiencing one of these cosmic expanders and tuning into its expansiveness will definitely recalibrate your vibration and create more alignment with the Highest.

I surround myself with as many expanders as possible, both human and nonhuman. My home is full of them. Everywhere I look, I see something that expands me: photos of people I love; sacred objects; flowers and plants; pictures of saints and spiritual teachers; colorful hangings and cloths; cards from my students; and much more.

It doesn't require money to surround yourself with expansive things. When I was in college, I was very poor, without a dollar to spare. Yet even back then, I understood this principle. I would decorate a cardboard box with a beautiful scarf I discovered for 50 cents at a thrift store. I'd tack photos cut out from magazines—waterfalls, beaches, mountains—up on the wall. I'd splurge on one flower a week.

What we see has a profound effect on us. It immediately shifts our vibration by either expanding it or contracting it. *When you look around at where and how you live, does what you see expand you or contract you?*

**In each moment, with each thought or emotion you follow,
you're creating expansion or contraction.**

**You can work yourself into a contractive collapse
by focusing on energies of contraction.
You can shift yourself into an expansive state
by focusing on expansive energies,
and partaking of an expansion snack.**

I call instant expanders *"expansion snacks."* Just as we may need a snack between meals to give us extra energy, so we need regular expansion snacks as part of our day, or when we find ourselves hungry for a vibrational boost. Most important, when you suspect you might be having a contraction attack and notice that you're upset or feeling negative, you need an immediate dose of expansion to raise your vibration.

**When you find yourself beginning to contract,
choose to do something that you know will create
immediate expansion.**

You can make an instant Soul Shift in just a few moments by doing expansive practices, taking expansive actions, and choosing expansive emotions. I suggest that you make a list of these for yourself, and carry it with you at all times. The questions that follow will help you articulate what expands you, as well as identify what contracts you.

Here are some important Soul Shift Recalibration Questions. These are designed for journaling and contemplation, not just in one sitting, but over time. My students spend months working with these questions that act like keys to open exciting doorways leading to a life of fulfillment, empowerment, and freedom in each moment. Please don't read them now and forget about them. They are one of the most essential practices I'll be offering you.

The answers to these questions will become your personal map to awakening.

Soul Shift Recalibration Questions

Who expands me?

Who contracts me?

What expands me?

What contracts me?

What experiences and activities expand me?

What experiences and activities contract me?

What thoughts expand me?

What thoughts contract me?

What feelings expand me?

What feelings contract me?

When do I feel most like an expander?

When do I feel most like a contractor?

Choices for expansion are always soul choices. They create space for the Highest in you to emerge. They have expansive consequences, not only for you, but for everyone around you. When you expand, you are a gift to the world.

THE GREAT EXPANDER: MORE LIGHT

Since I was 18, I've been running as fast as I could toward truth, not away from it. I've never tried to negotiate with it or modulate it, even when what I was seeing about myself or about a situation was terrifying or painful. My prayer was never, *Please—less light! I don't want to see what I'm seeing.* Instead, it was always, *More light! Show me more. What's behind that other door I see there? I want to see everything. More light!*

Light will always be your liberator.
When you look at yourself or a situation
and don't like what you see,
or don't understand what you see,
or are scared by what you see,
the solution is not to contract the amount of illumination,
but to do the opposite and expand it—
not to want less light, but to call in more light.

Imagine that you're trying to navigate around a dark house with an old flashlight whose batteries are almost dead. The bulb is very dim and hardly illuminates anything, so you keep bumping into things. You wouldn't decide that you want less light so that you don't have to see the obstacles in your path. *You would decide you need more light.*

Bringing more light to your process of transformation is going to expand you. Light is the Great Expander. Light brings life. When plants are exposed to the light, they grow. And we humans are drawn to the light because instinctively, we recognize its sacred gift:

Light creates expansion,
and the absence of light creates contraction.
The more light you can hold,
the more you can become a light for others.
When you shift, the world shifts.

When it becomes intolerable for you to continue in ways you have been living, thinking, and loving, pray and call on light to help illuminate your path of returning to your own wholeness. When you start to see, you make it possible for others to see. When your light grows brighter, it will spill over onto everyone around you, making it easier for them to travel their own road to awakening.

SOUL SHIFT PRACTICE: CALLING IN LIGHT

Whenever you're feeling lost, confused, frightened, resistant, conflicted, guilty, angry, or any other unpleasant or unwanted emotion, or when you find yourself thinking *I don't want to deal with this,* use this Soul Shift Practice of calling in more Light. Any time you want more illumination on an issue or problem, you can also use this practice. *Remember: Light creates an instant vibrational shift of expansion.*

ᏕᏬ CALLING IN LIGHT ᏕᏬ

Close your eyes. Take a few deep, slow, full breaths.

Place your hands in front of your heart area, close to your body, palms facing upward, one hand resting on top of the other, as if you're holding out your hands to receive something.

Now imagine placing the awareness of the issue, problem, or emotion into your hands, as if it is resting there like an object, as if you are offering it to be seen by someone.

Still imagining what's in your hands, allow yourself to fully feel the vibration of that issue, problem, or emotion in your body, as if you are one with it.

When you are ready, simply have the thought: "MORE LIGHT."

If you'd like, you can softly say those words out loud: "MORE LIGHT."

You can also imagine that you are asking for more Light from any Higher Beings you resonate with: from the angels, from Jesus, from Krishna, from Shiva, from Buddha, from the Goddess, from the Great Oneness.

Don't try to see anything, or imagine receiving anything, or visualize anything. Just be very still, surrendered, and open.

Sit for at least a few minutes like this, and whenever you feel ready to complete, take your hands and imagine placing whatever you were holding back in your heart, along with whatever Light was offered to you, even if you didn't feel anything.

Then fold your hands in prayer position in front of your heart, bow your head slightly, and say, "Thank you," out loud three times.

When you're finished, you can open your eyes.

Calling in Light is a very powerful practice to recalibrate your vibration from contraction to expansion. My experience is that it becomes even more effective over time. *Don't expect to do this Soul Shift Practice and immediately have everything magically transform. Just go through the sequence, and let go of any concern about the outcome.*

You may just notice more of a sense of calm, or a decrease in your anxiety or urgency about your situation, or an easing up of depression or despair—all signs of vibrational expansion. Perhaps in the hours and days that follow, you will become aware of having some new understandings or attitudes about whatever it was that you focused on.

Some people practice this every day, making it a part of their other spiritual rituals; others only do it when they feel the need. My students have had amazing results with this Soul Shift Practice. *The more closely you follow the instructions, and the less you instill any will, intention, or effort into it, the more profound it is going to be.*

Be on the lookout for more Light!

You are expanding your wisdom.
   You are contracting your ignorance.

You are expanding your knowledge.
   You are contracting your confusion.

You are expanding your hope.
   You are contracting your insecurity.

You are expanding your certainty.
   You are contracting your doubt.

You are expanding your freedom.
   You are contracting your bondage.

You are expanding your love.
   You are contracting your protections.

You are expanding your remembrance.
   You are contracting your forgetfulness.

You are expanding and expanding and expanding and expanding . . .

❀ 9 ❀

Mastery in Each Moment:
The Spiritual Practice of Choice

*"At any moment, you have a choice, that either leads you
closer to your spirit or further away from it."*
— Thich Nhat Hanh

Are you ready to learn how to use one of the most powerful magical forces that exists in the universe? It's an extraordinary advanced spiritual practice that will instantly shift you when you feel stuck, motivate you when you feel disheartened, rewire your vibrational programming, and recalibrate you in just moments from contraction to expansion. This special practice is the key to integrating all of the wisdom and understanding you've acquired, and is guaranteed to completely change your life. It is:

The practice of choice.

No, this isn't a clever trick with words. I'm completely serious when I say that **choice is one of the highest and most powerful spiritual practices available to us, and is crucial to integrated and grounded transformation.**

We've learned that Soul Shifts are transformative inner actions originating from and in alignment with the Highest spiritual truths. Rather than only focusing on changing things on the outside, we must take these inner actions and make powerful shifts in understanding, feeling, and consciousness from within. To take inner or outer action, however, first we need to practice choice.

When we think of spiritual practices, what comes to mind is usually prayer, meditation, going to a house of worship, chanting, visualization, and so on. We ask for grace, cosmic intervention, and miracles. We ask for guidance, for blessings, and for protection.

Choice is another kind of spiritual practice that says, "I am going to remember that I am the Ultimate Consciousness temporarily identified with this body and as this person; therefore, I can be a miraculous circuit for consciousness, wisdom, and power to flow out into my life. I'm going to be a vehicle for the life force to move through me. I am going to be the creator and shape my reality."

Every single moment of your life, you have the opportunity to practice choice. You have hundreds and hundreds of choices to make each day. I'm not just referring to the obvious ones, such as what to eat, what to wear, which task to work on first, whom to call, which program to watch on TV, and what time to go to bed, which are all behavioral or logistical choices. Some of the most important choices you make are invisible—they're the vibrational choices, the inner choices, and the Soul Shift choices.

Choice is essential to our evolution as an individual.
It takes the life force, God Consciousness, Divine Energy,
Cosmic Pulsation, Shakti, Chi, or whatever we wish to call it,
and moves it out into manifestation.
Choice is the miracle and blessing we've been seeking.
When we choose, we become the creator of our universe.

This may sound rather obvious. *I make choices,* you think. I'm sure you do—*except for the ways in which you don't.* For every choice you make, there are so many that you need to make and should make, but you haven't or don't:

You know that you're tired and in an irritated mood, and rather than choosing to take a break or a nap, meditate, shift your attitude, or do something to calm yourself down, you continue to snap at people and vibrate your agitation out to the world. *You didn't make a choice to feel better.*

You've been having stomach problems and have been advised by your physician to change your diet and cut out certain foods. You know you need to take charge of your health, but do nothing. *You didn't make a choice to take care of yourself.*

You're feeling upset about how someone is treating you. You watch yourself beginning to pull back emotionally and feel sorry for yourself. You know you should speak up and express how you're feeling to try to clear things up, but don't say anything. *You didn't make a choice to remain connected and not feel like a victim.*

Most people would not think these scenarios were examples of choices. In each case, it looks like you're doing nothing, but you're actually doing something: you're aware of how you're feeling, but aren't making a choice to change how you're feeling. Not choosing to make a choice is a choice that, in each case, has consequences.

> **You practice choice in each moment of your life.**
> **Even when you think you aren't choosing,**
> **you're *choosing to not choose.***
> **Not making a choice *is* the choice.**

When we begin to do transformation work, we often become an expert on noticing: "I noticed that I pulled away." "I notice that I haven't been asking for what I want." "I notice that lately I've been very critical with my children." "I notice I'm thinking a lot of negative thoughts." It's definitely important to notice how we're feeling and what's taking place in our lives. That's the first part of the Soul Shifts Mantra: *"I'm going to see what there is to see."*

Here's where we introduce the difference between *noticing* something and *choosing* something. **Once we see what there is to see, and know what there is to know about it, we are ready to shift: We need to move on to choice.**

SOUL SHIFT

SHIFT FROM JUST NOTICING WHAT IS HAPPENING TO CONSCIOUSLY CHOOSING IN EACH MOMENT

We don't just randomly wait for things to shift. Noticing what's happening should not be like noticing the weather. Whether it's raining or sunny outside, there's nothing we can do about it, but we *can* do something about what's happening to us on the inside and, in many ways, on the outside. **We shift from noticing to consciously choosing.**

We ask ourselves:
"What's the Highest choice for me in this moment?"
"What choice would raise me to the Highest vibration?"
"Is there another, more beneficial choice that I can make?"

It's not enough to notice that you're stuck.
You have to choose to get unstuck.

It's not enough to notice that you're shut down.
You have to choose to open.

It's not enough to notice that you've gotten off center.
You have to choose to find your way back to center.

It's not enough to notice that you've wandered into an old pattern.
You have to choose to find the exit out of it.

DOING THE CHANGE

"Do or do not. There is no try."
— Yoda, *The Empire Strikes Back*

One of my favorite treats as a little girl was to be allowed to ride in our car when it went through the automatic car wash. It felt magical to me as I sat in the backseat and the car began moving all on its own, pulled along by the mechanical track. I would squeal as the machinery squirted soap suds and water all over the vehicle, amazed that I wasn't getting wet. Fascinated, I'd stare out the window until I couldn't see anything because the whole vehicle had become engulfed in white foamy bubbles. Then, the swishers would suddenly appear—*thwack-thwack!*—slapping the car in an alarming fashion with their long, flowing curtains of cloth as they scrubbed it clean.

Next, I'd feel like I'd entered a South American rain forest, as torrents of water poured over the car to rinse off the cleanser. Finally, it was time for the blowers, and the whole vehicle would shake from the force of the air, while I'd marvel at the water droplets dancing along the car surface and then mysteriously vanishing into thin air. Then it was over and I'd see the flashing green light, indicating that the car was sparkling clean and we'd survived the journey.

On the way to teach a retreat in the High Desert of California not long ago, I stopped for gas at an exit, and to my delight, I saw an old-fashioned drive-through car wash across the street. Even though I'd just had my car washed at home a few days before, I had to treat myself. I think I was just as thrilled taking the ride through the car wash at 63 years of age as I was when I was 8!

Some people make the mistake of believing that the path of transformation and personal growth is like entering an automatic car wash, where everything's going to get done for them and the car's going to come out clean at the end. They imagine that they can sign up for the journey and sit back and enjoy the ride, assuming that no matter what they do, they'll emerge enlightened.

The path of awakening is not a cosmic car wash.
You don't get to sit back and be a passenger.
***You* are essential in the process of your transformation.**
It's not just being exposed to wisdom and insight that matters—
it's what you choose to do with it.

It's completely unrealistic to be exposed to knowledge from a teacher, seminar, book, support group, church, or spiritual community, and assume that simply because of that fortunate association, you'll magically and spontaneously grow. You have to bring your own offering to the process, an offering consisting of *the willingness to deeply contemplate; the openness to see beyond how you've been seeing; the commitment to keep excavating, even when what you're discovering about yourself makes you uncomfortable; and, perhaps most important of all, **the readiness to make choices that will shift your revelations into action.***

Once I watched a TV interview featuring a well-known actor who had just come out of a treatment program for an addiction. It was his first public appearance since he had entered rehab, and after making nervous introductory chitchat, the on-air reporter asked him, "Do you feel changed?"

The actor's answer was profound. He said:

"I don't think the idea is to feel the change.
It's to do the change."

I got chills when I heard this thoughtful response. It was something I'd been teaching for many years, but it was very moving to hear it through someone else' voice, especially someone who'd just spent almost two months isolated in rehab and was now faced with the challenging task of having to "do the change" he knew he needed to make.

Doing the change is more than just eloquently and passionately talking about what needs to change, and being able to identify and articulate the patterns and programming. Those are words. You may be feeling the longing to shift, and even believe that something inside of you has shifted, and it certainly may have. That's still not doing the change.

SOUL SHIFT

SHIFT FROM *NOTICING* WHAT NEEDS TO BE CHANGED TO CONSCIOUSLY *DOING* WHAT IT TAKES TO CHANGE

Doing the change means integrating, implementing, and applying what's happening to you on the inside by making new choices on the outside. It requires going beyond simply noticing what needs to happen, and choosing to make it happen.

This is much harder than conceptualizing a change. Often when I facilitate deep work for someone and they're able to see something they've never seen before, they'll say to me, "I get it." My response is always the same:

"Now let's see you do it."

"Getting it" is like what happens when someone gives you a heavy package. They hand it to you. You take it and say, *"I've got it."* So now, you've gotten the package, but what are you *doing* with it? Are you unwrapping it? Are you appreciating the contents of the package and using each item for its intended purpose?

Doing the change means showing up in a new way
as the change from moment to moment to moment:
communicating from the change, behaving from the change,
living from the change, loving from the change.
You can't change theoretically.
You can't transform in principle.
Shifts in understanding and awareness on the inside
need to be enacted on the outside, choice by choice.

There's a big difference between locating patterns and eliminating patterns, between having significant and genuine revelations and actually choosing the daily process of transformation. This Soul Shift is a crucial understanding for you as you make the transition from learning about yourself to transforming yourself, and as you master the practice of choice. *Locating your issues is not the same as working through your issues.*

SOUL SHIFT

SHIFT FROM STOPPING AT LOCATION AND REVELATION TO CHOOSING TRANSFORMATION

Revelation is not transformation. Locating your issues, your patterns, and your programming is important, but it's not the same as transmuting and transforming them. True transformation isn't an intellectual process of getting information about yourself and then being able to say, "I have all this good information about myself. I see things. I understand things." **This is collection. It has nothing to do with transformation.**

Figuring things out is not transformation.
Talking about what you've figured out is not transformation.
Transformation is energetic and vibrational.
It's a series of Soul Shifts that will rock your world.
It's radical.
It's noticeable.
You will not have to announce it.
You deserve nothing less.

WHY CAN'T I DO IT, OR WHY DON'T I DO IT?

*"Hell begins on that day when God grants us a clear vision
of all that we might have achieved, of all the gifts we wasted,
of all that we might have done
that we did not do."*
— Gian-Carlo Menotti

I recently received an e-mail from a reader complaining about the difficulty she was having making decisions in her life. She kept using the phrase "Why can't I?": *"Why can't I get more clients? Why can't I reach out to more people? Why can't I ask for what I want from my husband?"*

I'm sure you've heard this phrase often from people you love, and perhaps you've used it yourself. **The question "Why can't I?" really doesn't have an answer. That's because it's actually a complaint disguised as a question, a lament from a victimized point of view.** Think of one of yours right now, such as:

"Why can't I stick to my diet?"

"Why can't I find a job I like?"

"Why can't I get my kids to behave?"

"Why can't I say no to people?"

"Why can't I finish this project?"

"Why can't I stop eating junk?"

"Why can't I figure out why I'm afraid to let anyone get close?"

"Why can't I find a good plumber?"

Now, try taking just one of your "Why can't I?" statements, and changing the first few words:

Instead of: **"Why can't I say no to people?"**
Ask yourself: **"Why *don't* I say no to people?"**

Some examples:

Instead of: Why can't I find the right business partner?
                 Why *don't* I find the right business partner?

Instead of: Why can't I lose weight?
                 Why *don't* I lose weight?

Instead of: Why can't I express myself to others?
                 Why *don't* I express myself to others?

Instead of: Why can't I ask for what I want?
                 Why *don't* I ask for what I want?

"Why don't I?" is an actual question that can be answered. When you ask yourself "Why don't I?" suddenly the tables turn, and instead of feeling that the universe has singled you out for suffering and there's nothing you can do about it, you're actually exploring an issue.

SOUL SHIFT

SHIFT FROM ASKING YOURSELF "WHY CAN'T I?" TO ASKING YOURSELF "WHY DON'T I?"

When you ask yourself "Why don't I?," you make an instant shift into empowerment. For instance:

"Hmm, *why don't I express myself?* Maybe it's because I always was reprimanded as a child for speaking up. Maybe it's because I don't want people to get upset with me. These don't sound like very good reasons to keep stuffing my feelings."

Now you're seeing what there is to see, feeling what there is to feel, and knowing what there is to know. You've asked a conscious question, and you can dig deep as you look for the answers.

Can you see the difference? **"Why can't I?" is based on a vibration of helplessness, and powerlessness, and a resistance to taking responsibility.** When we ask "Why can't I?" we actually put ourselves in the position of being like a child. What do kids ask all the time?

"Why can't I stay up tonight and watch TV? Why can't I have that toy? Why can't I eat ice cream for breakfast? Why can't I pierce my ears like my older sister? Why can't I stay out late with my friends?"

When children ask those questions, they aren't actually expecting an answer, are they? "Why can't I?" is code for *"It's not fair!"* *"It's not fair* that I can't stay up and watch TV! *It's not fair* that I can't pierce my ears! *It's not fair* that I can't have that toy!"

Now look at your own "Why can't I?" questions from that point of view. *"It's not fair* that I have to look for a new business partner! *It's not fair* that I have to work so hard on this project! *It's not fair* that I am so afraid to ask for what I want!"

> **Finding the courage to ask yourself, "Why don't I?"**
> **will instantly shift you from feeling like a victim**
> **to feeling more in control.**
> **It's one of the most powerful transformational doorways**
> **you can walk through.**

"Why don't I say no more often instead of agreeing to do things and then resenting it? Why don't I show up on time? Why don't I face my uncomfortable feelings instead of stuffing them down? Why don't I ask for what I want instead of setting people up to disappoint me?" These are brave questions, and each one *does* have an answer.

I suggest you write out a list of your "Why can't I?" questions, and turn each one into a "Why don't I?" Then take some time to contemplate each item on your list and see what answers reveal themselves. You'll be making the choice to bring the light of consciousness to some areas of your life that have been vibrationally congested, loosening up the knots of unconsciousness, and dismantling old patterns that aren't serving your Highest.

GETTING UNSTUCK, ONE CHOICE AT A TIME

"Every morning I jump out of bed and step on a landmine.
The landmine is me.
After the explosion,
I spend the rest of the day putting the pieces together."
— Ray Bradbury

One of my least favorite words is *stuck*. We hear this word all the time. The sense that we are stuck or trapped in an unmoving state is directly related to our topic of choice.

Feeling stuck is a state of what I call "non-choosing." We're in a circumstance or emotional process for which we can't see an immediate solution. We're feeling powerless, and since nothing we think of doing in the moment can immediately solve the significant problem or issue, we end up doing nothing.

We're never stuck.
We're just making choices that don't serve us,
or we're choosing to not make any choices at all,
which means we're choosing non-choosing.

Most of the time when we feel stuck or stagnant, we're having a "spiritual tantrum." We're refusing to acknowledge that we have any choices, perhaps because we don't like the choices, and we're sitting on the floor waiting for someone to come along and pick us up, or for something to miraculously change.

You're never stuck as long as you have choice.

Every day you get to resurrect yourself from
however you fell down the day before.

Every hour you get to wake up from
however you went unconscious the hour before.

Every minute you get to redo
whatever you didn't do well the minute before.

SOUL SHIFT

❋

SHIFT FROM TRYING TO CHANGE EVERYTHING TO CHOOSING TO DO SOMETHING

This is a simple but powerful technique that can create an instant Soul Shift. Whenever you're feeling stuck, upset, confused, frightened, overwhelmed, or otherwise terrible, remember that in that moment, you can use the spiritual practice of choice. Say to yourself:

"Right now, let me choose to do *something*."

That's all. It's that simple. Right now, let me choose to do something.

Choose to meditate, choose to pray, choose to take a ten-minute walk, choose to drink some water, choose to call a friend, choose to take some deep breaths, choose to hug your dog, choose to do one item from your list of expansion snacks, choose to listen to one of your favorite songs, choose to look at photos of people you love, choose to make a list of five things you did right today, choose to wash your dishes, choose to call one person back, choose to make a list of things you can choose to do!

The moment you choose to do something, you shift yourself vibrationally from contraction to expansion. It doesn't even matter what you choose to do, as long as it's life-enhancing. The gift you'll give yourself is that you chose, you acted, you took charge of the moment and injected your will and energy into it. You will instantly feel better. That little bit of upliftment will encourage you to make another choice, and another—and before you know it, whatever darkness or lethargy you were battling will begin to lift.

Whenever you're going through a really fierce battle with despair or depression, you may need to use this technique every five minutes. I've done this many times in my life during times of shock or tragedy. *Right now, I'm choosing to walk over to the refrigerator and get a drink of juice. Now, I'm choosing to walk outside for one minute and take a few deep breaths. Now,*

I'm choosing to come back inside and wash these two dishes. Right now, I'm choosing to write in my journal.

Each of these choices lasts for one minute. Added together, you find you've had an hour of conscious life-enhancing choices. Just knowing that, you will feel stronger. **You may not feel any less pain, but you will feel less helplessness and contraction.**

There's an old saying: *"If you find yourself in a hole, the first thing to do is stop digging."* In order to stop digging, we need to make the *choice* to stop digging. Then we're free to make another, more expansive choice that will begin to get us out of the hole of contraction we've dug.

**When you feel stuck or stagnant, don't do nothing.
Make one choice.
When you make a choice,
you reconnect your circuitry with your will.
When you make a choice,
you expand yourself out of contraction.
When you make a choice,
you stir the energy that's been stagnant.
Just make one choice. Then make another.
Then make another.
Soon, you will feel the flow of the life force
moving through you again.**

Shift somewhere. Soon, you will see shifts in other places. Why? What are you really shifting by making a choice to do something? *You're shifting yourself. You're shifting your non-choosing. So when you shift how you interact with something, it's not just that situation that improves—you've* **improved.**

That choice to shift somewhere will make the next choice easier, and the next after that.

**When you shift anywhere,
it helps you shift everywhere.
When you choose somewhere,
it helps you choose everywhere.**

You can't make a choice for forever. You can only make a choice right now, and then again right now, and right now, and right now. Most people don't understand this, and scare themselves into being stuck and powerless.

For instance, let's say you've decided that you need to be more assertive and outgoing. This is an amorphous goal. It's global. There are no parameters of time and space to contain it. *You can't choose to be more assertive in general. Where would that happen? How would that happen?* So just the thought that you should do it depresses and discourages you.

What can you do instead? **You can make the choice to be more assertive for the next five minutes.** If your brother calls and asks if you can look up some information for him, you can choose to tell him that it's not a good time and you'll call him later. You'll have achieved your goal. You were assertive.

Then you make that choice again for the next five minutes. Then you make that choice again. Then you make that choice tomorrow. You're making choices in the moment. You aren't making it for your whole life, because it's overwhelming to try to even comprehend what that would look like.

> **Choice is a moment-by-moment practice.**
> **You can't globally change—**
> **you have to change in one moment.**
> **If you can choose in each moment, before you know it,**
> **it's a series of conscious moments,**
> **and then it's been a day of moments,**
> **and then it's been a year of conscious moments,**
> **and you're somewhere you never could have imagined.**

MAKING THE CHOICE FOR YOUR HIGHEST IN EVERY MOMENT

> *"The content of your character is your choice.*
> *Day by day, what you choose, what you think,*
> *and what you do, is who you become.*
> *Your integrity is your destiny . . .*
> *it is the light that guides your way."*
> — Heraclitus

No matter what else is happening, one of our greatest freedoms is that we always have a choice. Depending upon our circumstances, we may not always be able to fully exercise those choices in our outer life, *but on the inside, our freedom is unlimited.*

No one can take away your freedom
to make the Highest choice.
No one can take away your freedom
to make the most loving choice.
No one can take away your freedom
to make the most conscious choice.
That's true freedom.

When you make high choices,
you identify with the Highest in you,
and shift into that Highest.

Here is a very simple but stunningly profound Soul Shift Practice that will help you live every day with much more consciousness and awakening. It is the most powerful recalibration technique that I teach.

Whenever you're feeling anything less than centered, clear, and peaceful, whenever you're feeling anything unpleasant or undesirable, ask yourself:

"What am I choosing in this moment?"

For example, you notice that you're feeling angry with your partner. Ask yourself, "What am I choosing in this moment?" Then answer the question honestly. *Are you choosing connection or separation? Are you choosing judgment or compassion? Are you choosing stubbornness or trust? Are you choosing blame or forgiveness? What's actually happening?*

This is not a sarcastic question. It's not a judgmental question. It's an authentic question designed to guide you toward the truth.

The question is worded in a particular way for a reason. **You'll notice I didn't design it to ask, "What's happening in this moment?"** This would allow you to avoid taking responsibility for what you're doing and what you're choosing. **It doesn't matter what anyone else is doing or did to you. All that matters is for you to understand what you're choosing in the moment.**

"What am I choosing in this moment? Let me see, what am I actually choosing? Well, I've been sitting around feeling sorry for myself for the last two hours. I've been choosing to be cold to my partner and make sure he knows he upset me. What else am I choosing? I guess I'm choosing to go over a list in my head of everything he did wrong in the last few months. That means I'm choosing to condemn him and make myself right. I'm choosing to pull away. And I'm choosing to punish him. Ugh. This all sounds terrible. I can't believe I'm actually choosing to be this way."

Now you've become conscious of what you've been doing and what you've been choosing. Once you answer honestly, which may take a few tries, you'll probably be unhappy with what you've been choosing, perhaps even shocked. **That's the whole point of this technique—to force you to be conscious of what you've been choosing, to see what there is to see about it and feel what there is to feel.**

You can see that this practice has nothing to do with what you feel the other person did. It doesn't matter if they've been horrible. It only matters what you've been choosing. That's where your power is.

Here's something else to notice about this question: *"What am I choosing in this moment?" is a neutral question, isn't it? It has no opinion or preconceptions.* It moves you into a vibrationally neutral space, and when you're situated in a neutral place asking the question, guess what is happening? *You've already shifted.* **Just choosing to ask yourself the question shifted you vibrationally.** You're now in an empowered place of choice.

There's a second part to this practice. Once you answer "What am I choosing in this moment?" it's time to follow it with a new question:

"What do I *want* to choose in this moment?"

This second question is a powerful and instant expander. It lifts you up to your Highest in seconds. Your first answer might still be coming from your less than Highest, but watch what happens when you persist in asking the question.

"What do I want to choose in this moment? I want to choose to lock myself in the bedroom and watch TV all night because I'm so angry. I want to choose to make my partner suffer so he knows he hurt me. Yeah, I want him to hurt like he hurt me. *Actually, that sounds terrible. I don't really want to make him suffer.* I don't even want to keep fighting. I hate fighting. I just want to feel better. Let me start again: *What do I want to choose in this moment?*

"Well, I certainly don't want to feel this way, because I'm miserable. What do I want to choose? I guess I want to choose to feel better. I want to choose to be compassionate. I want to choose to not care that my partner was insensitive, and find a way to reconnect and maybe talk about it. *Even though I still feel angry, I want to choose to love."*

Can you see what happens when you contemplate what you *want* to choose? Asking yourself what you want raises you up to your Highest. By thinking about those things, you begin vibrating with their higher frequencies. With each thought and each emotion, you're already shifting. **The thought of what you want to choose makes the *choice actually happen in that moment*. The thought "I want to choose love"** *is* **the choice for love.**

There's another way to ask the second question that can help if you're really feeling stuck or resistant, or you can't think of what you want to choose:

"What is another, more enlightened choice I can make right now?"

If you forget every other Soul Shift Practice and only used this one, it could permanently transform you and change your life. This isn't something to do occasionally, or only under dire circumstances. I suggest you begin using these questions as consciousness expanders throughout your day. They are the express train back to your Highest.

"There is no path. Paths are made by walking."
— Antonio Machado

You have been given a sacred gift:
Every day you get to begin again
and be the re-creator.
You are the choice you make in each moment.
Choose wisely.
Choose joyfully.
Choose freedom.

❅ 10 ❅

Finding Your Way Back to the Highest

"May I rise to the highest pedestal."
— The Atharva Veda

The beautiful quote above is from one of the ancient Indian scriptures, the Atharva Veda, dictated almost 1,000 years before the birth of Christ. Where is the highest pedestal? It isn't a physical location, or a place of status in society. **It is within us. It is the pedestal of our Highest Consciousness, and of our true source and self.**

Every tradition teaches that within you is the Highest, whether you call that Highest God, Spirit, Christ, Allah, the Goddess, Divine Intelligence, or the Cosmic Pulsation. It isn't a concept. It's a vibrational reality. So to rise to the Highest means to align with it and vibrate as it.

The Highest in you isn't just the thought of the Highest.
It's the original and perfect vibrational blueprint of your soul.
You were designed to be an expression of the Highest.
When you vibrate with the Highest,
you've risen to the Highest pedestal.

How do we know when we have risen to our Highest? *By now, it should be clear: We are at our Highest when we are our most expansive, most connected, most vibrationally uplifting self.* Our Highest is a vibrational reality, and not simply an intellectual construct that we should think about in order to inspire ourselves and behave appropriately.

SOUL SHIFT
❂

SHIFT FROM THINKING ABOUT THE HIGHEST TO VIBRATING AS THE HIGHEST

Keeping your mind focused on God, Spirit, or uplifting ideas is fine as long as you remember that you're not imagining those realities to be somewhere outside of you, contemplating them the way you'd fondly remember a wonderful trip you took to a far-off destination, and hoping that you can get back there someday. **The Highest isn't anywhere else but right here, right now, not *in* you, but *as* you.**

Instead of thinking about consciousness being somewhere *in you*, remember that what you identify as "you" is actually an individual pulsation that's *in consciousness*. You *are* consciousness contained in a body.

We are souls with bodies, not bodies with souls. This Soul Shift is just a gentle reminder to remember what you mean when you tell yourself, "I want to be in my Highest." There's no distance to travel. It's just a shift in identification.

A few years ago while taking a walk by the ocean, I had a simple but profound revelation about suffering. It had been a very stressful day full of delays, disappointments, upsets, and agitated interactions with someone who worked for me. As I climbed the same hill I walked up each time I took this particular path, I found myself remembering yesterday's hike. I'd been happier, more relaxed, and definitely more vibrationally expanded.

Suddenly, I realized that nothing about me had changed in 24 hours—*I simply wasn't as fully connected to my Highest as usual because of the vibrational interference from my emotional agitation. I was suffering because I had partially disconnected.* **The Highest hadn't moved away from me. I'd moved away from it.**

Suffering is often a disconnection from your Highest vibration, which is *the* Highest vibration. Doesn't this make sense? Your natural essence and vibrational setting is love, wholeness, wisdom, and peace. To not be able to feel that, hold that, and broadcast that out to others creates an experience of suffering.

So much of our suffering comes from not vibrating at our Highest. We're not defective, cursed, bad, or beyond repair. We just aren't vibrating at our Highest frequency.

Can you see the difference between telling yourself, "I'm messed up," and instead saying, "I'm suffering right now because I'm not vibrating at my Highest"? It removes the wrongness and condemnation from what you're doing, and makes it more of a conscious choice. **It means that "I am capable of vibrating at my Highest, most uplifting frequency. I just wasn't doing it. I'm not a failure. I just need to be vibrationally recalibrated for my Highest to come through."**

This is the Soul Shift from seeing ourselves through the polarized eyes of right and wrong to understanding ourselves through the eyes of consciousness. Instead of judging ourselves as bad or weak, we objectively assess our actions as they relate to us at our Highest, versus us at our less than Highest:

"I wasn't at my Highest today when I was cold to my husband after he forgot to call me. I wasn't at my Highest this morning when I snapped at the kids as I got them off to school. I wasn't at my Highest last night when I watched four hours of reality shows instead of preparing my presentation for work. I wasn't at my Highest today when I silently berated myself for hours about not getting more done on my project at work. I wasn't at my Highest the other night on the phone with my mother when I became impatient with her reminiscing about her friend who passed away last year."

Can you see what happens when we have the thought *I wasn't at my Highest*? Which part of us has introduced that awareness? It's our Highest! It has intervened and tugged on our consciousness as if to lovingly say, "You might want to pay attention to what's happening right now."

True freedom means the freedom to choose to feel, speak, and act from your Highest in every moment.

More and more, we've been learning to rise to our Highest pedestal and vibration. However, we not only need to learn how to live as our Highest, but to find our way vibrationally back to our Highest once we realize we've unknowingly drifted away from it.

USING YOUR COMPASS OF CONSCIOUSNESS

"One never goes so far as when one doesn't know where one is going."
— Johann Wolfgang von Goethe

Earlier in the book we talked about how small things make a big difference, and introduced the idea of how we often drift off course in life, both in small ways and in very serious ways. Now it's time to understand this principle of drifting as it pertains to how we drift from our Highest. **I call this "vibrational drifting," because you're not actually moving anywhere on the outside, but on the inside, you're drifting away from vibrating in your Highest**—drifting from your wisdom, from your connectedness, from your steadiness, and from your love. No one can see you vibrationally drifting, but eventually they feel it, and so do you.

SOUL SHIFT

SHIFT FROM JUST TRYING TO BE IN YOUR HIGHEST TO NOTICING WHEN, HOW, AND WHY YOU DRIFT FROM YOUR HIGHEST

**Being conscious doesn't just mean knowing what you need to do
in order to be at your best,
but also noticing when you *were* at your best
and then suddenly drifted away.**

What causes you to vibrationally drift? That's really what we've been exploring on our Soul Shifts journey. It could be that you're vibrationally impacted by a person in your life in a less than positive way; it might be that your own programming or habits of unconsciousness short-circuited your connection to your most expanded self; it could also be any one of the many other things we've discussed. Either an incident happens, or someone comes along, or something comes up within you, and you start to veer off course, just a little bit at first. *Slowly, your small driftings add up, and you find yourself in emotional territory you absolutely did not plan on visiting.*

You drift off course because it takes a tremendous amount of energy to hold the ship of consciousness steady. It takes focus, strength, clarity, and courage to be unwavering when you set a course for your freedom. Seeking the Highest is like sailing into direct sunlight—the light of consciousness and self-discovery is very bright, and you can easily be tempted to look away or close your eyes and say, "This is too hard."

This is where your Soul Shifts come in. *Each one I've offered you is a "compass of consciousness" that will point you in the right direction, a compass of consciousness that guides you back to your Highest when you've drifted off course.* They're designed to help you make the vibrational adjustments necessary to steer yourself to your ultimate destination of true freedom.

**Once you realize that you've drifted
and need to use your compass of consciousness,
you're already changing course.**

**Once you say to yourself,
"I'm not feeling centered in my Highest, and I need to shift back,"
you're already shifting.**

**Once you notice that you're not vibrating at your Highest,
you're already shifting back to your Highest.**

Your compass of consciousness will never steer you in the wrong direction.

Rising to Your Highest: Climbing the Ladder of Light

*"We live that our souls may grow.
The development of your soul is the purpose of your existence.
God Almighty is trying to obtain some decent association for Himself."*
— John G. Lake

Earlier we talked about the practice of choice. Now we integrate that understanding with our intention to live in the Highest in each moment.

No matter what the specific circumstances, in every moment you have one choice to make. Here is a new Soul Shift Recalibration Question:

"Am I going to be in my Highest or not?"

This is actually the only question you ever really need to ask yourself because it will serve as your compass of consciousness. "Am I going to speak from my Highest or not? Am I going to choose from my Highest or not? Am I going to do this task from my Highest or not? Am I going to love from my Highest or not? Am I going to respond to this person who is not in *their* Highest from my Highest or not?"

You can fill in the blank after the first part of the phrase in order to personalize this for any situation:

"Am I going to _____ from my Highest or not?"

This is a really powerful recalibrator. My experience is that it works on just about everything and anything.

Here are some of the more unusual situations in which my students have used this Soul Shift Recalibration Question. These are real examples of questions they actually asked themselves in order to shift into their Highest:

"Am I going to fire my employee from my Highest or not?"

"Am I going to surf this wave from my Highest or not?"

"Am I going to go through this speed-dating lunch from my Highest or not?"

"Am I going to visit my mother from my Highest or not?"

"Am I going to plan my wedding from my Highest or not?"

I have to admit that I just love this Soul Shift Recalibrator. It's worded exactly as I meant it to be, in order to bypass any places you may be feeling stuck or confused, and take you on the express elevator to your Highest.

Here's how it works: *Asking yourself if you're going to do something from your Highest instantly sends a message to your brain to access what that Highest might be. Your brain opens the file that says "My Highest," and all of that neurological information is suddenly available. You're now vibrating at your Highest, and all you did was ask one question!*

Even a short visit to your Highest
will instantly change everything.

Naturally, you've had many experiences when you've been at your Highest, vibrating from your Highest, loving from your Highest, and seeing from your Highest. You know what it feels like. *It's important to remind yourself that the Highest doesn't mean the perfect.* It means the Highest for you, the wisest for you, the most loving for you. Highest means higher than you were before, knowing that as you continue to transform, your Highest will continue to expand.

Here is the Soul Shift Practice called "Choice for the Highest." You can use it along with or separate from the recalibration questions I just introduced.

The question "Am I going to do this from my Highest or not?" shifts you out of contraction into a more expanded consciousness. These new contemplations go one step further, and help you more specifically articulate how your Highest Self would behave and think.

Soul Shift Practice: Choice for the Highest

What would it look like right now to be in my Highest?

What is the Highest thought about this situation?

Imagine that you're watching a movie about a hero who needs to make an important decision. He moves through a huge, unruly crowd of people all calling out to him with requests and instructions, demanding that he pay attention to what they have to say. Undaunted, the hero pushes them aside, and finally comes to his destination—the quiet sanctuary of the wise sage. He enters and sits down with this great master, seeking only his counsel, for he knows it will be the Highest and most true wisdom.

This is how you experience yourself every day. There's always a boisterous crowd of thoughts and feelings clamoring for your attention. Your emotions are saying one thing. Your ego is loudly pressuring you to take its side. Your patterns and programming are spouting off old recorded opinions from long ago.

When you ask yourself, "What would it look like to be in my Highest? What is the Highest thought about this?" it's as if you're pushing aside the mob of emotions and taking yourself into the temple of your heart to your own great guide, your great representative of the Source, your great inner teacher. You're asking your Highest what the Highest choice would be, and letting that counsel be what guides you.

This is a beautiful and really effective way to bring yourself back from any drifting you've done, or just to refocus you on your most expanded self. If you like, you can even *imagine a representative of what you consider the Highest vibration in a person or being, and visualize yourself sitting with that person* and asking, "What would it look like right now for me to be in my Highest?" You're sitting with Jesus, Buddha, Kuan Yin, or whomever or whatever resonates as the Highest for you.

It takes only a minute to close your eyes, imagine yourself having this cosmic conversation, and ask these Soul Shift questions. In that minute, you will have found your way back to your Highest.

All of the specific Soul Shifts and recalibration questions that I've highlighted in the book are inner actions that will realign you with your own Highest vibration. **Whenever you're feeling off center, contracted, or less than fulfilled, you need to make a Soul Shift. Look through the list at the back of the book and find one that resonates with you in the moment. Use it as a compass of consciousness, put it into practice, and you'll be going in the right direction.**

I tell my students that in each moment, we're standing in a spot where there's a ladder of light above us and a ladder of darkness below, a ladder of expansion above us and a ladder of contraction below. There's the hand of an angel trying to pull us up and the hand of something else trying to pull us down. *In each moment, we have a choice.*

The question is: *Which ladder does your hand grab on to?*

I have spent my life reaching out my hand for the Highest. No matter what other forces were pulling on me, I've always clung tightly to the ladder of light, and climbed as fast and as high as I could.

Even when you're writhing around in confusion, even when you've drifted, reach out for the Highest. Just have the thought, *I'm reaching out for the Highest,* and you will feel something reaching back to pull you up out of the quicksand of your forgetfulness.

PROTECTING YOUR HIGHEST

A few months ago, I saw an amazing TV documentary about bald eagles, which are an endangered species. Bald eagles are monogamous and mate for life. They build huge nests called eyries in tall trees or in the side of cliffs. Female bald eagles lay two or three eggs at a time, and both parents have a very strict regimen of protecting the nest from predators for the 35 days of gestation.

The filmmaker partnered with some researchers who actually placed several cameras in an eagle's nest. The documentary showed breathtaking footage of the female sitting on her eggs, and then her partner came right next to her. She moved just the tiniest bit over, and then he moved the tiniest bit in her direction, until, without the eggs being unprotected for even a second, she was free to fly, to hunt. Now the male was in charge, keeping the eggs covered from predators—ravens, gulls, and buzzards—that would come and steal the little baby eagle eggs for food, killing the developing eaglets.

These eagles will fight to the death to fiercely protect the nest. They do not leave what is precious unguarded or exposed to potential harm. I was grateful and fascinated to witness these majestic eagles and to be reminded of this important teaching: ***We each need to protect our nests of transformation.***

Imagine in our metaphor that the nest is your growing wisdom, your love expanding from the melting of your old frozen patterns, and deepening healing. When anything grows, it's vulnerable—a child, a plant, an idea, a tender feeling. These are the vulnerable eggs of consciousness that are hatching to bring forth incredible gifts into your life. While they are still expanding and integrating, you must protect them from those things that would harm them, those predators that would steal what is precious from you.

**The beginning of the unfolding of your own wisdom,
your own expansion, and your own healing
is a tender time, and tender times call for protection.**

What are those predators? Some of them are from inside yourself—your fear, doubt, criticism, and skepticism that begin to eat away at your hope, courage, and inner accomplishments a little bit at a time, until you notice that you're wavering in your commitment to freedom. *This is you not protecting yourself from yourself.* Some of the predators are from the outside, people whose vibration disturbs yours and threatens to pull it down into a less expanded and uplifting frequency.

What threatens the vibration of your growing transformation? Perhaps it's a friend who pulls you into gossiping every time you talk. Perhaps it's a particular topic of conversation in which you engage with someone at work that always leaves you feeling drained and angry. Perhaps it's a certain kind of movie or TV program that, while entertaining, agitates your vibration and doesn't protect your sense of serenity.

I'm not suggesting you need to announce to someone that you're protecting yourself from them and are therefore canceling your lunch date. Protecting your wisdom means that you're loving and respecting who you are, the path you're on, and everything that's blossoming inside of you.

**Protection is not a pushing away.
It is an act of love.
It means protecting something you see as valuable.
It is a way to honor the Highest that is unfolding in you.**

We must love ourselves and value our journey enough to protect that which is trying to grow and hatch within us. Ask yourself:

**"Am I aligning myself with people who support the Highest in me?"
"Am I in relationship with people in whose
presence I rise to my Highest?"**

It's much harder to grow, to change, to shift, and to recalibrate yourself when you're with people who are not wanting to align with the Highest in you, aren't interested in the Highest in themselves, and in fact, *want your "not Highest parts" to keep their "not Highest parts" company.*

It will be challenging for you to stay in your Highest Self,
your most loving self, and your most wise self
if you're trying to harmonize with someone who's aligned with
their most judgmental self, their most contracted self,
or their most negative self.
You can't successfully do both.

I have a saying: *"You can't walk through the mud and not get some on your feet, even if it's not your mud, and even if it's mud you're quite fond of."*

What are some of the ways you get sucked into or seduced into the mud?

* A friend calls you gossiping about somebody else, and you allow yourself to get pulled into participating in that energy, and then after the phone call, you notice, *I feel slimed. I'm exhausted.*

* You share an exciting new idea with someone who appears enthusiastic on the surface, but they plant bombs of doubt in you by things they say, or the face they make, and afterward *you feel insecure and somehow exposed.*

* Someone you know is always angry or outraged about everything, making cutting sarcastic comments and blaming anyone and everyone. *You stumble away from these conversations feeling beat-up,* even though none of the negativity was directed at you.

The mud isn't always obvious. Sometimes it's subtle. It can even be wrapped in lovely paper and decorated with bows, but when you touch it, it's still mud. Yes, you can continue to wash it off with the cleanser of your own uplifting vibration, but that's an investment of a lot of time and energy that would be better used in uplifting pursuits.

Making this assessment doesn't mean you don't love someone. There are many people in my life for whom I have deep love, but with whom I spend little or no time or rarely speak to because the influence they have on me is not one that is uplifting. *I value my consciousness and my vibrational field, and am fiercely protective about what's allowed to enter it.*

From the Highest point of view, participating in a vibrational dance with someone else's muddy consciousness not only doesn't serve you, but it doesn't even serve them. It simply reinforces and enables the way they're functioning. *The most loving thing you can do is to not feed their pattern, and model a more enlightened alternative for them.*

**The best thing you can do for everyone in your life
is to operate from your Highest possible vibration.
Your choice to be in the Highest
can recalibrate other people to their Highest.
This is actually the true meaning of love,
and the true purpose of service.**

Soul Shift Recalibration Questions

**Who in my life helps to support
my alignment with my Highest?**

**Who in my life makes it more difficult
for me to align with my Highest?**

ALIGNING YOURSELF WITH THE HIGHEST:
SOUL SHIFT RECALIBRATION PRACTICES

How can you experience more of the Highest in your life, not just once in a while, but every day? How can you find those moments of expansion that will recalibrate you to your Highest, as well as find your way back to the Highest when you've drifted away? Here are some other easy-to-use Soul Shifts Practices that I've created for you. They're powerful tools that will help you find your way back to your Highest and stay there.

⌬ THE SOUL SHIFT INSTANT RECALIBRATOR ⌬

Sometimes we need something that slaps us awake and cuts through everything. Here it is! I created the Soul Shift Instant Recalibrator to help my students when they find themselves drifting from their Highest and lingering in emotional or behavioral places they know they shouldn't be. It's a very simple but powerful question that you ask yourself:

"DO I HAVE TIME FOR THIS?"

Naturally this question doesn't refer to your schedule, as in "Do I have time to stop for coffee?" but means *"Do I have time in my life for this contracted, less than positive situation?"*

When do you use this Soul Shift Instant Recalibrator? You use it whenever you find yourself in any state less than your Highest. For example:

You find yourself obsessed with worrying about what someone you barely know or don't care for thinks of you; you're upset with someone about a petty misunderstanding; you're berating yourself for making a mistake in how you handled a situation that happened days ago, but haven't let it go; you're annoyed that someone didn't get back to you exactly when they said they would; you're drawn into the middle of an argument between two people, a fight that has nothing to do with you.

Do you have time for these things? The answer, of course, is, *No you don't!*

Once you determine that you don't have time for something, you'll be motivated to make a different choice. So you could ask yourself "Do I have time for this?" and then when you realize you don't, you can ask your other Soul Shift question: "What is the Highest choice I can make for myself in this moment?" It's really that simple.

When you ask yourself "Do I have time for this?" it's helpful to articulate what the "this" is. "This" is usually not something that is supporting you to be in your Highest. Once you're clear about that, it's easy to decide you aren't going to waste your time on it. You make a choice for your Highest.

Some examples of "this" might be: *blame; self-righteousness; anxiety; being reluctant to tell someone no; paranoia about things totally out of your control; arguing about superficial things; the attempt to convince, fix, or control someone who you know is not going to budge; stubbornly insisting that something inconsequential is done your way; and so many other scenarios that you don't have time for!*

In the beginning of this practice, I suggest that you write out the Soul Shift Instant Recalibrator and put little signs or sticky notes everywhere, not because you'd forget the wording of the question, *but because you'd forget to even ask yourself the question!*

Many of my students have shared that this is one of the most practical and powerful techniques I've taught them. It cuts to the chase and "bottom line's" everything, doesn't it?

ᕲᕳ SOUL SHIFT PRACTICE: ᕲᕳ
TAKING THE ELEVATOR
TO YOUR PENTHOUSE OF CONSCIOUSNESS

Imagine that your consciousness is like a high-rise building. At the very bottom of the building is the basement in which there are no windows, and no light entering from outside. The basement is where the garbage for the building is processed, where the trash drops down to from chutes on the upper floors.

At the very top of the building is the penthouse. It's full of light streaming in from the windows, and sunshine can enter unobstructed by any other tall structures. From the penthouse, you can see for miles and miles around with a huge vantage point in every direction, since nothing is blocking your view. It is quieter up at the penthouse because you're away from the street noise, and because you're so high up, you can accurately assess everything—the traffic patterns, the weather—*anything there is to see, you can see.*

Between the basement and the penthouse, there is everything else, all of the other floors. The building has an elevator to take you to whatever floor you want. You can push the UP button and go all the way to the top. You can push the DOWN button and descend to the bottom. You could get off of the elevator anywhere in between the two.

Our consciousness is just like a high-rise building. We have our Highest floor—our penthouse—where there is light and vision and clarity; and we have our lowest floor—our basement—where it's dark and cut off from the world; and many floors in between. *The good news is that we also have an elevator called choice that will take us wherever we want to go.*

In every moment of our life, we get to decide on which floor we'd like to reside. That's what the Soul Shift Practice of choosing the Highest is all about. Do we want to spend the day in the basement of our consciousness, where all of our vibrational and emotional trash is waiting to be removed? Do we want to sulk by ourselves in the dark? Or do we want to find the elevator and push the UP button?

If you're having a difficult day and know that you aren't in your Highest because of the quality of your thoughts and emotions, *you don't have to stay there in the basement, or on one of the lower floors of your consciousness: You can get in the elevator and go "up." Where are you going? As high as you can go.*

Here's the exercise:

ᑭᑫᑫ TAKING THE ELEVATOR ᑫᑫᑭ
TO YOUR PENTHOUSE OF CONSCIOUSNESS

Close your eyes and visualize yourself standing in an elevator in front of a huge panel of buttons. Imagine seeing the button that says "P," for penthouse, for the Highest, and with great intention and commitment, see yourself pushing that button. (It helps to actually put out your index finger as if you're pushing an invisible button.) Feel yourself rising and rising, perhaps visualizing it's a glass elevator and you can see yourself getting higher and higher above your life.

Then picture the doors of the choice elevator opening, and see yourself walking out into your penthouse of consciousness. It's good to spend time at some point imagining what your penthouse would look like. Perhaps it's a temple or sacred space. Perhaps it's filled with inspiring and uplifting objects or reminders of your Highest. Perhaps great divine beings *are there waiting for you. Maybe it's not a room in the building but a separate whole world somewhere, such as in the mountains or on a tropical island. **When you're in that penthouse of consciousness, you align with your Highest truth, your Highest wisdom, and your Highest love.***

*It could happen that, when you imagine getting into your elevator from whatever lower state you're in, it stops somewhere that feels a little better, but still isn't your Highest. Maybe ten minutes pass, and you realize that you're not happy with this floor. Just imagine getting back in your elevator, and pushing the UP button once more. **"I know there are higher floors than this inside of me. How high can I go?"** Once you're there, you'll have no interest in going down to the basement again.*

This is a really fantastic technique. **It can shift you in just a matter of minutes, because you do have a penthouse of consciousness, one that actually keeps getting raised higher and higher as you do this work.** Naturally you're not "going" anywhere, but are using your mind to shift to higher vibrational frequencies that already exist within you.

You can practice this while you're sitting in a business meeting and realize that you've been stuck in the basement. You can do this before an important gathering, social event, or phone call. You can use this in the middle of an argument with your partner, or when you're feeling down or agitated. You can also do this as a regular practice in the morning before you start your day, simply to recalibrate yourself to the Highest.

Here's another Soul Shifts reminder:

When something comes up, lift up!

By now you understand the principles of vibrational transformation, so you can see that establishing a habit of "going up" to your penthouse of consciousness is simply an enjoyable way to recalibrate yourself. **Eventually, as a result of practicing this and the other Soul Shift techniques, you won't have to consciously remind yourself to shift: you'll begin shifting automatically without even realizing you're doing it.**

Soon you'll be *living* in the penthouse, and will only need to use your elevator if you somehow go unconscious or develop a bad case of sleep-walking, and find yourself wandering around on some strange floor of awareness far below where you're used to living!

∼ SOUL SHIFT PRACTICE: ∼
TAKING A TWO-MINUTE PILGRIMAGE

Most of us wait to be uplifted, like waiting for the sun to come out, or waiting for something to be delivered to us. We love it when it happens, but it seems out of our control. An essential Soul Shift understanding is that it only takes a moment to be your own "uplifter"—to lift yourself up.

SOUL SHIFT

SHIFT FROM WAITING TO BE UPLIFTED TO LIFTING YOURSELF UP

It's delightful to contemplate taking a pilgrimage to an ancient temple, or a famous cathedral, or a spectacular sacred spot in nature. However, our everyday lives don't usually allow for these kinds of marvelous spiritual journeys. Isn't a sacred place simply one in which we experience upliftment, expansion, silence, and a reminder of the Highest? You don't need to travel thousands of miles to India, Tibet, Rome, Peru, Israel, or anywhere else to experience a pilgrimage to the Highest. *You already have all of the ingredients to create one right in your own home.*

Here is a practice I call the "Two-minute Pilgrimage." It's very simple, and is based on our understanding of what we know vibrationally expands and uplifts us.

⟨⟩TAKING A TWO-MINUTE PILGRIMAGE ⟨⟩

For two minutes, do or experience something with the thought and intention that you're taking a sacred pilgrimage.

For instance:

Two minutes reading passages from an inspirational book, as if you're receiving the wisdom of a wise being.

Two minutes listening to healing music with your eyes closed, as if you've come to a special place to be vibrationally recalibrated.

Two minutes looking at a photo album of your family, children, or friends, as if you're opening to the vibration of love and blessings pouring off of the pictures.

Two minutes standing in your yard or by a tree on your street, as if you're receiving the blessings of Divine Intelligence through nature.

As you can see, I'm not simply saying "read a book" or "look at a picture," but rather, experience that activity as if it were a sacred pilgrimage. Formally begin and end your two-minute pilgrimage just as you would a physical pilgrimage:

When you go to a sacred place or enter a sanctuary, you approach it with reverence, and open yourself in a particular way. So instead of just looking at a photo, you approach it with reverence, perhaps folding your hands in front of your heart and honoring those you love. Instead of just reading a book, you approach it with reverence, opening yourself to receive the wisdom as if you're having an audience with a great being. When you're finished, you formally offer gratitude for what you just experienced, and go about your day.

If you'd like, you can create a few spots in your home that you designate as sacred places of pilgrimage. These don't have to be elaborate or large in scale: It could be several photos of people you love set next to a candle. It could be a place where you have a few treasured inspirational books sitting on a special cloth. It could be a photo on the wall of something that uplifts you. ***Remember not to see these as objects, but as pilgrimage spots.***

My house has dozens upon dozens of pilgrimage sites: altars with sacred objects; special groupings of photos; flowers and plants reminding me of the exquisiteness of nature. I don't practice a two-minute pilgrimage at each location every day, but I have many sacred sites from which to choose! I get to ask myself, *"Which sacred place do I want to visit today?"*

This is a really wonderful practice, and figuring out the different two-minute pilgrimages is a process in itself, as it forces you to contemplate what raises your vibration to the Highest. Even if you've never done anything like this before, I suggest you try it for a while. **Remember that it isn't the photo, the altar, the mountain, or the journey that's magically shifting you. It's what happens inside of you as you have the intention of aligning yourself with the Highest.**

༄ SOUL SHIFT PRACTICE: ༄
MASTERY MOMENTS:
MAKING THE CHOICE FOR THE HIGHEST

Can you find one moment in the last few days during which you made a choice from your Highest? Perhaps you were cross or impatient with one of your kids and caught yourself, took a breath, and instead of scolding them, gave them a hug. Perhaps you were thinking about what to eat and were deciding between something junky and something healthy, and chose what was healthy. Perhaps you began to criticize yourself, judge yourself, or be hard on yourself, and stopped to feel some compassion for yourself and what a challenging situation you were in. Perhaps you noticed yourself feeling self-pity, like no one cared about you, and decided to reach out by phone to a few friends who were thrilled to hear your voice.

It's very important to recognize these experiences. **They're what I call "mastery moments," in which you're integrating the Highest you into your life.**

Here is what's exciting to understand: **if you can choose to be in your Highest one time, even for one minute, you can do it for another minute, and another and another. If you can choose to see or interpret or respond from your Highest, you can do it over and over again.**

Each choice for the Highest not only elevates us
in just that moment,
but it makes the next choice for the Highest easier,
and the next after that,
because we're starting out from a higher vantage point.

This is what it means to keep yourself aligned with the Highest—vibrating with the Highest thought about a situation, the Highest behavior, the Highest understanding. We all have our Highest and, of course, we all have our lowest. We all have the more awakened aspects of ourselves, and then we have our more unconscious aspects that are still reluctant to get out of bed!

Even on a difficult day, or during a difficult situation, or when you're dealing with a difficult person, *you have freedom.* You have the freedom to make a choice for your Highest.

You Are the Answer to Your Own Prayers

"God has entrusted me with myself."
— Epictetus

One of the most beautiful verses in the Bible is Psalm 121: "I will lift up mine eyes unto the hills, from whence cometh my help."

I *will* lift my eyes. I lift them up from their contracted gaze looking down at the darkness, staring down at my smallness, and identifying with my limitations, and I raise them up to the hills, to the heights, to my heights, to the sacred, to the Highest.

I will lift my eyes to see things from the Highest consciousness, and from there to know the truth.

Help is there. Love is there. Healing is there. Grace is there. But I need to do something to connect with it. "I will lift" up my eyes means I don't just sit there and wait for grace to come down and rescue me. I will do it.

I will choose it. I will commit to it. *I see the path before me, and I will follow it back to my own mountaintop of consciousness.*

**In each moment, you are the answer to your own prayers.
You have the ability to recalibrate yourself, to choose the Highest,
to vibrate as the Highest, and to embody the Highest.**

Not only are you the answer to your own prayers, but you are meant to be the answer to someone else's prayers. At this crucial time on the planet, none of us, including me, can indulge in taking a vacation from being in our Highest or from serving the world in any way we can. We can't assume that surely, someone else will hold down the fort while we linger just a bit longer in forgetfulness or spiritual laziness. Our awakened presence, your awakened presence, is not just requested, but necessary.

**When you reunite with your Highest,
you can offer the Highest to each person.**

**When you offer the Highest to each person,
it brings out the Highest in that person,
who can offer the Highest to the next person,
who can offer the Highest to the next person.**

And this is the way that we change the world.

PART FOUR

LIVING YOUR SOUL SHIFTS

❧ 11 ❧

Soul Accomplishments and Your Cosmic Curriculum

"In the course of our lifetime, there is one person we must meet . . .
who is this person? It is the true self."
— Sekkei Harada

I remember when, at the end of my last year in high school, those of us in the graduating class were asked to choose a goal we wanted to achieve. The list was published for everyone to see. Most of the items were predictable, such as: "Become a doctor," "Get married and have two children," "Start my own business," "Buy a home in Florida," "Get elected to public office," and "Become a well-known artist."

My contribution was: *"Be free."*

At the time, I wasn't even sure what it meant to be free, but I knew it was what I wanted. There were no self-help books in those days, no motivational TV programs or transformational seminars. "Living as an awakened human" wasn't on a list of possible career paths from which we could choose, but it was the only one that interested me.

I recall being included on another list: The names of students who were voted "Most likely to succeed." Naturally, by "succeed" my classmates meant to be known for something or make money at something—external goals. Some of you may remember the other humorous categories seniors were asked to vote for: "Most likely to get married right away," "Most likely to get arrested," "Most likely to become famous," and so on. While I was happy at the time to at least be in a respectable category, if I could have projected myself into the future, I'd have preferred to be named **"Most likely to wake up"**!

You too must have been on the *"Most likely to wake up"* list that put you on the schedule for your Cosmic Alarm Clock to go off, and as you wake up, you need to adjust the way you value yourself and the events of your life journey.

So what *are* you here for?

What is your cosmic curriculum and the purpose of your Earth journey?

And how will you know you've accomplished that purpose?

Here is our Soul Shifts answer:

What if, from the Highest vantage point of consciousness, the purpose of your journey is not for you to become anything, get anything, or acquire anything, but rather *to transcend your limitations and heal those contractions that have made you forget who you are—* an individual expression of great light and love?

What if you are here to gather and acquire the wisdom that will elevate and uplift your soul, so that each day you can say, *"I'm wiser than I was yesterday. I see more clearly than I saw yesterday. I understand more than I understood yesterday"*?

What if *your true accomplishments happen in your character, in your heart, and in your soul,* and cannot and should not be measured by the limited constructs of the world?

What if you had the following soul goal every day?

> Today I want to live as the most awakened, loving
> human being I can be.
> I want to stay awake
> and be more awake at the end of the day
> than I was when the day began.

For a seeker of truth, that accomplishment becomes one of the most treasured attainments we would ever hope to achieve. It's what I call a "soul accomplishment."

SOUL SHIFT

SHIFT FROM FOCUSING ONLY ON EXTERNAL GOALS AND ACCOMPLISHMENTS TO HONORING YOUR SOUL ACCOMPLISHMENTS

**Everything we've been exploring in *Soul Shifts*
has been about soul accomplishments—
transforming, remembering, healing, relinquishing,
expanding, serving, awakening, loving,
making a positive vibrational contribution.**

**You know you've made a soul accomplishment
when the reward you receive is lasting.
Nothing and no one can ever take it away from you.**

What are soul accomplishments? When you evaluate your day, how will you know you've truly achieved those things you should be proud of? You've made great soul accomplishments if you can say any of the following:

"Today I thought deeply about things."

"I saw something about myself that I didn't want to face, but kept looking until I understood it."

"I caught myself going into contraction and chose to do something else to create expansion."

"I realized I was shutting off and reached out to reconnect."

"I expressed appreciation for people I loved."

"I forgave myself."

"I lightened up about something."

"I had compassion for someone I previously would have judged."

"I handled something a little bit better."

"I chose the Highest thought and shifted my attitude about an issue."

"I loved myself even though I wasn't perfect."

"I remembered to be grateful for being alive."

"I took a two-minute pilgrimage to my heart."

"I was conscious."

"I didn't go back to sleep."

These are profound soul accomplishments. The other things that occurred on the outside are just the karmic events of the day. One day you make more money; one day you make less money. One day your job is calm; one day it's chaotic. One day your home life is peaceful; one day it's contentious. If you evaluate your success based on those ever-changing external circumstances, you'll be setting yourself up for unhappiness.

This is exactly how we often sabotage our feeling of accomplishment: **We believe that to feel good about ourselves means we need more of something. We have to get more or do more, and when we don't, we conclude that we've failed.**

Nothing's wrong with outer achievements. I have earned many of them myself, and enjoy helping others manifest their own dreams. However, our material goals become a problem when they overshadow the quest for our soul goals, *those inner attainments that aren't about achievement or acquisition, but about true mastery.*

Every day, I see wonderful, conscious people who have attained great personal mastery yet suffer and condemn themselves because they don't feel successful, all because their achievements don't fit the picture of how they think success is supposed to look. They're living lives of authenticity, compassion, service, humility, gratitude, and grace. All of these are astonishing soul accomplishments, but since they can't be measured or valued in traditional terms—money, prestige, possessions—they're discounted.

We can begin to recalibrate this understanding with our next Soul Shift.

SOUL SHIFT

SHIFT FROM ALWAYS TRYING TO GET MORE AND DO MORE ON THE OUTSIDE TO BECOMING MORE ON THE INSIDE

There's nothing wrong with wanting "more," except that we're usually focusing on more of the wrong things rather than those qualities and choices that would bring us closer to our Highest.

Is there really a way to be more without getting more? Of course there is! Every day you can be more. You may not be able to acquire or do more, but you can always *be* more. **That's because true soul accomplishments don't depend on anyone else but you.**

**"More" has to start inside of you:
You can be more giving; you can be more compassionate;
you can be more forgiving; you can be more grateful;
you can be more courageous; you can be more loving.**

To see yourself, the darkness and the light, and to shift and shift and shift—this is an unbelievable honoring of the Highest. This is a great soul moment. And these are great soul accomplishments for which you deserve to be honored.

I call this "seeing yourself through God's eyes." (Instead of *God*, feel free to use *Spirit, the Divine,* or any other term you wish.) Do you really think that some great Cosmic Being or Intelligence, whatever you imagine it to be, would say, *"You know, I don't think those sales numbers are really good. Hmm, she didn't close that deal today. Did I see her eating two portions of ice cream? What about that cellulite—that's unattractive. What a messy desk—that certainly doesn't present a good case for her soul. No, I don't think she's doing that well."*

This imaginary scenario should help you see the absurdity of how much you beat yourself up for simply being human. Naturally, the thought of a Higher Power judging you as a failure because of the things for which you judge yourself is ridiculous—but so is your habit of disqualifying your soul accomplishments.

RECOGNIZING AND HONORING YOUR SOUL ACCOMPLISHMENTS

One of the Soul Shifts Practices I suggest you try is to *make a list of your soul accomplishments.*

This is meant to be an uplifting, powerful exercise to create an immediate shift as you look at yourself through the eyes of Spirit, rather than the eyes of your parents, or your competitive best friend from college, or your nemesis at work, or your critics, real or imaginary. This isn't something to do in one sitting and then conclude that you're finished. *Noticing your soul accomplishments should be an ongoing process and an ever-present part of your life.*

༄ HERE ARE SOME OF MY ༄
PERSONAL SOUL ACCOMPLISHMENTS:

Keeping my heart fully open to the fullness of loving, no matter how many times I have been hurt or had to let go of a dream, and never shutting down or shutting off for one moment of my life.

Teaching from a place of hope, inspiration, and complete dedication, even during times when I was personally experiencing despair and loss.

Having the tenacity, patience, and fortitude to stand by something or someone even with no immediate reward or progress, and not let go of my conviction that it was the right thing to do.

Knowing when it was time to help both of my dogs leave their bodies and go forward on their journey, even though I wanted to hold on.

Turning down opportunities for more fame or fortune when the projects were not in alignment with the Highest for me, even though it meant having less income and a much less glamorous lifestyle than most of my colleagues.

Giving myself time and space to go through profound rebirth several times in my life; rather than pushing myself to write a book every year in order to be commercially successful, I instead waited for the right moments to birth new wisdom.

Being willing to teach, write, and speak about meditation and the spiritual path long before it was acceptable or popular.

Learning how, when it was necessary, to let go of situations, people, and attachments in every area of my life, and move forward without looking back.

Taking time away from my career trajectory to study with my spiritual teachers, deepen and stabilize my experiences of awakening, and cultivate the expansion of my consciousness.

Never giving anything less than 100 percent effort, even when no one else is watching, and always approaching everything with the utmost of sincerity.

Learning that sometimes love needs to be fierce.

Never giving up.

Being willing to share this list with you.

Right now, if nothing else ever changed in your life, you have many soul accomplishments for which to honor yourself. Honor yourself for the choice to be awake and conscious. Honor yourself for the choice to open, to feel, to see, and to shift. Honor yourself for the ways in which you've served and loved others. Honor yourself for your moments of revelation and humility. Honor yourself for reading this book, and every book you've ever read to guide you on your path to freedom.

Just a few minutes ago, one of my students sent me an e-mail. It said: *"I cherish who I am becoming."* I love this message, and it is a wonderful contemplation to remind you to cherish the unfolding of your magnificent self.

Don't wait to honor yourself until you become
who you think you should be.
Honor who you're becoming.

Love: The Great Soul Shifter

"Where there is great love, there are always miracles."
— Willa Cather

What is one of our greatest and most important soul accomplishments? I believe it is *to love*. Love is the great expander, the great solution, and the great service to humanity. For this reason, it's the ultimate vibrational remedy, and the most magnificent Soul Shifter.

When you're in the space and vibration of love, you spontaneously align with and vibrate at your Highest. **Choosing love, you can live in your Highest soul accomplishment every day.**

I frequently give out small cards at my seminars with this statement printed on it:

THE WORLD IS WAITING FOR MY LOVE.

This isn't meant to be just an uplifting affirmation. There *are* actually people you haven't met who are waiting for their appointment with you: a chance encounter that gives them courage; a conversation at just the right moment containing wisdom they need to hear; an offering of love and compassion from your heart that guides them to be kinder to themselves. Your job is to prepare yourself so that when these moments arrive, you're ready to serve from your Highest.

SOUL SHIFT

SHIFT FROM SEEING WHERE YOU'RE RECEIVING LOVE TO SEEING WHERE YOU CAN OFFER LOVE

Love is the highest form of service. Part of the job of an awakening human being is to look for it and recognize it, and then to be the deliverer of it to others. That means shifting from walking around seeing where you're getting love, to seeing where you can offer it.

"If you would lift me, you must be on higher ground."
— Ralph Waldo Emerson

When I ask myself who's made the most significant difference in my own life, I realize that it hasn't been leaders in the traditional sense of the word. Rather, it's been those individuals who have led me back to truth, to wholeness, to love, and to my Highest Self. *One thing all of these people have in common is that the way they led me and loved me was through their ability to move me.*

Take a moment and remember a time you felt moved by someone or something. Perhaps it was hearing someone give a motivational speech or sermon, watching an interview or story about someone very courageous on television, attending a concert by a talented artist or musician, seeing a compelling film, or being present at a life-changing event such as the birth of a child, or the death of a loved one.

What actually happens inside of you that makes you feel you have been "moved"?

* When someone moves you, something they say or do "moves" you out of your smallness and into a more expanded, loving place.

* When something moves you, it transmits a vibration of beauty, harmony, magic, or miracles, and "moves" you out of limitation to an experience of wonder and gratitude.

* When someone moves you, something they say or do "moves" you away from numbness, fear, or despair, and closer to your courage, passion, and vision.

* When someone moves you, the vibration of their love, kindness, or strength temporarily melts and "moves" your blocks or resistance out of the way, so suddenly your inner path is clearer from vibrational debris, and you can move yourself toward your Highest.

To be moved by something doesn't simply mean that you have an emotional reaction—*it's a vibrational reaction, an actual shift in your energy.* Something impacts you energetically, and because of it, you begin

fferently. That difference is characterized by more expansion,
iousness, and more love.

**To move someone is to move them up,
away from their darkness or fear
and closer to the light, closer to their Highest,
and closer to Spirit.**

Here's some wonderful news: *When you continually move yourself back to your own Highest, your vibration will spontaneously move others up to their Highest. Isn't this what loving someone should be—that in your presence they rise to their Highest and most awakened Self?*

WHEN THERE'S NOTHING ELSE YOU CAN DO BUT LOVE

"Love means to love that which is unlovable; or it is no virtue at all."
— Attributed to G. K. Chesterton

One of the most difficult lessons I've had to learn on my own journey has been to watch someone I love suffering, and to not be able to fix their pain. Whether a person's ordeal is physical, emotional, or circumstantial, I want to do something; I want to make it all better; I want to chase away their darkness. This has been one of the great spiritual tests and challenges in my life, as I know it has been for so many of us—**to surrender to the fact that sometimes there's nothing else you can do for someone but love them.**

It took me a long time to accept the fact that sometimes love looks like not doing anything. At first, this was a shocking thought to me. Many times we think, *If I love someone, I should . . .* , and then we have a long list of to-dos: *I should help them. I should protect them. I should heal them. I should make them happy.*

**We can't save people.
We can only love them.
But that love *is* enough.**

What if sometimes love means just being, not doing anything except loving, because in those situations there is absolutely nothing else we can do?

244

Think of someone in your life whom you wish you could help or heal but haven't been able to. It could be your partner, a child, a parent, or a friend. You wish you could fix something for that person inside or outside of them. You wish you could make something happen. You wish you could make them feel better about themselves, or have them see the truth, or give them courage or confidence. You wish you could take away their pain or heal their body. You wish you could open their heart, break down their walls, wash away their shame, smash their stubbornness, dissolve their anger, or have them see the light. You've tried, but you can't.

The feeling of *I can't help you* can break your heart.
Yet it's very important to understand
that even if there's nothing else you can do, you can love.
You can always love.
That love will and does mean something.
Loving someone always, *always* makes a vibrational difference,
whether you can see it or not.

Once someone I loved very much went through a time of great darkness. There was nothing I could do to help, and no way I could fight his battle for him. Over and over, I would say, "My heart is breaking because I can't help you."

His response was always the same: "But you are helping me. You're helping me so much."

"How am I helping you?" I'd ask in tearful frustration. "You're still suffering."

"You're helping me because you still love me," he explained, "and because I know you're here for me, and I'm not alone."

I had a hard time accepting this answer, because to me, it looked like my love wasn't doing anything. The truth, however, was that my love wasn't doing the thing *I* wanted it to do or thought it should, *but it was doing something.* It was keeping him from drowning in hopelessness. It was keeping him from collapsing into total despair. My love was like a flame he stored deep in his heart, and when he was ready, he used the inextinguishable glow from that flame to make his way out of the darkness back to light.

Right now, I'm sure you are on someone's list of the people they feel are there for them. Right now, knowing you exist, just feeling

your presence in their life is making someone somewhere feel grate-ful, blessed, and comforted. The fact that they know you're there for them is one of the greatest gifts you could ever give that person. They don't feel alone. They feel your love, and they're strengthened by you. *That is everything.* That is a great soul accomplishment.

> Any moment of triumph in your life, invisible or visible,
> has been a moment in which there was
> a tremendous amount of love.
> To triumph, you must choose love.
> When you do, it will lead you forward,
> and lead you home.

What would happen if each day, you made just one soul commit-ment: *that no matter what else occurred, or what other goals you had, you were going to choose to be in your Highest and bring more love to every situation?*

If you did just that one thing, you would find yourself and the peo-ple around you miraculously shifting, and you'd be celebrating true soul accomplishments.

> Know that you are waking up.
> Know that you are opening up.
> Know that you are rising up.
>
> These are the great triumphs of your soul.

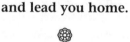

❦ 12 ❦

Sacred Love, Sacred Time

"Do not be seduced into seeing each other merely as the human shell.
Rather, see the soul, the consciousness within . . .
When you see each other as the Divine and eternal beings that you are,
you will never cease to wonder and to glory in the coming together."
— Emmanuel

I was fast asleep in my hotel room in Mumbai, India, when the phone rang. It was March 5, 2006, the day after my birthday. I'd been on a three-week pilgrimage to the country that feels like my spiritual home, and had four more days of temple visits planned before I was scheduled to fly back to California. My mother's trembling voice was on the other end of the line, telling me that my stepfather was in the hospital and had only days to live. I spent the rest of the night making arrangements to cancel the remainder of my trip, and took the next flight back to the U.S. Within 24 hours, I found myself at my stepfather's bedside.

My mother, Phyllis, and my stepfather, Dan, met when I was 12 years old, and were as deeply in love over 40 years later as they had been at the very beginning. They spent all of their time together and were virtually inseparable. Mom and Dan lived a very simple and modest life, but were abundantly wealthy in joy and devotion. Dan and I shared two very important things: *We had the same birthday, March 4, and we both adored my mother, who had the biggest heart of anyone I've ever known.*

For many years, my stepfather had valiantly battled cancer, supported by my mother's unconditional love. To them, every day was a gift, especially since Dan had originally been given only a few months to live, and 11 years later, he was still alive.

It had been a while since I'd seen Dan, and as I sat next to him holding his fragile hand in mine, I could see that he weighed practically nothing and that his body was contracting so his soul could be set free. He was on a morphine drip for his pain, but knew exactly what was happening, and in his selfless and humble way, apologized that I'd had to cut my trip short.

As Dan lay on what we all knew was his deathbed, the only thing he wanted to talk about was how much he loved my mother. Over and over, he told us how happy she'd made him, and how he couldn't have wanted a better life. *"I'm not afraid of dying,"* he said to me when she left the room. *"I just don't want to leave Phyllis."*

My heart broke as I watched my mom keep this final vigil over her beloved, wetting his dry lips with an ice cube and stroking his thin arm, which had held her in such a safe embrace for so many priceless years. **She was doing what she'd always done for most of her life, what she'd taught me to do—being so amazingly brave and relentlessly loving in the face of so much pain.** I knew what she was thinking: *Will I wake up tomorrow and be able to give him a good-morning kiss? How many more minutes do I have to hold his hand? How many more times will I hear him say my name?* No moment was too small to cherish or too unimportant to waste.

I left for a few hours to freshen up, and when I returned, my mother looked upset. "Dan's doing strange things," she told me. "He keeps thrashing around on the bed, raising his arms up in the air, and asking for a cup. I think he wants something to drink, but every time I offer it, he gets more agitated."

"Maybe it's the effect of the morphine," I reassured her. "Let me watch him while you go to the cafeteria. You can come right back." I went back to sit by Dan's bedside, hoping that I could figure out what was happening.

Suddenly, he opened his eyes, saw me, and said my name. Then he raised his frail arms up in the air and mumbled something over and over while staring at the ceiling. I bent down closer to him so that I could hear what he was trying to say. "What is it, Dan? What do you want?" I asked.

He repeated what he'd been saying, but this time, I heard it clearly:

"I want to go up. I want to go up."

Dan had always insisted that he was an atheist, and before he got sick, I used to tease him and predict that one day, when he left his body and found himself conscious on the Other Side, he'd think of me and say,

"Barbara was right after all." Now we had arrived at that moment, and I understood what was happening—**his soul was beginning the process of separating from the body. He could already sense that there was an "up," maybe could even see it, and wanted to go there but didn't know how.**

"Yes, Dan," I reassured him softly. *"That's right. You're going to go up! Anytime you're ready, you can go. Don't worry, sweetheart. You won't have to do it alone—you'll have help. You're going to do it perfectly! You know how to do this, because you've done it before. You're going to go up."*

I could feel Dan's soul immediately relaxing as some part of him understood what I was saying. His put his arms down, stopped thrashing, and became very calm. Then, to my surprise, he reached his hand out over the hospital-bed railing toward me, as if he wanted to make sure I knew that he was grateful I'd helped him get ready to "go up." I gently took his bony fingers in mine. He was almost gone.

Even in the middle of terrible grief, we can often find sweetness and, surprisingly, humor. As I waited for my mother to return, I couldn't help but smile, now realizing why she'd been so confused. My mom was very hard of hearing, and absolutely hated wearing her hearing aids. So when Dan was mumbling, *"I want to go up,"* she'd thought she heard him say, *"I want a cup."* She would shout back, "Do you want juice?!" obviously frustrating poor Dan, who would then repeat himself, to no avail.

Later, the hospice nurses told me my mother had been bugging them for cups of juice for days that, of course, Dan wouldn't drink since he wasn't thirsty. *He was just ready to go home.*

At one point while Dan slept, we went outside in the hall, and tears began to pour down my mother's face. "I don't want him to see me cry," she confessed.

"Why, Mommy?"

"I'm trying to be strong and cheerful for him," she said. "I don't want him to be scared."

"He doesn't need you to be strong right now. He is already being readied for his Great Journey Home," I explained. I told her about what had taken place when she was gone, and that he said he wanted to "go up." She sobbed in my arms as she realized what Dan had actually been trying to tell her over the past two days.

"Do you think I should tell him it's okay to go now?" she asked. "That it's okay to go up?"

"If you feel ready to do that, I believe he's ready. *But don't try to be strong, Mommy. He needs your whole heart. If you push down your pain, you'll push down the love. Don't keep any of it to yourself. Give him every last drop of love to take with him.*"

My mother went back in the room and asked me to come with her. She got on the bed with Dan, carefully put her arms around him, and wept as she told him how much she adored him, how proud she was of him, how he had given her everything she ever could have wanted. She told him that she didn't want him to suffer anymore, and it was okay to go up. "I'll be fine, baby," she kept saying, even though I knew she didn't believe it. "You can go."

And the next morning, he did.

Those last few days were some of the most sacred of my life. They were sacred because every second counted. They were sacred because only truth existed between each of us and all of us. They were sacred because Dan gave me the privilege and good-bye gift of witnessing his moment of remembrance that there was an "up." Most of all, they were sacred because in the end, nothing mattered but love.

I'd visited so many ancient temples and shrines on my trip to India, and had innumerable moving and uplifting spiritual experiences. My last stop was going to be one of the most magnificent temples of all, and had been canceled when I found out that Dan was dying. Instead, my last stop on the journey ended up being that hospital room in Philadelphia.

Instead of golden and marble statues, exquisite beauty, and colorful decorations, I was surrounded by antiseptic starkness and institutional green walls. Instead of fragrant garlands of exotic flowers and the intoxicating aroma of incense, I was breathing in the atmosphere of decay and death. Instead of the hypnotic and soothing sound of Brahman priests chanting 3,000-year-old hymns and mantras, I was listening to game shows blaring on the lounge television, and cold, perfunctory announcements and pages for doctors blasting out of the loudspeaker. **In spite of** all this, it was and always will be one of the most sacred pilgrimages I will take in this lifetime.

Looking back, I should have known that the love my mother and stepfather shared was unbreakable by time and space. Less than 18 months later, after being totally healthy her whole life, my mother was diagnosed with a highly aggressive form of cancer, and within a few short months, she too went "up." I was and still am utterly heartbroken to not have her here on Earth with me. I miss her terribly, and sob even now as I write this—for myself, but not for her. *She's exactly where she wants to be, together with her true love.*

YOUR SACRED GIFT OF TIME

"Begin at once to live, and count each separate day as a separate life."
— Seneca

What I've shared with you about my mother and Dan was not only a story about love, but a story to help you make a Soul Shift about time. The average human being has been given the gift of approximately 28,000 days on this planet in this body. This adds up to about 448,000 waking hours. This gift of time that we are given passes so very quickly. As we grow older and reach the age where we have more years behind us than we do ahead of us, we wish we had more of this gift of time that seems to be shrinking before our very eyes.

Knowing that this is the truth, you must ask yourself these Soul Shift questions:

Soul Shift Recalibration Questions

Do I have any time to waste?

Do I have any time to throw away in unconsciousness?

Do I have any time to live in forgetfulness or denial?

What are your answers to these questions? If some divine power came to you right now and said, *"Listen, you have to give up thousands of your allotted days on Earth, or tens of thousands of your hours. Somebody else needs them. I know you're supposed to have 28,000 days, but you need to give up 9,000 of those days. Can you spare them?"* The answer to this, of course, would be an emphatic, **"No!** No, I don't have time to waste. No, I don't have time to throw away on unconsciousness. No, I don't have time to live in forgetfulness or denial. And no, I don't want to give up days or even hours of my time."

Yet this is exactly what many of us do. We throw time away—days, hours, minutes of our most treasured gift gone, gone as if we have all the time in the world . . . and we don't.

In each moment, then, we remember the Highest: *Can I afford to waste this day? Can I afford to waste this hour? Can I afford to waste this moment?* This doesn't mean that we don't take time to relax, enjoy ourselves, or sleep. It means to never forget the truth:

Time spent in ways that do not support you in the Highest is really time wasted.

I know I'm offering you a very strong and perhaps fiery message, but it's one I need to share with you as we think about what it really means to live a conscious and fulfilled life. How many thousands of hours have you spent feeling angry, feeling like a victim, feeling like it's unfair, going on strike, shutting off, shutting down, pushing love away, ignoring feelings inside of you, keeping yourself stuck in resentment, blame, judgment, or revenge? How many thousands of hours have you spent stuck in pursuits of vanity or indulgence or superficiality?

Throwing away these hours would be like willingly inviting someone to steal all of your money and savings, and then telling yourself that you don't care. *It's actually worse, because you can always get more money, but you can never get more time. Time is far more precious than money.* Many billionaires have lain on their deathbeds realizing that in spite of all their wealth, they were powerless to buy one more day with their family, or even one more minute of time.

**This is our greatest denial as a soul:
that we have more time than we actually do;
that we can somehow afford to squander it;
that we somehow can throw it away
or spend it on doing or feeling things that waste its value,
as if we had an infinite amount.**

When we disrespect time, we not only disrespect ourselves, but I believe we disrespect what we might call God, Spirit, or Cosmic Intelligence. We're disrespecting that which gave us time, as if we're saying, "Thanks anyway for this life and this time, but it really isn't worth that much to me, so I'm not going to treasure it."

**Never tell yourself that something doesn't matter,
because *it all matters.*
Every moment that you're alive is a miracle,
and every moment matters.**

Right now, today, someone is being told that they have a limited amount of time to live. They would give anything for all the days or hours you may have thrown in the trash. **They would take your leftovers in a hot second.**

If you knew you had one more day with someone you loved who has been gone—a parent, a grandparent, a child, a brother or sister, your own animal companion—wouldn't that be priceless? That extra 24 hours would be a treasure, and you wouldn't waste a moment of it.

You have that 24 hours now and, God willing, another and another and another. Take in the joy of that miraculous revelation. *I am here! I am alive!* Make this the day that changes everything. Gather up your gift of time and hold it tightly in your arms. Protect it. Honor it. *It is sacred.*

FROM MEASURING TO MARVELING

*"If we could see the miracle of a single flower clearly,
our whole life would change."*
— Jack Kornfield

One of the greatest blessings pain and loss offer us is their remarkable ability to put everything in perspective, and remind us of what is truly important. I experienced this so profoundly a year after my stepfather died when my mother was diagnosed with cancer and given just a few months to live. She'd been healthy and vital, and wasn't even feeling ill at the time. I'd been prepared for Dan's passing, but my mom's sudden death sentence shook me to my core.

I'd always had a timeless soul bond with my mother. As she began to fade and I realized that she would be leaving her body soon, something astonishing and almost surreal began to happen. **I started to vicariously experience everything through her eyes and heart, as if she were living my life with me, showing it to me through the perspective of someone who had very few days left on the planet.**

I remember the first time it happened: I was sitting outside on my patio one morning, eating a peach. All of a sudden it hit me that in a matter of weeks, she wouldn't be here. She wouldn't be able to enjoy a delicious, sweet peach as she always had. In that moment, I experienced eating the peach as a miracle. Everything about it seemed to be sacred. I wept as I felt both the joy of being alive and the grief of knowing that my mom was about to leave me.

After that, day after day, everything I tasted, saw, felt, and heard, I experienced as if I were my mother:

I remember walking by the ocean, feeling the sun warming my face and the tender breeze blowing through my hair, and realizing that soon my mother, who'd grown up at the seashore and adored the ocean, would never see it again in this lifetime, would never smell the sweetness of the salt air, or hear the seagulls serenading her.

I remember looking at the flowers in my garden, decorating my backyard like a collection of colorful, living jewels, and realizing that soon my mother, who for as long as I could remember had loved gardening, would never again have the joy of putting her hands in the earth, of tenderly planting her bulbs and seeds and watering them with her favorite old watering can.

During those heartbreaking weeks, every single moment of my life changed. I'd always been in a place of tremendous grace and gratitude, but now, *each small experience was elevated and exalted by the thought of losing it.* Everything seemed magical, significant, precious, and devastating to imagine never experiencing again.

Even when we believe that we're very conscious,
we take so much for granted.
We overlook ordinary delights simply because
they're so abundant.
We forget to notice the miraculous because
it's so omnipresent.
If you would allow yourself to experience the
full vibrational impact of being alive on this planet,
you'd live in a sanctified state of perpetual awe.

My mother had always lived as the embodiment of generosity and unconditional love. Somehow, in those heart-wrenching days leading up to her death, she gave me as much as she had in life. **Even though she has left her body, that sanctified state of perpetual awe has never left me. It was her final and everlasting gift.**

I want to offer you one more Soul Shift that can profoundly improve your relationship with time.

SOUL SHIFT

SHIFT FROM MERELY MEASURING TIME TO MARVELING AT YOUR BLESSINGS

To truly experience life's fullness,
you have to go beyond just noticing something
to really experiencing it,
beyond just measuring something's value
to marveling at it.
You have to allow yourself to be awestruck.

Researchers at Stanford University recently published a scientific study about the value of experiencing awe. They found it to be an experience so visually or conceptually expansive that we have to reconfigure our consciousness to be able to even register the experience. I loved what they concluded: *that regular exposure to awe actually transforms us.* The impact is residual, creating an actual shift in consciousness, reflected in increased feelings of well-being and compassion toward others.

In essence, what the research reveals is that
when we allow ourselves to marvel and experience awe,
we create an actual, measurable Soul Shift.

What does it mean to marvel at something? It means to experience it with our heart, and not just our mind. Noticing that the peach is sweet and being grateful for it is fine. Marveling at it requires that you open fully to really "see" the peach and experience the miracle of it. **Marveling at life's miracles is one of the highest forms of love.**

In order to marvel and experience awe, we need to practice seeing things as my mother's death taught me to see them: *with eyes not jaded by our habitual exposure to life's wonders; with a heart not numbed to the miraculous just because it's always around us; and with our soul wide open, inviting everything to vibrationally vanquish us, embrace us, and thrill us.*

Here is a Soul Shift recalibration exercise that will help you practice marveling. It only takes a few minutes:

SOUL SHIFT PRACTICE: HOW TO MARVEL

Now, or when you have time, find a piece of fruit and hold it in your hand. Then, return to this page and follow these instructions.

Allow your awareness to be totally on the fruit and nothing else.

Look deeply at its amazing color—orange or red or purple. How delightful it is to look at!

How different it would be if it had been brown or gray!

Allow the vibration of the color to penetrate your eyes. Drink it in.

Now, think about where this exact piece of fruit came from—a tiny seed in the ground, invisible, containing the intelligence to produce this delicious fruit you're holding now.

Visualize the "orange essence" or "apple essence" mysteriously present in the seed, like a vibrational blueprint that would one day be a fruit you would hold in your hand.

Now see the tree that sprouted from that seed, tiny at first, its branches just bare brown twigs. Look at your fruit, and know it was already present in that seedling.

Feel the tree roots drinking the water from the ground and sending it up into the branches to nourish the leaves and blossoms that were forming.

Imagine the flower withering, and within it, the tiny bud of fruit beginning to form.

Feel the sun shining bright and hot on the little fruit bud, filling it with life so it could keep expanding. Imagine as you hold your fruit, you can feel the warmth and love of the sun still vibrating in it.

Now see your ripe fruit waiting patiently on the tree. It knew when to stop growing at the perfect time. Feel its enjoyment of its own fullness.

Picture someone getting up before dawn, driving to the orchard, and working hard to carefully pick your piece of fruit for you.

See your fruit being placed in a crate, and traveling many miles in one truck after another on its way to you. Feel the drivers, the people unloading the box in the store, the person who arranged it on the shelf, until finally, there you were.

All of the things you just contemplated and felt into—from the person who planted the fruit tree perhaps hundreds of years ago and is no longer alive, to that pulsation of consciousness designed to look like a fruit whose blueprint manifested it, to the journey the fruit took to get to you—all of these were meant for this moment, when you are holding the fruit in your hand.

Gaze at the fruit one last time, and if you like, take a bite of it, or eat a slice. As you do, relive the entire journey all over again from its invisible origins, *and realize that you are eating consciousness in a fruit costume.*

If you allowed yourself to experience all of this fully, then right now you are marveling . . .

This moment is what's sacred.
You are what's sacred.

❀ 13 ❀

Shifting into Gratitude
and Opening to Grace

*"We can only be said to be alive in those moments
when our hearts are conscious of our treasure."*
— Thornton Wilder

Right now, think of someone or something for which you feel really grateful. It could be your children, your partner, the home you live in, or the work you're privileged to do. It could be your devoted animal companions or loving human companions. It could be the recovery you've made from an illness, a door of opportunity that's opened for you, or someone who's made an enormous difference in your life. It could be a beautiful place you've had the privilege of visiting in the outside world, or a sacred place you've touched inside of yourself.

Place your awareness in the center of your chest, around your heart, and notice for a moment what you're experiencing when you're feeling grateful. Do you feel more open or closed? Open. Do you feel more contracted or expanded? Expanded. Do you feel more agitated or peaceful? Peaceful.

I'm not asking you to notice the thoughts you have about the person or thing for which you're grateful. Instead, I'm asking you to **feel what the actual vibration of tuning in to gratitude does to you: It expands you; it opens you; it ushers you into a momentary state of peace and contentment. It brings you immediately back to your Highest.**

I often hear people say that as part of their intention to live an awakened life, they "practice an attitude of gratitude." I'm sure you've heard this phrase, or even used it yourself. What does this mean to most of us? It means we try to be positive, to acknowledge the good things that are happening, to verbalize what we are grateful for, and to have a positive attitude toward life.

It is time to make a Soul Shift from thinking of gratitude as a mental or intellectual way of looking at things—an attitude—to understanding gratitude as a dynamic vibrational experience.

SOUL SHIFT

SHIFT FROM TRYING TO HAVE AN ATTITUDE OF GRATITUDE TO LIVING GRATITUDE AS A VIBRATIONAL EXPERIENCE

Simply put, gratitude is not an attitude. It's one of the *transformative inner actions I spoke of when I defined Soul Shifts, an action originating from and in alignment with the highest spiritual truths.* It's an *opening up* in the presence of something that we value.

We can't *experience* gratitude in our head. That's not the *feeling* of it, but rather the *thought*. The actual experience of gratitude occurs first in the heart, and is the result of our choosing to take that auspicious inner action, to make a Soul Shift.

**Gratitude is not an attitude in our mind.
Gratitude is an internal experience of fullness
and expansion in the heart,
an expansion that spontaneously arises
from the recognition of love, of goodness, and of grace.
In its highest form, therefore, gratitude is not a practice.
It is a living expression of our own expanded consciousness.**

When we understand the vibrational mechanics of gratitude, we realize that *it is one of the easiest and most effective ways to experience an instant Soul Shift.* We've seen how important it is to practice vibrational "expanders" in our life—how expansion energetically opens us, recalibrates us, and aligns us with the Highest part of our self. **Like love, gratitude is a powerful expander. We choose to enter into the experience of gratitude, then, not just because we believe it is a good or spiritual thing to do, but because it is a Soul Shift Practice that immediately raises us up to our highest vibration.**

GRATITUDE BY APPOINTMENT VS. GRATITUDE BEYOND CONDITIONS

I know a lot of sincere people who practice what I call "appointment gratitude": *"Every morning when I get up, I'm going to say three gratitude statements,"* or *"At the end of the day, I'm going to write down five things I'm grateful for,"* or *"Once a month, my friends and I get together and do a gratitude circle, sharing what we are thankful for."* There's absolutely nothing wrong with such practices—they can be a meaningful way to begin or end a day, or to honor a gathering with friends. I incorporate many such practices in my teaching and seminars.

However, one of the problems that can occur when we tell ourselves we're doing gratitude practices is that we think of being grateful as a spiritual appointment or exercise, rather than a consistent state of consciousness. I love what mystery writer Jacqueline Winspear says on the subject: *"Grace isn't a little prayer you chant before receiving a meal. It's a way to live."*

**Gratitude should be a *state of consciousness* we inhabit,
not just a practice on our "spiritual to-do list."
Seeing things from a place of abundance and fullness
shouldn't be an enlightened assignment for a special occasion
or a few minutes a day.
Gratitude consciousness allows us to vibrationally interact with
the world and the people around us in such a way that,
moment by moment, it produces a powerful experience
of love and expansion for us and everyone in our vibrational field.**

Being a spiritual adult means living in a state of "gratitude beyond conditions."

SOUL SHIFT

SHIFT FROM CONDITIONAL GRATITUDE TO GRATITUDE BEYOND CONDITIONS

Many of us give ourselves permission to experience gratitude when we're happy with the way things are going, with the way people are treating us, and with what the universe is bringing to our doorstep. *It's easy to be grateful when we approve of what's taking place in our life.* But what happens when people are doing things that hurt us? What happens when we're faced with circumstances that are painful or challenging? What happens when events unfold that we don't understand or feel are terribly unfair?

Our spiritual intention to have a consciousness of gratitude means absolutely nothing if we're not living it. *It means nothing if our gratitude is conditional.* It means nothing if, when the slightest thing goes wrong, we become angry with Spirit. It means nothing if, when we don't have something turn out as we hoped it would, we angrily conclude that the universe is against us, and forget everything good that blesses us each day.

BEING UNCOMFORTABLE AND BEING GRATEFUL

"The truth that many people never understand, until it is too late,
is that the more you try to avoid suffering, the more you suffer,
because smaller and more insignificant things begin to torture you,
in proportion to your fear of being hurt."
— Thomas Merton

One of the most human qualities we all share is an aversion to pain and a desire for pleasure. It's natural to want to feel good, and to want *not* to feel bad. From the time we were babies, our natural, human response to discomfort was to get mad. That's what babies do.

Imagine an infant lying in their crib, happy, carefree, and adorable, goo-goo, ga-ga. Suddenly, something changes: there's a little dump in their diaper, or their blanket falls off and they're chilly, or they're suddenly hungry, or their big brother took away their rattle. The baby starts to scream: "Whaaaa! *I was happy in a state of bliss and comfort, and now I'm uncomfortable. I hate this! Whaaaa! I'm going to cry and scream until you fix it and make me comfortable again!*"

Young children, and even teenagers, demonstrate this same pattern when their pleasure is taken away, whether it's no more ice cream, or no more time playing online games, or no more staying out until 3 A.M. As conscious adults, however, our everyday reactions should not be controlled by our pain or our pleasure, but by our consciousness.

The brilliant words I quoted above from the late American Catholic writer and mystic Thomas Merton speak powerfully to how our very aversion to any pain can create pain. My observation is: *When we become terrified of feeling discomfort, we lose any tolerance we have for enduring what is not comfortable or pleasant.*

This, by the way, is what addictions are about. Those of you who have had challenges with addiction in your life probably have been plagued by a "feels good or feels bad" mind-set, which often is the cause for the need to anaesthetize the "bad" feelings with alcohol, drugs, food, and so forth. I've actually had many students and clients free themselves from addictive habits once and for all by realizing that, whenever they experience "not good" feelings, they don't have to try to immediately get rid of them. *Instead, they can choose to see, feel, and know what's taking place, and use what they discover as doorways to more healing and consciousness.*

> **What feels good or what feels bad are not always**
> **correct and accurate measurements to use on the spiritual path.**
> **Sometimes things that don't feel good are good for us,**
> **and things that feel good are bad for us.**

Remember that it's our "black-and-white" and "either-or" thinking that causes us to swing from one stance to another: *I'm uncomfortable, so life is terrible,* or *Things are great with me, so I'm grateful and trust the universe.* What if instead, we practiced the Soul Shift of looking at this from a more expanded point of view?

> **You can be in discomfort and still be grateful.**
> **You can acknowledge that you are in**
> **an uncomfortable or unhappy time,**
> **but also allow your consciousness to notice and feel gratitude**
> **for the lessons you are learning,**
> **or the friends who are supporting you,**
> **or the unexpected blessings your challenge is bringing you.**

Imagine that you cut yourself and a piece of glass has become buried deep in your hand, causing it to bleed badly. You go to the emergency room, and the physician on call tells you that he'll have to remove the glass in order to clean your wound and stitch it up. He needs to use a very sharp scalpel to dig the glass out, and prepares you for the procedure.

As you lie there during the removal process, you're feeling two very contradictory things happening inside of you at the same time: The first is that it really, really hurts, and you're miserable! The second is that you're also very, very grateful. Your mind is going through thoughts something like this:

Thank God I got here and somebody knows what they are doing. Ouch, it hurts! Thank God the doctor is helping me. Ouch, this is killing me! I'm so grateful that my friend was with me and knew where to come. Jeez, the doctor is torturing me!

Is what's happening a good thing or not? It's good for you to have the surgeon remove the glass, but it sure doesn't feel good. You hate what is happening to you during the procedure, but you're very grateful for it.

SOUL SHIFT

SHIFT FROM DISQUALIFYING YOUR GRATITUDE DURING CHALLENGING TIMES TO UNDERSTANDING THAT YOU CAN BE BOTH GRATEFUL *AND* UNCOMFORTABLE AT THE SAME TIME

This Soul Shift offers us a profound and expanded approach to gratitude. It will create possibilities for you that haven't existed before—*a way to transmute the vibrationally contractive energy of challenges by adding the vibrationally expansive energy of gratitude.*

Don't abandon your gratitude just because you're temporarily unhappy or uncomfortable.

You need to find your gratitude even when you're suffering, frightened, or in pain.
That's actually when you need it the most.

BEING GRATEFUL FOR WHAT ISN'T HAPPENING

"The best things in life are not only free, they are mostly invisible."
— Thaddeus Golas

We've all heard platitudes that tell us not to get upset about "the small stuff," but as I'm sure you know, this is easier said than done. This is one of the great blessings of gratitude—**being in a constant state of gratitude helps us put things into a true perspective.**

Something is seen as small in proportion to something else that is bigger. For example, you may have grown up in a house that you thought was a normal size until you visited a friend's home that was enormous. Suddenly, your house seemed tiny by comparison. So we have to put our attention on bigger things for something else to be seen as insignificant.

This is where gratitude comes in. We've seen that it creates vibrational expansion, which helps us to rise up and above those things that would weigh us down. When we are consistently saturated with gratitude, we spontaneously put things in their proper perspective.

When we practice noticing the big things we're grateful for, the small things, annoyances, and disappointments won't overwhelm us so easily. We remember how we are blessed in every moment and won't get caught in the small pettiness of life that can suck the joy right out of us, not to mention make everyone who has to be around us miserable, too.

Gratitude blesses you.
It opens you so that more can come in.
It literally expands the vibrational space around you.
When you're living in that expansive space,
more of everything will flow into your life.

One day around the time I began writing this book, I suddenly heard a horrible commotion outside. The sounds of drilling, smashing, revving truck engines, and shouting came pouring through my window. When I went outside to find out what was happening, I was horrified: right across the street from me, a neighbor had started a massive renovation project on his home. His property was full of jackhammers, cement mixers, and noisy equipment of all kinds.

No, not now! I thought to myself in disbelief. My office windows are always open (warm California!) and look out onto what is usually a fairly quiet residential street. Naturally, I could hear everything that was going on. I was just immersing myself in 12 hours a day of intense writing, and needed peace and serenity.

Week after week, and even during weekends, the interminable construction went on. I'd dread the moment every morning when I'd inevitably hear the parade of trucks arriving across the street. I always listen to special, uplifting, instrumental music when I write, and so my new practice was to play it loud enough to try to drown out the terrible racket. I'm sure the neighbors and workers wondered what was going on, and thought that there was a strange New Age temple across the street. I didn't care. I just wanted the noise to stop.

One day, I sat down to write as usual, and after a few moments passed, I noticed that I felt strange. Something didn't seem right. Then, it hit me: *It was quiet.* I hurried outside, and sure enough, the trucks were gone. The major construction was complete. Peace had returned to the neighborhood, and to my office.

That day, along with the joy of writing, I felt continual waves of gratitude pouring through me. "Thank God it's so still," I kept saying to myself. "Thank God I can hear the birds singing. Thank God I can write in peace."

I was experiencing gratitude for what *wasn't* happening. This is what I call "gratitude for the absence of things."

Gratitude for the absence of things is just as important as gratitude for the presence of things. We tend to look for situations, people, or possessions for which we can be grateful. *However, you can also practice having a consciousness of gratitude for things that no longer exist*—for instance, circumstances or individuals that have been removed from our lives by our own will, or by fate, or by divine intervention.

SOUL SHIFT

SHIFT FROM ONLY BEING GRATEFUL FOR WHAT'S PRESENT TO ALSO BEING GRATEFUL FOR WHAT IS ABSENT

Think of a situation or circumstance that used to exist in your life, but no longer does.

Now feel how grateful you are for its absence.

For example, perhaps for many months you were working on a huge project at work, pressured to meet a deadline. Day and night, it was all you could think about. Finally, you finished. For one day, you might feel grateful for what you accomplished, but normally by the next day, you're already on to the next thing. Instead, you can be grateful for the absence of the deadline. Each morning when you wake up, you can celebrate the absence of the pressure: No deadline today!

Perhaps after years of battling with your old car, you finally invested in a new one. Normally for the first few days after getting a new vehicle, you feel excited and consciously enjoy all of the new features, but then you get used to it. Instead, you can prolong that vibrationally expansive experience of gratitude by noticing the absence of things: the absence of the squealing brakes; the absence of the jammed door; the absence of the dented fender and scratched paint; the absence of the worn seat cushion.

The absence of things often offers us enormous blessings.
Instead of just looking for the presence of something
for which you want to be grateful,
look for the absence of things that you're grateful are *not* present.

I'd like to introduce a wonderful Soul Shift Recalibration Practice called:

"Celebrating the Absence of Things."

Each day, pay attention to the gifts you're receiving from the absence of things. Here are some examples:

The absence of pain after you heal from an injury or illness.

The absence of a dog's incessant barking when your neighbor moves.

The absence of tension from a person who no longer works with you.

The absence of rain and cold weather when the sun finally comes out.

The absence of traffic on the freeway on the drive home.

The absence of ants invading your kitchen when they finally disappear.

The absence of the dirty dishes in your sink when you've finally cleaned them.

The absence of dirty diapers when your child is finally potty-trained.

The absence of piles of unwashed laundry after they're fresh and folded.

The absence of the lawn you don't have to tend now that you've moved from a house to an apartment.

The absence of your cold and stuffy nose now that you can breathe normally.

The absence of the chaos in your closet after you've finally organized it.

The absence of the tension between you and your partner after you kiss and make up.

Celebrating the absence of things is not a one-time event. We can make it a habitual part of our consciousness as we pay attention to our world. Several months have passed now since my neighbor's construction mercifully terminated, for instance. Still, many times each day, I take a moment to savor the absence of noise and the delicious silence.

THE GRACE OF RECEIVING

"We are loved, and we have always been loved.
It is not a question of merit or accomplishment.
The Divine Love is here.
We need only unclench our fists and open to it."
— Jeanette Berson

We can't talk about gratitude without shifting our understanding of *receiving.* I know many people who consider themselves to be very conscious and evolved, and are constantly articulating and declaring their gratitude. Yet, in actuality, they're highly resistant receivers.

Receiving is the action that allows us to fully experience gratitude. We can have a feeling of gratitude within ourselves that no one else can see or feel because attitudes are invisible. However, when we practice the action of receiving, our gratitude is an enlivened experience that the giver can witness and feel vibrationally and energetically.

SOUL SHIFT

SHIFT FROM THE IDEA THAT YOU'RE RECEIVING TO THE *VIBRATIONAL EXPERIENCE* OF RECEIVING

Receiving anything—
a compliment, love, wisdom, help, a gift—
is the *action* of being grateful
and honoring what is being offered to us.

When we allow ourselves to be emotionally impacted
and vibrationally penetrated by the giver,
we are engaged in a true act of gratitude.

Some of you may be having a startling revelation right now, as it dawns on you that perhaps you haven't been truly receiving for most of your life. You've been *noting* that people have been trying to give to you. You express your verbal appreciation to them for what they're offering.

However, you don't allow yourself to fully vibrationally receive it, or show others that act of receiving. Acknowledging what people are offering to you is not the same as allowing them to see and feel you receive what they're offering to you.

Three of the greatest blessings in my life were my animal companions: my cat, Luna, and my two Bichon Frises, Bijou and Shanti. They were my beloveds in little white fur bodies, and have now all returned to their angelic forms in another realm.

My youngest dog, Shanti, was a mischievous little girl with many humorous and adorable quirks. Whenever I gave her a treat, such as a dog biscuit, she would never eat it in front of me. First, she'd look away as if to convince me that she really didn't care if she got the treat or not. Then she'd quickly snatch it up in her mouth and race away to another part of the house, where she would either eat the treat alone when no one was watching, or hide it to be retrieved later. Shanti would never allow anyone to see her enjoying the treat in the moment.

My other dog, Bijou, who was a very advanced soul and extremely present, would watch her do this with serene amusement, and then kiss my hand that held the treat out to him so that I'd be sure to know that he was grateful. Then, quietly and elegantly, he would eat the treat in front of me, allowing me to enjoy his delight.

I am grateful to my animal teachers for this wonderful lesson about receiving. So many of us are just like Shanti—*when we are offered the treat of love or wisdom or delight, we "take the biscuit and run away"*—*perhaps not physically, but energetically.* **We emotionally "nibble" in private on what we've received, and do feel grateful for it. But we don't let the giver see how much we genuinely enjoy their offering.** Perhaps you've had friends, relatives, work associates, or loved ones like this, who didn't let you know how much they treasure you by allowing you to *see* and *experience* them fully receiving your love in the moment, to see them be moved by you or melted by you.

Imagine that you brought someone you loved a bouquet of flowers. "Here," you say, "I got these for you because I love you." Now imagine that, rather than taking the flowers from you, they reply, "Oh, thanks, just lay them down on the table." They don't inhale the fragrance of the flowers, or comment on how beautiful they are, or put them in a vase of water.

How would you feel? *You'd feel as if what you offered was not received,* even though they physically had the flowers right there. You were given intellectual recognition that they saw and appreciated your offering, *but you can't see them receive it because they are not letting you see them feeling it.* They are not enjoying the "biscuit"!

This is what it feels like to others when you don't receive. It's like a kind of emotional hoarding. There are unopened packages that people have given you. You know you got them, but you haven't opened them. A part of you is feeling, *I'm not going to let you see how you're impacting me.* There is a vibrational pushback to the love, or the wisdom, or the help—in essence to the flow of Divine Energy that is attempting to be delivered to you. **It's actually a form of emotional stinginess to not receive.**

What kind of receiver are you?

Do you hide your treats from the universe
and nibble them alone,
or do you let the people in your life see you
just basking in their love?

Do you let your partner see you being moved
and touched
by the things they do for you?

Do you let your animal companions see how much
you're in delight being around them?

Do you allow your children to feel you melt
when they offer you affection or sweetness?

Do you give yourself permission
to be moved on a daily basis?

This is the way to live with a generous
and grateful heart.

I would like to invite you to contemplate becoming a "gracious receiver."

SOUL SHIFT

SHIFT FROM BEING A RELUCTANT AND RESISTANT RECEIVER TO A GRACIOUS RECEIVER

Learning to be a gracious receiver is not about becoming more verbally effusive, or complimenting the other person. It's the energy of *allowing yourself to vibrationally receive someone's love, and allowing that love to reverberate inside of you.* When you fully receive, someone else can tell, because they can feel the vibration of your receiving in their own heart.

HOW RECEIVING CREATES ABUNDANCE

"If the only prayer you say in your life is 'thank you,'
that would suffice."
— Meister Eckhart

When most people think of the word *abundance,* they associate it with desires such as: *I want a beautiful home and possessions. I want lots of clients. I want money. I want love.* But the wanting is just the first step in creating abundance. Having something manifest is the second step. The third, and probably most important step, is the receiving.

Many of us are good "wanters,"
but we may not be good receivers.

We all have a lot of practice wanting, but when we begin to get the things we wanted, we are often so unskilled at receiving that it's almost as if we never got them at all.

Appreciation is a form of abundance. Receiving is a form of abundance. **When you are a good receiver, the universe wants to offer you more.**

Imagine that you're giving somebody you love a foot massage, and they just sit there silently, not making a sound. You ask, "How is it?" and they answer, "It's okay." All of a sudden, you start to think, *My hands hurt. I think I've done this for long enough.* And you stop.

Now, what if when you asked how it felt, that same person said, "Oh my gosh, this is the best foot massage I've ever experienced. I am in ecstasy." You probably would think, *Okay, then I won't stop. Let's do it for another 15 minutes.* **Their full and grateful receiving would create the desire for more to flow out from you.** It is human nature to want to feel as if we're making an impact.

When you block your energetic door for receiving, it creates a tremendous contraction and tension inside of you. Have you ever watched someone trying to give their young child a spoonful of bitter medicine? The child crunches up their face, squeezes their eyes shut, and bites down on their lips, all in the hopes that they can resist receiving the terrible concoction. Their mouth is closed in defiance, and their energy field closes off as well.

Receiving has the opposite effect: *It expands you. It opens you.* Think about what it takes to receive something—you have to open your hands, or you have to open your mouth, or you have to open your front door. Opening is an expansive action, and that includes what occurs when we open on the inside.

When we're in the habit of receiving,
we are also cultivating the habit of opening.
The more we open vibrationally,
the more space we make for receiving everything.

Several years ago, I was shopping at a grocery store near my home. I'd just returned from a seminar and was feeling overwhelmed with gratitude for my students, for the privilege of being a teacher, and for the powerful healing that had taken place at this event for all who had attended.

As I stood in the checkout line, I noticed the woman in front of me counting out small coins from a dirty plastic bag to pay for her only purchase, a can of soda. She was strangely dressed, appearing to be one of the homeless people who often congregated in the store parking lot.

As soon as I paid for my purchases, I rushed out of the store, hoping to find her and give her the $20 I had left in my wallet so she could buy herself a hot meal. I drove a few blocks and caught up with her as she was pushing her shopping cart full of possessions along the street.

I got out of my car and approached her with the cash. "I saw you at the store," I explained, "and I don't want to offend you, but I thought you might need some money for food, so please accept this offering that I hope will help."

I'll never forget what happened next.

The homeless woman glared at me, and then glared at the bill in my hand as she shouted, *"Twenty dollars! Twenty dollars! That's nothing! If you don't have a Ben Franklin* [slang for a $100 bill], *I don't even want your $$##&&** 20 dollars."* And as I watched in amazement, she walked away.

I drove home shaken and saddened by the experience. The next week, I saw this woman again outside of the same store, and realized that there was no way I was going to try to offer her money. The thought of approaching her contracted me terribly. Instead, I saw an elderly man to whom I often gave money, and handed him $20, for which he thanked me profusely.

As I walked to my car, I felt sorry for the poor woman. I remember wondering at the time if perhaps that was why she was so lost—*she couldn't receive.* Who knows what her pride had cost her in her life? Even more telling to me, however, was the reaction I'd had: *To not have my offering received didn't make me want to offer it again.*

This is such a powerful lesson for us as we contemplate the relationship between the action of receiving and gratitude. **My observation is that when we are stingy with our gratitude to the universe by not being a gracious receiver, the universe will be stingy with us. Just like me, it will offer its gifts elsewhere.** *When the flow of water is blocked by a wall or an object, it changes its direction and flows around it.*

Are you a grateful receiver? When you receive $100, do you think of it as a blessing, or do you become angry that it isn't $1,000? When you receive one opportunity in a week, do you feel grateful, or do you feel resentful that you didn't receive more?

Not receiving rips people off:

When you don't receive, you are blocking people from having grace flow through you to them.

When you don't receive, you are blocking people from having wisdom flow from them to you.

When you don't receive, you are not allowing someone to experience their own value.

When you don't receive, you are not allowing someone to experience what a difference they make.

When you don't receive, you are not allowing somebody else to be your hero.

It's essential to learn how to become a good receiver. Yet you can't just decide, "Okay, I'm really going to receive right now. See, I'm sitting here and really concentrating on trying to receive."

Just as we've seen with all of our other Soul Shifts, receiving isn't something you *do* as much as what happens when you *stop doing* those things that collide with your receiving. **Once you vibrationally eliminate those attitudes and patterns that block your ability to receive, and they are out of the way, receiving will just happen.**

Receiving happens in the heart when the heart opens.
It is the natural result of allowing yourself to open enough
and be vulnerable enough to fully feel
how someone has touched you, moved you, and impacted you.

BLESSINGS OR BURDENS?

"We wait for God to bless us while God waits for us to accept the blessing."
— Betsy Otter Thompson

Whenever I share the story about the homeless woman, most people respond in the same way. *"I can't understand that negative attitude. People should be grateful for what they receive. How could she be insulted by your trying to help her?"* These are understandable responses. Perhaps, then, you'll be surprised by what I'm going to say next:

Every day, all of us experience things that are actually our blessings, but that in our mind, we've somehow turned into our burdens.

I'm sure I don't do that, you may be thinking. Oh no? Read on . . .

"I just got home from work, and my children want to play with me and show me what they made at school today. I'm soooo tired. Oh well, I guess I have to spend a little time with them. Maybe if I turn on the TV, they'll get distracted, and I can at least look at my iPad while they play." **Blessing or burden?**

"There is absolutely nothing in the refrigerator. Why can't I just have a Saturday morning to rest? I suppose I should go out to the supermarket and stock up on everything I need for the week. But I hate shopping on the weekend—it's always so crowded." **Blessing or burden?**

"Look at this closet—it's a disaster! There are so many clothes jammed in everywhere that I can't find anything. And look at that huge bundle of things to take to the dry cleaners. I'd better at least get some of these piles off of the floor." **Blessing or burden?**

"My mother called again last night to ask how my presentation to my boss went. These conversations are so frustrating. I mean, she doesn't understand what I do at all, but she insists on knowing when I have an important meeting and telling me how wonderful I'll be. It's not like I'm ten years old anymore." **Blessing or burden?**

"What? The dog has to go out again? That's the second time tonight. Come on, Lucy, can't you wait until morning? Jeez, having an old dog is getting to be such a drag. I haven't had a good night's sleep in a year." **Blessing or burden?**

We often lose perspective about what is real and true and precious in life, and allow a veil of forgetfulness to fall over our eyes:

A family who loves you is a blessing, not a burden.

Having to buy all the food you want whenever you want it, and knowing that fresh, healthy food is readily available with no shortages, is a blessing, not a burden.

A closet stuffed full of beautiful clothes is a blessing, not a burden.

A mother who is still alive, cares how you are every day, and is proud of you is a blessing, not a burden.

An animal companion who is braving old age and discomfort to last a little longer and give you unconditional love and companionship is a blessing, not a burden.

And this work of seeing, digging, recalibrating, and healing is a blessing, not a burden.

SOUL SHIFT

SHIFT FROM BEMOANING THINGS AS BURDENS TO CHERISHING THEM AS BLESSINGS

It's so easy to allow our gratitude for the blessings and abundance in life to be swallowed up by the contractive habits of grumbling, complaining, and whining about situations, possessions, and people whose existence we should be cherishing. Every person who has lost a child would never have the thought that playing with their kids was a burden, and would give everything they had for one more day of being tired while they got to be with their children. Every person around the world who's hungry or starving would gladly make the trip to the crowded supermarket to buy all the food they wanted, and would in fact feel as if they'd died and gone to heaven.

Every impoverished person who owns just a few threadbare garments to wear would happily sit in a messy, unruly closet overflowing with clothing and feel that they were in a dream that was too good to be true. Everyone, like me, who's lost a mother or father (or both) would tolerate any amount of boring phone calls filled with love, praise, and pride, and would pray for just one more priceless conversation. Everyone whose beloved animal companion is gone would weep with joy to care for their aging devoted fur angel for one more precious night.

When we decide that something is a burden,
we draw all of the grace and joy out of it.
When we see something as a blessing,
we stop experiencing it as effortful and allow it to expand us.
The same task or experience can uplift or exhaust us,
depending on how we hold it in our heart.

277

Can you look at the things you've been feeling burdened by and transmute them into blessings?

You can burden or bless yourself in this lifetime. The limited ego will always see burdens. Your Highest Self will always see blessings.
Every moment you choose—blessing or burden?
This Soul Shift alone can change your life.

You are part of the Great Miracle unfolding around you.
Delight in this!
Open yourself to grace.

❧ 14 ❧

Why You're Here:
Making a Vibrational Difference

"It would be frightening to think that in all the cosmos,
which is so harmonious, so complete and equal to itself,
that only human life is happening randomly,
that only one's destiny lacks meaning."
— Mircea Eliade

My grandparents and great-grandparents were immigrants who, like tens of millions of others, came from many parts of the world to America around the beginning of the 20th century. After long sea voyages on overcrowded ships, they arrived at Ellis Island, carrying not much more than a damp, worn scrap of paper on which someone had written a strange-sounding address in an unfamiliar city, along with the name of a distant relative or a friend of a friend—all they had to guide them forward.

That piece of paper was priceless, because it meant entry, it meant hope, it meant freedom, and it meant a new life with unimaginable possibilities. I know that I, and many of us who now live in North America, are alive because of those precious scraps of paper, and the courage and vision of those who clutched them to their heart, praying that they would find their new purpose here.

I believe that, if you're reading these words, you've arrived here on this earth, at this time, and in this life because you too have something you are supposed to do. You too have an invisible piece of paper stored in your heart, guiding you toward your destination.

Perhaps you've always known what's written on that tiny piece of paper, and have never questioned it or faltered from your assignment. Perhaps you've been trying to decipher the message that's been placed in your soul and figure out what you're supposed to do. Perhaps you've misplaced that cosmic piece of paper, and have been suffering knowing that it's there somewhere, yet feeling lost without its direction. Perhaps you read one side of that paper years ago, and diligently followed the instructions, only to recently discover that there's more written on the other side so you're going to have to totally change your direction.

"How can I change the world? How can I discover my purpose? How can I find a way to do something important and significant that really makes a difference?" These are the questions that cry out from the hearts of all sincere seekers. I understand them because they were my own questions when I began my spiritual journey. They burned in my heart like a relentless fire that demanded my attention. *What was I going to do? What was I supposed to do?*

Within those very questions lies the doorway into our next Soul Shift. The key is in the word *do,* and the belief that only when you *do* something, create something, influence something, fix something, or heal something, will you be making a difference.

You've come to understand that you're a vibrational being having a profound vibrational effect on everyone and everything around you in every circumstance. Therefore, it follows that *you're already doing something that makes an enormous difference.*

Making a difference is not about having a purpose,
or successfully completing a project.
It is the inevitable consequence of your consciousness
in every moment.
Your vibration is *always* making a difference.
The question is: What kind of difference are you making?

SOUL SHIFT

SHIFT FROM TRYING TO FIGURE OUT HOW TO MAKE A DIFFERENCE TO REALIZING THAT YOU'RE *ALREADY ALWAYS* MAKING A DIFFERENCE

Whether you know it or not, you're making a difference every minute of every day. When you're home with your family or friends, when you leave the house and go somewhere, when you pass by strangers on the street or walk through a store, your vibration is always making a difference, even when you don't want it to. **Your presence makes a difference one interaction at a time, one thought at a time, one choice at a time, one heart at a time.**

> **It is not as if one day, when you feel ready,**
> **you'll finally start making a difference.**
> ***You are already making a difference***
> ***beyond anything you can imagine.***
> **You can't *not* make a difference.**

This is such a radical Soul Shift, and one that can literally transform your experience of yourself, your life, and your own personal fulfillment. *Many of us tend to associate making a difference with some kind of decision.* We decide we're going to make our mark on the world and, in turn, hope to achieve some level of fame or notoriety, or earn a lot of money, or have people know about us and admire us. If these external validations are present, we feel that we are absolutely making a difference.

Setting and achieving measurable goals is admirable. Having a vision and seeing it come to fruition in a way others can witness is very gratifying. However, you don't need to do these things in order to make a difference.

Our new Soul Shift reminds us that we don't actually have a choice about whether or not we want to make a difference in the world around us. By definition, as vibrational beings in vibrational relationships with everything, we must inevitably make a difference. We do inexorably make a difference. Even if we decide that we don't want to make a difference, we will anyway!

The Vibrational Gift of Your Presence

"Behold, he spreads his light around him."
— Job 36:30

How do you want to impact people? What do you hope they will experience in your presence? *I know that I've always wanted to give people the experience of my heart, of my love, of my light, and of the Highest when they are in my presence, to uplift them.* Isn't this what we all want—to have people feel better and higher and happier in our presence?

You're used to hearing the word *uplift,* but take a moment to contemplate its structure: "up-lift; to lift up." We all like the idea of being able to uplift others, which should mean that we are able to "lift them up." Your energetic presence not only affects others, but it can actually serve them, change them, and recalibrate them.

This is the work of all great healers—*to raise the vibration of the world by how we are vibrating.* We're meant to be living as great beings, and therefore, we're meant to be "uplifters."

Our real work is to raise our own vibration to such a high frequency that in our presence people feel uplifted—
"lifted up" by who we are.
By recalibrating ourselves to the Highest vibration,
we'll be giving a gift of the Highest to everyone.
What greater way is there to serve others than by uplifting them?
Understanding this, we suddenly, joyfully, realize that,
in each moment, we can be living our Highest purpose.

SOUL SHIFT

SHIFT FROM LOOKING FOR YOUR PURPOSE, OR THINKING YOU
HAVE TO POSTPONE FULFILLING YOUR PURPOSE,
TO LIVING YOUR PURPOSE *RIGHT NOW IN EACH MOMENT*

These are not just inspiring words, or an encouraging way to think about your life. **I believe that the Highest purpose for each and every one of us is to be a conduit for light and an ambassador of love, as much love as possible in every moment.** When you start to understand that you can be (and in fact are) a channel for something greater—for light, for love, for compassion, for God, for Christ consciousness, for Divine Energy, or for whatever the Highest is for you—it dawns on you that this *is* your ultimate purpose in life.

Right after that amazing revelation, a second, even more spectacular revelation emerges: **If your true purpose is to uplift the world through uplifting your vibration—to be an uplifter—then you can start living your purpose immediately!** Of course it's important to set and fulfill your tangible life goals, but you don't have to wait until you finish your degree, or reach a certain amount of people in your business, or write a book, or build your website, or any of the other things you tell yourself you need to do before you can make a difference. You're already fulfilling that purpose by taking this Soul Shifts journey and beginning to recalibrate your vibration so that you can be a vibrational beacon of love.

When you're in your Highest, you're naturally a vibrational lighthouse for people. Your own state of uplifted energy encourages others to lift themselves as high as they can go. Living in the vibration of love, you become a walking blessing to others in invisible and mysterious ways.

I'm frequently asked to describe what it is that I do as a teacher. Simply put, *it's my service to the world to keep my heart open. It's my service to the world to vibrate at my Highest. It's my service to the world to live in the vibrational space of love so that I can invite others to join me there.* This is my one true job, purpose, and profession. In fact, I believe that no matter what else we do in this world, it should be *everyone's* profession.

What is your Highest purpose every day?
It's to vibrate with as much love as possible
in each situation and in every moment.
Whatever your profession, education, or circumstance,
nothing you could do would be more healing
and uplifting to others
than to walk around the world with
an open and loving heart.

You don't need a business card proclaiming that you're a teacher or a leader, or that you're here to transform the planet. It doesn't matter what you do to earn your income. You could be a hairstylist, a gardener, a nurse, a lawyer, a salesperson, a yoga teacher, or a chef, but if you're doing your best to be in your Highest, then you'll have a second and very important job: *You'll be a vibrational ambassador of the Highest!*

You don't have to make a difference in the world for a living. You can make a difference in the world by the way you live.

Your New Assignment: Offering Your Blessings

"Do all the good you can, by all the means you can, in all the ways you can, in all the places you can, at all the times you can, to all the people you can, as long as you ever can."
— Attributed to John Wesley, Founder of Methodism

All over this planet, there are great beings who give their lives to serve the world by creating positive, uplifting vibrations. In India, China, Tibet, Burma, Bhutan, and Nepal, for example, there are Brahman priests, Vedic priests, Yogis, Hindu monks, and Tibetan monks and lamas who live in remote and isolated ashrams and monasteries, far away from everything. They never leave. They dedicate themselves every day to chanting mantras, meditating and performing sacred rituals for the sake of humanity.

There are Roman Catholic monasteries throughout the world where cloistered monks and nuns live in total seclusion, praying for humankind. No one will ever know the names of these devoted ones. They don't get paid. They own no possessions. They lead lives of dedicated and selfless service in order to vibrationally hold up humankind.

In this very moment, there are also people desperately praying for those blessings, praying for hope, praying for compassion, praying to feel they're not alone. In this very moment, there are people praying for light, praying for grace, praying that their prayer might be heard.

Just as great saints meditate in caves and temples and offer prayers for the world every day, just as monks, nuns, and swamis sit in ashrams and monasteries and offer prayers for the world every day, so too you can become someone who offers blessings.

Several years ago while I was deep in meditation, a longing suddenly arose to create a blessing prayer for the planet, one that I could teach my students, one that would raise the vibration of the person offering the prayer and have a focus for their energy of compassion and love. When I emerged from meditating, the words of a beautiful blessing rose up from within me. I rushed to write down the sentences before I forgot them, and was humbled to read what I had received.

"The Soul Shifts Blessing Prayer for the Planet" is a powerful practice you can offer to the world and all who inhabit it. **When you offer this blessing, you will shift your identification into your Highest, and lift yourself up to your most elevated vibration.**

Here are some suggestions to help you experience the power of this Blessing Prayer:

* You may want to read this prayer once silently, without speaking the words out loud. As you read each phrase, allow yourself to feel and vibrate with the meaning, and offer that feeling along with your intention.

Then you can say the blessing aloud, moving that energy from the meaning in your heart out into the spoken words. Saying the words reverently from your heart, and not simply repeating them from your intellect, will open you as you make your offering.

* I suggest you read or recite the words very slowly. Remember that these are not just sentences I composed, but rather are powerful vibrational packages. Let the vibration of your love shower down upon the earth, upon those beings you speak of, and know that as you think it and offer it, it is becoming so.

* You may want to visualize what you are saying and add that dimension to the blessing. For instance, as you think about the phrase "may all who suffer now be comforted," allow yourself to feel those people, visualize them in different countries, and see the conditions of their suffering. Imagine that you are actually showering love and healing upon them, like showers of light.

* It's sometimes helpful to have a physical representation of the planet when you offer this Blessing Prayer. My students use a small glass marble-sized replica of Earth that you can easily find online. You can also use a photo of our globe taken from space. You can hold the globe or photo in your hands and look at it, or even place it close to your heart like you would hold the most precious child. I always imagine that I am tenderly embracing the planet, pouring my love energy into it.

* **Some people like to light a candle at the beginning of this Blessing Prayer Ritual to represent the Divine Light they are calling forth.**

* **You may want to set a special time during which you offer your Blessing Prayer,** perhaps in the morning, or as a part of your own prayer or meditation practice, or before bed. Sometimes people do this prayer when they are out in nature, or after learning of a tragedy or disaster in the world.

* **This is a powerful practice to do together with other people, as it expands the scope of the vibrational circuitry through which the blessing can travel.** In the virtual community of my students and readers, people from all over the world come together every day on a special phone conference line for five minutes at noon Pacific time to do this prayer. When you do this at that time, you can know that you're joining tens of thousands of people who are practicing this blessing ritual, and that you're a part of a global healing network.

* **I have many students who have included this blessing as a family ritual with their children,** such as grace before a meal or bedtime prayers. The children love to take part in the "sending love to the planet" practice so that they can feel they are making a difference, and are excited to take turns holding the globe or photo.

Here is the prayer:

THE SOUL SHIFTS BLESSING PRAYER
FOR THE PLANET

I offer my blessings to the planet Earth,
my home while I am in this body.

May grace now shower upon the world and restore it to peace.
May all who suffer now be comforted and healed.

May all who are oppressed now be liberated,
and their dignity redeemed.

May all who are lost in forgetfulness now awaken from
the Great Sleep
and return to remembrance.

May all beings now live together in perfect harmony.
May all souls now align with their Highest.

May all souls now find their way back to love,
and may that love be All That Is.

May the One Perfect Light now triumph over all darkness
in all people and all places,
seen and unseen,
And may that One Perfect Light prevail for all time.

May there be peace.

May there be peace.

May there be peace.

Each time you offer this Blessing Prayer, you will be a healer. You will be an uplifter. You will be a blessing. No matter what else you do that day, you will be living your purpose.

As you've opened yourself to this Soul Shifts journey, whether you know it or not, you have made a difference and blessed the planet.

As you've allowed your heart to be purified, whether you know it or not, you have made a difference and blessed the planet.

As you've chosen light over darkness, whether you know it or not, you have made a difference and blessed the planet.

In this moment,
know that you are a courageous lightworker.
In this moment,
know that you are and can *always* be a bringer of grace.
In this moment,
remember why you are here on this earth—
to become a walking, breathing blessing.

This will be your greatest soul accomplishment.

❧ 15 ❧

Your Legacy of Love

"Those who realize that all life is One
are at home everywhere
and see themselves in all beings."
— Taittreya Upanishad

When we spend our life being a student, we're always on the lookout for teachers and come to understand that they appear in many unexpected forms. On my last trip to India, for instance, I encountered many amazing teachers in very unlikely places, most of whom will never know that they were teaching me anything at all.

One afternoon, returning from a temple visit, we passed through a village where the main activity was the making of bricks. Our driver stopped the car so that we could get out and watch the workers, who consisted of a mixed group of men, women, and children. Several elderly women were doing what appeared to be backbreaking work, scooping up a special mixture of mud and clay, putting it into molds, and carefully scraping off the excess so that when the mold was removed, a soft brick remained. These fresh bricks would then sit in the sun drying for days until someone else would take them away for the next step of preparation.

One particular woman caught my eye. She looked as if she was in her 70s, but was probably closer to 50. She was wearing a tattered cotton sari that had probably been a bright yellow color originally, but was now faded into a pale dull shade that looked like weathered sand. *I knew that this is what she had been doing her whole life, every day, year after year—hunched over a hole in the hot sun, turning mud into bricks.* And for every thousand of these bricks, her family earned the equivalent of about $5.50.

This was her karma, to be born into poverty in India, to spend her entire life making bricks for other people's houses, for large, air-conditioned buildings far away that she would never see, all so she and her children could have enough food to survive and a safe place to sleep. That was her accomplishment. My eyes filled with tears of humble gratitude as I thought of my own life, my own good fortune, and I sent blessings to this Indian sister, praying that her next life would bring her more ease.

There was something else I saw that day, something even more important. I sensed by watching this woman that, in spite of the harsh conditions, the monotony, and the hardship, she was content. I could hear her softly chanting the name of Sita, the devoted wife of Lord Rama. I watched her use a scrap of cloth to very carefully wipe the extra mud off of the mold. *She was proud of her bricks. They were hers. She had made them with her own hands.*

In many ways, you and I have nothing in common with that woman, and yet in other ways we have everything in common with her. **Each of us is standing in the hot sun of our own mysterious path, making bricks of wisdom, bricks of self-discovery, bricks of compassion, and bricks of love. It's hard work, and it's uncomfortable work, and at times it's even frightening and backbreaking work. Yet, like her, in spite of how arduous it can be, we continue, knowing that our labor has been building our own road to freedom within.**

Often when I'm experiencing a challenging moment, I conjure up the image of this woman from a tiny unnamed village in a remote part of Southern India. I can see her tired, lined face, her sun-darkened skin, her gnarled hands and deformed back—but I can also see her peace as she gazes with a contented smile at the growing pile of bricks she has made. At these times, I thank her for unknowingly being my teacher, and for reminding me of what I'm now reminding you—**that each challenging Soul Shift, each courageous experience of healing, every bravely unearthed revelation, each painful but necessary relinquishment, each humble moment of forgiveness—each is a brick of victory, a brick of freedom, a brick of ascension that, when combined together, are building your new palace of awakened consciousness.**

At the beginning of this book, I shared my dream about the obstacle that looked like an enormous wall but was really a doorway to the other side, and the key that opened it. *In the same way, this may have appeared to simply be a book filled with words, but it truly is a doorway, one that hopefully*

has already and will continue to offer you vibrational pathways leading to realms of fulfillment beyond your imagination.

I hope with all my heart that you put what I've offered you on this journey into practice. Use the recalibration techniques, do the exercises, continue your journaling, and go back and reread the suggestions about how to use the book in the Introduction. They'll make more sense now, and will guide you as you reread and digest the wisdom.

The particular Soul Shifts I've offered you are ones that reflect what I believe to be universal spiritual truths and vibrational principles. They've been my map to travel farther than I ever imagined I could travel—to wisdom, healing, freedom, and awakening. However, your own personal Soul Shifts will reveal themselves in miraculous ways. *Watch for them. Recognize them when they happen. Write them down, contemplate them, and don't forget to celebrate your seeing.*

**The universe is always trying to lovingly shift us,
speaking to us through a flower, a song, the shape of clouds,
what someone says, what we see in the news,
speaking to us through the words of those we love, and of course,
and mostly, through the silent whispers of our own heart.
Listen . . .**

*"When you plant a seed of love,
it is you that blossoms."*
— Ma Jaya Sati Bhagavati

This is a story about another kind of teacher, as we travel from a brickmaker in India to a tree in California.

In 1876, a sailor returning from a long sea voyage to Australia landed in Santa Barbara harbor. Among his many souvenirs, he brought back a tiny seedling he'd found on his trip. He wasn't even sure what kind of plant it was or what it might grow into, but he kept it with his belongings.

Some of the local children were down at the wharf, excited to witness the large clipper ship's arrival from such a faraway place. The sailor noticed a sweet, wide-eyed little girl standing nearby and, on the spur of the moment, decided to give her the seedling as a gift. "What am I supposed to do with this?" the girl asked, puzzled by the strange leafy present. The sailor replied, *"Plant it and see what happens."*

The girl went home and planted the seedling in her yard. Soon her family moved away—but before she left, she gave the little plant to a good friend, who transplanted it to a spot a few blocks from the ocean.

What happened to that seedling? *Today it's known as the Moreton Bay Fig Tree, and it's the largest tree of its kind in North America.* It stands 80 feet tall, and the span of the leaves from one end to the other is almost 200 feet wide—two-thirds the length of a football field. This spectacular tree provides 21,000 square feet of shade, and the root system covers a full acre of ground. It's estimated that 10,000 people could fit standing under the tree. It's amazing to behold.

This tree started out as an impromptu gift of kindness and good-heartedness from a sailor who saw a curious little girl and decided to give her something from his travels, knowing that she would probably never get to take a voyage halfway around the world as he had. Decades later, that gift, which didn't seem like much at the time, has offered millions of people experiences of joy, wonder, and delight. They've sat under the tree with their loved ones, used it for shelter in rainstorms, and picnicked in its shade. The tree has been the site of first kisses, engagements, marriages, memorial services, reunions, and rendezvous.

Hundreds of thousands of birds have perched in its lush branches, and a million songs have been sung among its leaves. Generations of squirrels and chipmunks have made it their playground. **All of this love, life, and celebration came from one tiny seedling transported from Australia, and offered with love.**

When the sailor gave the seedling to the little girl, she probably thought it was interesting, although it didn't look like much—just a few green leaves on a tiny stalk. She never could have imagined how big it would become. As for the sailor, I'm sure he couldn't possibly have envisioned that one day, nearly 150 years later, people from all over the world would be reading about his gift in a book.

The Moreton Bay Fig Tree is a wonderful teacher for us as we come to the final pages of *Soul Shifts,* reminding us of these truths:

We may think that we know what we're getting when we receive an offering of wisdom, but we really don't have any idea of the abundance of the gift that's been given.

We may think we've fathomed the full depths of our mind, our heart, and our soul, but there are endless realms of astonishment and wonder with whose existence we aren't yet familiar that will astound us once they're discovered.

We may think we understand how those seeds of knowledge and truth will grow, but the scope of what will happen to us and in us is beyond anything we can even imagine.

Sometimes our revelations don't look like much. Our shifts in understanding seem interesting, but we can't imagine that they could be *that* life changing. Just as a gardener gazes lovingly at her seeds and then plants them, knowing that they'll bloom and grow into amazing wonders, so I have a wonderful vision of what can and will bloom for you from the seedling of this *Soul Shifts* journey. *Plant it and see what happens.*

Plant your gathered seeds of truth, of healing,
and of courageous seeing deep within your awareness.
Water them carefully and diligently with your contemplations,
your commitment, and your courage.
Be patient.
Even now, something miraculous is happening.
Your seeds are putting down roots of illumination.
Grace is helping them grow.
One day, sooner than you think,
you will be sitting under the magnificent, spreading branches
of your own miraculous tree of wisdom and love.

Your Legacy of Love

*"Go running through this world,
Giving love, giving love . . ."*
— Hafiz, from "If the Falling of a Hoof,"
The Gift (translated by Daniel Ladinsky)

Whether we've been on this earth for 18 years or 80, each of us finds ourselves contemplating the journey we've taken since we were born. From deep within our soul, questions call out to us, compelling us to search for answers: *How have we lived? How have we loved? What have we learned? What have we contributed to the world around us? What will we leave behind when we cross the threshold to the life beyond this life? What will our legacy be?*

When my mother was dying, I thought a lot about the meaning of *legacy*. My relationship with her transcended the traditional roles of mother and daughter. From the beginning, we gave each other strength in mysterious ways, and we both knew this in the way that old soul friends know things they never need to speak of, but that make them trust one another completely.

Phyllis was my refuge of safety in what was a very painful childhood. She'd miscarried twice before me, and spent most of her pregnancy lying alone in bed hoping I would survive. Once I was born, she loved me unconditionally. I have deep, sweet, subtle memories of being kissed, hugged and held, and told how special I was—and I believed her.

Even as a young girl, I sensed that I was my mother's light in her own dark times of betrayal from and disappointment in my father. She was dignified and courageous when most women still didn't know how to be courageous. **One of the greatest lessons I learned from watching her was to *never, ever let hardship harden my heart*. If you feel my love coming through these pages, it's because of her.**

As soon as I became successful, I did whatever I could to compensate for the poor circumstances we experienced when I was a child, to pamper my mother and give her everything that would make her life easier and more joyful. Something I never gave her, however, was grandchildren. I'd consciously chosen not to have children so that I could fully dedicate my life to this work as a teacher. In my mother's typically loving way, she understood and accepted my decision, and never once made me feel wrong for it.

Now, with no warning, she was leaving me. I hastily prepared to fly home to Philadelphia, knowing she didn't have much time left, hoping her mind would still be clear by the time I arrived. There was only one thing I wanted to make sure I did when I saw her—*to tell her about the legacy she was leaving behind, not of grandchildren, but of love*. I'd asked my students and friends to write my mother letters expressing how their lives had changed because of my work—which meant because of her—and created a beautiful large book that I titled *Legacy of Love*.

I spent several precious but heartbreaking days at home with my mother before I had to go back to work. On the last night of my visit, I sat down with her, put my arm around her thin shoulder, and showed her the book I'd made. She was very frail from massive radiation treatments and didn't say much, but tears poured down her face as I reverently turned the pages and read each one out loud, sharing the tributes from those whose lives she'd touched and transformed through me—her legacy.

One month later, my beloved mother passed away. This is the letter I read to her that night, and read again when I gave her eulogy:

My Dearest Mommy,

Most parents look toward their children to give them a sense of legacy, the feeling of having passed on the best of themselves to those who come after them—their children, grandchildren, and great-grand-children. In this way, they feel they are truly living forever, even when they no longer inhabit their body in this lifetime.

Dearest Mommy, I know at this time on your own journey, you find yourself in circumstances that none of us ever truly understand but must inevitably accept, and that you've been looking deeply at yourself and the life you've lived.

*As your only daughter and the recipient of your female lineage, you know I chose not to have children of my own, and because of that, the female lineage ends with me. **Instead, I was called to serve humanity, knowing that my purpose was to teach and awaken as many people as I could. This commitment asked many sacrifices of me, sacrifices I was happy and privileged to make.***

*And so, although I cannot give you a legacy of grandchildren and those who would come after them, I do have a legacy to offer you. **To me, it is the highest legacy of all—the legacy of love.***

***For through you and from you, I have learned what it means to love unconditionally, to serve selflessly, and to live with a pure heart and generous spirit.** This was your true legacy to me, and through God's grace, I have passed this legacy of love on to millions and millions of people.*

This book contains some expressions of that legacy—messages to you from my students and friends about how you have impacted them, their families, and their lives in ways that can only be called true blessings.

I offer you their words in this time of your transition. May they give you deep peace and fulfillment as you look upon your life. May you carry them with you as you journey forward into the light. And may you always, always know that I will love you forever beyond time and space, and that we are one.

Your Daughter in Love,

Barbara

I count writing and reading this letter to my mother as one of my great soul accomplishments. I made sure she knew about her remarkable legacy of love, and I am certain that it gave her peace as she crossed over.

Perhaps there are people in *your* life who are still alive, and need to know what legacy they've passed on to you *before* they leave the earth.

Don't wait until someone you love is gone to honor them.
Don't postpone sharing your gratitude until they're
no longer here to receive the gift of your words.
Tell them *now*, whether they're young or old.
We never know when someone's time on Earth will be over.

What will your own legacy be? **One of the most profound Soul Shifts we need to make each day is to contemplate our legacy, not what we'll leave when we've departed from the planet, but *the legacy we're leaving right now,* today, and tomorrow and the next day.** This is what our Soul Shifts journey has been about, understanding that each day, we leave a legacy on this world, and that our freedom and our responsibility is in choosing what that legacy will be.

Here, then, is our final Soul Shift.

SOUL SHIFT

SHIFT FROM CONTEMPLATING THE LEGACY YOU WANT TO LEAVE AT THE END OF YOUR LIFE TO CONTEMPLATING THE LEGACY YOU'RE LEAVING TODAY

Each morning, ask yourself:

"What legacy will I leave today?

**How will the world be different at the end of this day
because of my choices and actions?"**

Think about this throughout your day, focusing not on the work or tasks you did or did not get done, but rather, as we've seen in these pages, *the vibrational mark you leave on everyone and everything.*

What is the greatest legacy? You should know by now what my answer is going to be: *love.* When we're in a moment of love, we are the biggest, most formidable force that there is. *We're as big as we can get when we are vibrating with love. We could not get any bigger.*

Don't look for the gift. Be the gift.
Don't look for the hope. Be the hope.
Don't look for the light. Be the light.
Don't look for the miracle. Be the miracle.
Don't look for the blessing. Be the blessing.
Don't look for the love. Be the love.

"Love says: 'I am everything.'
Wisdom says: 'I am nothing.'
Between the two my life flows."
— Nisargadatta Maharaj

So, my dear ones, we come to the end of our pilgrimage, but hopefully not the end of *your* pilgrimage. How has your journey been? Can you feel things being rearranged inside of you, shifting, adjusting, recalibrating, expanding, opening, and melting? Are you beginning to sense some mystical currents of remembrance stirring deep within your heart? Are you experiencing some fresh, new joy as you understand that you *have* woken up, and are making your Great Return back to wholeness?

The story of a true spiritual pilgrimage is one that, in fact, cannot be told. It is silent, invisible, and indescribable. Words attempt to articulate what the mind believes that it's comprehended. *However, it is in the inner temple—the temple of the heart—where something profound and miraculous has occurred.* In that sacred space, beyond the senses, beyond language itself, the nectar of the journey is mysteriously revealed. To drink of that nectar is to taste awe, to taste reverence, and to taste peace.

When I was 18, it was that taste of the Divine that fueled the fire of my longing for ultimate freedom, and formally began my path in this lifetime as a spiritual seeker. It was that taste of the Divine that led me to this moment here with you. **The true nature of that taste is grace itself, for when we experience it, we want more, and nothing else but the Highest will do. Thus, we are propelled forward on the path, not allowing anything to stop us from our journey home.**

It has always been this way for me, and so now, at the end of my pilgrimage of birthing Soul Shifts, it remains.

FROM MY HEART TO YOURS

*"The tide of my love
Has risen so high let me flood over
You."*

— Hafiz, from "An Infant in Your Arms,"
The Gift (translated by Daniel Ladinsky)

Writing this for you has been what can only be described as a surrender to love. More than any other work I've brought forth, *Soul Shifts* has required me to let go of everything to make space for the love that was waiting to come through, **not love for anything or anyone, but love that contains everything and everyone.**

This love is not what we think of when we imagine love as happy and joyful. This love contains joy and agony, betrayal and compassion, relinquishment and redemption, humility and triumph all at once. *It is completely full because it encompasses everything, leaving nothing that is human out, and then goes beyond that, exploding into what I can only describe as sublime. It is love for the imperfection of humanity that, at the same time, does not disqualify us from our divinity.*

The imperfect container still holds what is perfect.

Like this, I have been a humble, trembling chalice receiving so much love, so much compassion, and so much grace, all meant to be offered to you. There were many times in which I've simply wept from the impact of the waves of energy pouring into me, many times the tears would not stop as I felt the pain of the world, my pain, *our* pain, our battle with our own darkness and our longing for the light, and many times I could feel the heavy, hurting hearts of so many beautiful, frightened souls trying to fight their way out of the web of forgetfulness. *"Hang on!"* I wanted to cry out. *"Hang on! You are not alone. We will do this together."*

Most of all, I prayed that in spite of many harsh and unforgiving winds that unexpectedly stormed into my life and shook me to my roots, this container of my soul would be strong enough, steady enough, and fearless enough to not spill one precious drop of what was meant for you.

If you've received my words and the transmission of love and wisdom they contain, then you can feel me, *as I am feeling you now, as I have been feeling you.* You are the faceless, nameless beloved, my inspiration, the one whom I've been serving without knowing who you are—yet miraculously, here you are, sitting with me in the innermost realms of my heart as I write, your soul keeping my soul company. This is the mystery of what I do.

"We're all just walking each other home."
— Ram Dass

You are part of something profound that is happening, you and so many others of us on the planet. We are in a mystical, vibrational relationship with one another, a relationship in which we are energetically connected from the innermost realms of the true spiritual heart.

This is the ultimate Soul Shift:
the Great Remembrance and the Great Reunion
with our own Highest and most true Self.

When each of us opens, we all open.
When each of us heals, we all heal.
When each of us shifts, we all shift.

When each of us ascends, we all ascend.
When each of us enters into the vibration of love,
we all vibrate as love.
In this way, the coming together of our true hearts heals the world.

These are my Highest blessings for you. Receive them from my heart to your heart:

May you remember who you truly are as a soul, and what you are here to do in this body, in this life, and at this time on Earth.

May all of your sincere intentions for freedom, for healing, and for liberation be received and sanctified by grace.

May all obstacles within you and without be now removed so that light may enter.

May you bravely shift your way back to wholeness.

May you be free from suffering. May you be at peace.

May you be a blessing to the world and to everyone you meet wherever you go, whatever you do, in each and every moment.

May people thank God for you.

May you live in such a way that you become the gift, the hope, the miracle, the blessing, and the love to your family, your friends, and the world.

May the highest light in you shine like an eternal sun, so brightly that you yourself are dazzled by its brilliance.

May you know yourself as that light, and remember that you are already nothing but that light. Only light.

May you awaken. May you awaken. May you awaken.

Thank you for keeping our appointment, and for giving me the immeasurable privilege of sharing my love with you through these words.

**In the place beyond conditions and causation
and time and space,
I am with you.**
And there is always and only love.

Your Soul Shifts

SHIFT FROM SEARCHING TO OPENING

SHIFT FROM SEEKING TO SEEING

SHIFT FROM MODULATING YOUR SEEING
TO SEEING EVERYTHING

SHIFT FROM SEARCHING TO REMEMBERING

SHIFT FROM THINKING ABOUT TRANSFORMATION
TO LIVING IT

SHIFT FROM TRYING TO CONTROL THE OUTSIDE
TO SHIFTING YOURSELF FROM THE INSIDE OUT

SHIFT FROM MANAGEMENT TO MASTERY

SHIFT FROM FORWARD TO WITHIN,
AND FROM FARTHER TO DEEPER

SHIFT FROM POSITIVE THINKING
TO POSITIVE VIBRATING

SHIFT FROM THINKING OF YOURSELF AS
AN EMOTIONAL/INTELLECTUAL BEING
TO UNDERSTANDING THAT YOU ARE A VIBRATIONAL BEING

SHIFT FROM THINKING OF YOUR RELATIONSHIPS
AND INTERACTIONS WITH PEOPLE AS EMOTIONAL
TO UNDERSTANDING THAT ALL OF YOUR INTERACTIONS
ARE PRIMARILY *VIBRATIONAL*

SHIFT FROM SEEING YOUR PAST AS A SERIES OF
EMOTIONAL EVENTS
TO UNDERSTANDING THEM AS *VIBRATIONAL EVENTS*
THAT HAD A *VIBRATIONAL IMPACT* ON YOU

SHIFT FROM ONLY SPEAKING YOUR TRUTH
TO VIBRATING YOUR TRUTH

SHIFT FROM ASKING YOURSELF "ARE PEOPLE LIKING ME?"
TO "HOW AM I VIBRATING?"

SHIFT FROM MASTERING YOUR PERFORMANCE
TO MASTERING YOUR PRESENCE

SHIFT FROM PICKING AND CHOOSING
WHEN TO BE CONSCIOUS
TO REMEMBERING THAT EVERYTHING COUNTS

SHIFT FROM "ALL OR NOTHING" THINKING
TO UNDERSTANDING THAT EVERYTHING IS EVERYTHING

SHIFT FROM TRYING TO LOOK GOOD
TO CULTIVATING VIBRATIONAL CREDIBILITY

SHIFT FROM THINKING OF MASTERY AS
AN ATTITUDE AND AN INTENTION TO BE EXCELLENT
TO MAKING MASTERY AN ACTUAL PRACTICE AND A HABIT

SHIFT FROM LOOKING FOR GREATNESS
TO PREPARING YOURSELF FOR GREATNESS

SHIFT FROM CONTRACTION TO EXPANSION
BY CULTIVATING EXPANSION
AND ELIMINATING CONTRACTION

SHIFT FROM TRYING TO RESIST OR REMOVE EMOTIONS,
PATTERNS, OR UNDESIRABLE ENERGIES
TO CREATING CONDITIONS OF EXPANSION SO THAT THESE
ENERGIES CAN VIBRATIONALLY UNWIND AND DISSOLVE

SHIFT FROM WAITING PASSIVELY TO SEE
WHICH PART OF YOU WILL TRIUMPH
TO SIDING WITH AND CHEERING ON YOUR EXPANSION TEAM

SHIFT FROM JUDGING SITUATIONS AND EVENTS
AS GOOD OR BAD
TO ASSESSING THEIR VIBRATIONAL IMPACT ON YOU

SHIFT FROM JUST NOTICING WHAT IS HAPPENING
TO CONSCIOUSLY CHOOSING IN EACH MOMENT

SHIFT FROM *NOTICING* WHAT NEEDS TO BE CHANGED
TO CONSCIOUSLY *DOING* WHAT IT TAKES TO CHANGE

SHIFT FROM STOPPING AT LOCATION AND REVELATION
TO CHOOSING TRANSFORMATION

SHIFT FROM ASKING YOURSELF "WHY CAN'T I?"
TO ASKING YOURSELF "WHY DON'T I?"

SHIFT FROM TRYING TO CHANGE EVERYTHING
TO CHOOSING TO DO SOMETHING

SHIFT FROM THINKING ABOUT THE HIGHEST
TO VIBRATING AS THE HIGHEST

SHIFT FROM JUST TRYING TO BE IN YOUR HIGHEST
TO NOTICING WHEN, HOW, AND WHY
YOU DRIFT FROM YOUR HIGHEST

SHIFT FROM WAITING TO BE UPLIFTED
TO LIFTING YOURSELF UP

SHIFT FROM FOCUSING ONLY ON EXTERNAL GOALS
AND ACCOMPLISHMENTS
TO HONORING YOUR SOUL ACCOMPLISHMENTS

SHIFT FROM ALWAYS TRYING TO GET MORE AND DO MORE
ON THE OUTSIDE
TO BECOMING MORE ON THE INSIDE

SHIFT FROM SEEING WHERE YOU'RE RECEIVING LOVE
TO SEEING WHERE YOU CAN OFFER LOVE

SHIFT FROM MERELY MEASURING TIME
TO MARVELING AT YOUR BLESSINGS

SHIFT FROM TRYING TO HAVE AN ATTITUDE OF GRATITUDE
TO LIVING GRATITUDE AS A VIBRATIONAL EXPERIENCE

SHIFT FROM CONDITIONAL GRATITUDE
TO GRATITUDE BEYOND CONDITIONS

SHIFT FROM DISQUALIFYING YOUR GRATITUDE
DURING CHALLENGING TIMES
TO UNDERSTANDING THAT YOU CAN BE
BOTH GRATEFUL *AND* UNCOMFORTABLE AT THE SAME TIME

SHIFT FROM ONLY BEING GRATEFUL FOR WHAT'S PRESENT
TO ALSO BEING GRATEFUL FOR WHAT IS ABSENT

SHIFT FROM THE IDEA THAT YOU'RE RECEIVING
TO THE *VIBRATIONAL EXPERIENCE* OF RECEIVING

SHIFT FROM BEING A RELUCTANT AND RESISTANT RECEIVER
TO A GRACIOUS RECEIVER

SHIFT FROM BEMOANING THINGS AS BURDENS
TO CHERISHING THEM AS BLESSINGS

SHIFT FROM TRYING TO FIGURE OUT HOW TO
MAKE A DIFFERENCE
TO REALIZING THAT YOU'RE *ALREADY ALWAYS*
MAKING A DIFFERENCE

SHIFT FROM LOOKING FOR YOUR PURPOSE, OR THINKING YOU
HAVE TO POSTPONE FULFILLING YOUR PURPOSE,
TO LIVING YOUR PURPOSE *RIGHT NOW IN EACH MOMENT*

SHIFT FROM CONTEMPLATING THE LEGACY
YOU WANT TO LEAVE AT THE END OF YOUR LIFE
TO CONTEMPLATING THE LEGACY YOU'RE LEAVING TODAY

THE
SOUL SHIFTS
MANTRA

TODAY I AM GOING TO SEE WHAT THERE IS TO SEE,
TO FEEL WHAT THERE IS TO FEEL,
AND TO KNOW WHAT THERE IS TO KNOW.

ACKNOWLEDGMENTS

It is my honor to name those who have loved me, guided me, prepared me, inspired me, supported me, and sustained me while I birthed this book.

Deepest gratitude to my spiritual teachers, guides, and protectors, divine and human, in this world and beyond:

His Holiness Maharishi Mahesh Yogi and *Gurumayi Chidvilasananda,* for the priceless and prayed-for gifts of awakening, liberation, and unending grace, without which I would not have been able to fulfill my promise in this lifetime.

My beloved mother, Phyllis Garshman, and my stepfather, Dan Garshman, for teaching me so much even as you departed your physical forms, and embracing me every day with unconditional love from the other side.

My precious animal companions in heaven, Bijou, Shanti, and Luna, for being my now and forever angels.

My former husband, Doug Henning, for unmistakable magical signs that you are watching over me from above and, once again, helping to facilitate my metamorphosis.

All those divine invisible ones whose names I do not know, but whose presence I feel with me always. I am humbled to be a vehicle for your beneficent wisdom.

Deepest gratitude to honored helpers, healers, supporters, and heart family:

Lenna and Alan Wagner, for eternal bonds, timeless friendship, always being by my side, and loving me in all of my many mysterious forms.

Marisa Morin, my ancient soul friend and mentor, for being my bridge to the highest love and light and always pointing the way home.

Dr. and Master Zhi Gang Sha, for soul healing and miracles.

Dr. Sat Kaur Khalsa, Chakrapani Ullal, Mark Lerner, Dr. Neil Kobrin, Chantal Evrard, Rashani Rea, Mahinanani Laughlin, and *Brent Bahr,* for compassion, maps, and timely healing.

Alison Betts, for almost two decades of unmatched support and loyalty, transcending all conditions.

Rose and Jack Herschorn of The Sacred Space, for our reunion just at the right time and being my treasured Santa Barbara family.

Gail Kingsbury, for helping me birth my new expansion and always being there.

Jim Kwik, for your brilliance and inspiration.

Bill Gladstone and Waterside Productions, for recognizing who I really am, understanding the need for *Soul Shifts,* and shepherding me in the right direction.

The wonderful people at Hay House, for your dedication to serving the world, and generously sharing your expertise with me, especially *Louise Hay* for forging the path, *Reid Tracy* for once again giving me the opportunity to share the message and transmission of this book with so many people, *Patty Gift* for honoring my words and wisdom, and *Margarete Nielsen* for her deeply appreciated support and enthusiasm.

T. Harv Eker, Brendon Burchard, Rick Frishman, Mark Victor Hansen, Craig Duswalt, Debbie Allen, and *Demian Lichtenstein,* for generously helping me share my message on stage and in film with so many new people over the past nine years.

Everyone who works for and with my company, Shakti Communications, for being my steady pillars of service and helping me serve so many others.

And most of all, my beloved students from all over the world, past and present, who kept their promise to find me again as I kept my promise to find you. Thank you for remembering me. You are my cherished blessings.

About the Author

Dr. Barbara De Angelis is one of the most influential teachers of our time in the field of personal and spiritual transformation. As a renowned author, speaker, and media personality, she is legendary as one of the first people who helped popularize the self-help movement in the 1980s, and for over four decades has reached tens of millions of people with her inspirational messages about how to create a life of true freedom, mastery, and awakening.

Dr. De Angelis has written 14 best-selling books that have sold over 10 million copies and been published in 25 languages, including four #1 *New York Times* bestsellers. She has starred in her own television shows on *CNN, CBS,* and *PBS*; and has been a frequent guest on *The Oprah Winfrey Show,* the *TODAY* show, and *Good Morning America.* She was the creator and producer of the award-winning infomercial *Making Love Work,* which was seen throughout the world by hundreds of millions of people and was the most successful relationships program of its kind.

Dr. De Angelis is known for being one of the most moving and inspirational female speakers in the world, and is among only five women ever honored as one of the most outstanding speakers of the century by Toastmasters International. She has been a featured presenter at countless conferences along with such luminaries as His Holiness the Dalai Lama, Sir Richard Branson, Deepak Chopra, Wayne Dyer, Louise Hay, and many other great teachers.

Dr. De Angelis credits her dedication and unrelenting commitment to her own personal journey as the source of all that has come through her. She is a serious seeker who has deeply immersed herself in spiritual practice and study from the age of 18 and spent many years in residence with several of the most renowned spiritual masters of our time.

Dr. De Angelis is President of Shakti Communications, Inc., dedicated to bringing enlightened messages to the world through her work. She offers seminars, retreats, online courses, and training programs to all those longing to live a life of mastery, fulfillment, and freedom. She is delighted to be a resident of Santa Barbara, California.

❧ SPREAD THE LOVE AND ❧ MAKE A DIFFERENCE

Dear Reader,

I hope that *Soul Shifts* has inspired you to honor your own journey and helped you realize how much of a difference you are always making in the world. Remember: *You may not be able to do something for everyone, but you can do something for someone. Each day, in some small way, you can leave the world a better place than the day before.*

One immediate way you can do this is to share *Soul Shifts* with as many people as possible. **Someone you know needs this book right now, and I need your help getting it to that person:**

* Someone who is ready for a deeper understanding of the events in their life

* Someone going through relationship or work challenges or a reevaluation

* Someone at a turning point who wants to make a change

* Someone undergoing deep physical or emotional healing

* Someone who feels stuck, confused, or afraid to take the next step

* Someone interested in deepening their spiritual perspective

* Someone who you know needs to make a Soul Shift

I've created another easy and immediate way that you can make a difference in addition to recommending *Soul Shifts.* Go to this web address:

www.SoulShifts.com/spreadthelove

We will help you *e-mail a free excerpt* from *Soul Shifts* to *as many people as you wish* without ordering anything. To thank you for your help, we'll give you a *year's free subscription* to my monthly e-newsletter.

Please take a moment to think of all the people whose lives you can touch by sharing the information in *Soul Shifts.* Thank you for joining with me as we invite all those around us to wake up and, together, uplift the vibration of our planet.

SPREAD THE LOVE

In service to your highest and with deep gratitude,

Barbara

More from Dr. Barbara De Angelis

Live Seminars, Retreats & Online Courses

Barbara De Angelis is delighted to offer *live Soul Shifts seminars and retreats*, as well as many other workshops throughout North America for those interested in having a deep in-person transformational experience. In addition, her many *online courses and live tele-seminars, all taught personally by Barbara*, are a convenient way you can work with her from anywhere in the world to gain more valuable wisdom and practical support to create the awakened life you deserve. Please contact us to see a list of courses and to learn more.

Listen to Dr. De Angelis on Hay House Radio

Tune in each week to hear Barbara live on *Hay House Radio,* streaming on the Internet 24/7. Visit HayHouseRadio.com® for more information.

Join a Soul Shifts Mastery Group

Dr. De Angelis has created *Soul Shifts Mastery Groups,* facilitated by her trained, advanced students and designed to connect you with other *Soul Shifts* readers and seekers around the world. To learn more, please go to:

www.soulshifts.com/masterygroups

Share Your Soul Shifts Story

Dr. De Angelis would love to hear about the impact *Soul Shifts* has had in your life and to hear about your own Soul Shifts. Please send your stories to:

Stories@SoulShifts.com

Speaking Engagements

Over the past 35 years, Dr. De Angelis has been a highly sought-after motivational speaker, giving hundreds of presentations to major corporations, conferences, conventions, hospitals, and churches. Recently she was honored with the prestigious Toastmasters International Golden Gavel as one of the outstanding speakers of the century, and is known for sharing her eloquence, passion, and powerful presence with her audiences. To inquire about booking Dr. De Angelis, please contact us at:

Booking@BarbaraDeAngelis.com

Contact Information

Please contact us to:

* See a schedule of Dr. De Angelis's upcoming live seminars and appearances.
* Sign up for Dr. De Angelis's *free* newsletter.
* Register for exciting online courses taught personally by Barbara.
* Listen to *free* inspiring audio wisdom and messages.
* Receive invitations to *free* calls with Barbara, bonus gifts, and discounts.
* Read *free* excerpts from her other best-selling books.
* Book Dr. De Angelis for an appearance or event.
* Find out how you can join a *Soul Shifts Mastery Group.*
* Become part of the *Soul Shifts Online Community.*

FOR INFORMATION, GO TO:

www.SoulShifts.com©

or

www.BarbaraDeAngelis.com©

PHONE: (855) 8WISDOM (toll-free) or (310) 996-5586

E-MAIL: info@SoulShifts.com

Follow Dr. De Angelis on Twitter: @drbdeangelis

Facebook: DrBarbaraDeAngelis

We hope you enjoyed this Hay House book.
If you'd like to receive our online catalog featuring additional information
on Hay House books and products, or if you'd like to find out more about the
Hay Foundation, please contact:

Hay House, Inc., P.O. Box 5100, Carlsbad, CA 92018-5100
(760) 431-7695 or (800) 654-5126
(760) 431-6948 (fax) or (800) 650-5115 (fax)
www.hayhouse.com® • www.hayfoundation.org

Published and distributed in Australia by:
Hay House Australia Pty. Ltd., 18/36 Ralph St., Alexandria NSW 2015
Phone: 612-9669-4299 • *Fax:* 612-9669-4144 • www.hayhouse.com.au

Published and distributed in the United Kingdom by:
Hay House UK, Ltd., Astley House, 33 Notting Hill Gate, London W11 3JQ
Phone: 44-20-3675-2450 • *Fax:* 44-20-3675-2451 • www.hayhouse.co.uk

Published and distributed in the Republic of South Africa by:
Hay House SA (Pty), Ltd., P.O. Box 990, Witkoppen 2068
Phone/Fax: 27-11-467-8904 • www.hayhouse.co.za

Published in India by: Hay House Publishers India, Muskaan Complex,
Plot No. 3, B-2, Vasant Kunj, New Delhi 110 070 • *Phone:* 91-11-4176-1620
Fax: 91-11-4176-1630 • www.hayhouse.co.in

Distributed in Canada by:
Raincoast Books, 2440 Viking Way, Richmond, B.C. V6V 1N2
Phone: 1-800-663-5714 • *Fax:* 1-800-565-3770 • www.raincoast.com

Take Your Soul on a Vacation

Visit www.HealYourLife.com® to regroup, recharge,
and reconnect with your own magnificence. Featuring blogs, mind-body-spirit
news, and life-changing wisdom from Louise Hay and friends.

Visit www.HealYourLife.com today!